The Arimaspian Eye

SUNY Series,
The Margins of Literature

Mihai I. Spariosu, Editor

The Arimaspian Eye

David Lynn Hall

STATE UNIVERSITY OF NEW YORK PRESS

Cover painting, "Men of Myopia," by Steve Hastings,
Cover illustration copyright © 1992 by Steve Hastings

Production: Ruth Fisher
Marketing: Theresa A. Swierzowski

Published by
State University of New York Press, Albany

© 1992   State University of New York

Library of Congress Cataloging-in-Publication Data

Hall, David L.
     The Arimaspian eye / David Lynn Hall.
         p.   cm. — (SUNY series, the margins of literature)
     ISBN 0–7914–1307–1 (acid-free). : ISBN 0–7914–1308–X (pbk. : acid
     -free)
     I. Title. II. Series.
     PS3558.A3655A88   1992
     813'.54—dc20   76331
                                                                  91–45682
                                                                      CIP

10 9 8 7 6 5 4 3 2 1

This is a novel of ideas. Flatly to say that it is a work of fiction would needlessly call into question the value of those ideas. To claim, on the other hand, that the text is factual, in whole or in part, would, after tedious reflections on the meaning of "facticity," likely be judged a lie. Let's just say, in sympathy with the Buddhists whose spirit infuses this work that, as "the dharmas are empty" and the world itself only an illusion, the characters, events, and situations depicted inside this book have precisely the same ontological status as those which are naively purported to exist beyond its pages.

For Stephanie
...never yet, nor any longer mine

I would have offered you a name,
and filled that vacant space with sounds
of lulling whispers, laughter, and sweet sighs.

—Anonymous

Contents

I

Karla and Company

1

"I can play the clarinet."

He thought that she probably could. "What's your name?"

"Zenaida."

He asked her to spell it. "What would you like, Zenaida?"

"Could I just rest for a moment? I think I am tired."

"Would you like some water?"

"Champagne, I think. You have champagne?"

"Yes, I do. Will you be all right if I leave for just a few seconds?" He didn't like leaving the room. He remembered what happened when he left Honey alone.

"Of course. I shall acquaint myself with my new bed. With these walls, the painting. Rouault, isn't it?"

He would never adjust to this. "Yes, it is. When I come back you can tell me what you think of it. OK?"

"If it pleases you."

"It would please me very much." He hurried to the kitchen. He decided on the better of the two champagnes. Zenaida would probably have some knowledge of wines. The thought made him dizzy. And Christ, she could play the clarinet. He *knew* that she could. He ran tap water over the bottle, put it in the freezer and called to her: "Can you wait a few minutes, Zenaida? I'll chill the champagne." No reply. He hurried to the bedroom.

"I am not given to shouting," she said. She touched his arm. "You must have a name, too."

"My name is Michael. I'm a friend of Adrienne." He wondered why he hadn't said that he was Karla's friend.

"Ah."

"You know Adrienne?"

"I know no one. No one. But, I am known. I need to be known by you, I think. Does...Adrienne know me?"

Michael was ashamed to look at her body. She had made no attempt to cover herself. Was she even aware that she was naked? He stood by the bed wearing only a tee shirt. She didn't seem to notice him any longer. But she must have, for as soon as he became erect she turned her head to one side and closed her eyes. At the same time she put both hands on the insides of her thighs just above her knees and opened her legs.

It was a hot summer afternoon, but her body remained completely cool and dry. Her breathing was shallow, quiet. She made no sound at all. Toward the end he felt her legs begin to quiver. Her eyes never opened, but when he moved away from her she turned her head from the wall, placed her hands on her knees and held her legs firmly together.

"Champagne, Zenaida?" His whisper occasioned the slightest smile.

"Champagne. Yes."

Michael returned with two glasses. Zenaida was gone. Collie was sitting on the floor.

"Did you fuck her?"

"Who?"

"There was someone here."

"Yes, Collie. She said her name was Zenaida."

"Fuck *me*. Fuck me on this floor. On this rug. This...*rug*." She was tearing at the shag carpet with both hands.

She called herself Collie Frankee Mackovich.

2

Michael had been seeing Karla for almost two years before the members of her "company" announced themselves. First Honey, then the creature who would be called "Adrienne," both in a single evening. Several weeks later Collie appeared, a woman seemingly wrought in detail from his most intense sexual fantasies. Last of all, Zenaida, the concert clarinetist.

The most bizarre happenings are often the easiest to accept. When Tertullian insisted, "Credo, quia absurdum est," he celebrated one of the most fundamental of human traits. We find our strangest experiences difficult to doubt; their unusual character makes them seem somehow more, not less real.

Routinely ordered everyday events, allow us to ease our grip, let our attention wander. After all, they will remain dependable without our support. Prodigies, on the other hand, demand our participation and engagement. We are compelled to believe them because they are so—there is no other word—*obvious*.

Were Michael standing before his usual audience when this insight came to him, he would doubtless proceed to reveal the original meaning of "obvious." The word derives from *ob*, "against," and *via*, "way." "Something is obvious," he might have said, "when it stands in the way, when it *confronts* us."

Honey's initial appearance was just that sort of obvious event. On that first evening, after several minutes of conversation with the lisping child Karla had become, Michael found himself treating Honey ("Honey ith my name," she had announced, without Michael asking) like the five-year old she claimed to be. ("I'm five. Thath juth ath old ath I am. How old are you?")

3

Though equally "obvious," Michael had greater difficulty accepting the next birth. Honey was describing her favorite game. After some moments Michael realized that she was talking about hopscotch, though it sounded more like "hop-stop" when Honey said it. Right in the middle of a sentence, Honey sat up in bed (Karla and Michael had been lying in bed; they had just made love) and said in a rapid, mechanical whisper: "I'm going now. Good-bye, Mithter Michael." Then she closed her eyes and leaned her head back against her pillow.

When Honey/Karla opened her eyes, she was neither Honey nor Karla.

"You sick bastard. What do you think you're doing? You asshole pervert!"

"Karla?" Michael spoke Karla's name, but he knew this was not Karla. He began to think he had let things get out of control.

"Who are *you*?" Michael asked.

"Listen, Michael…"

He wasn't surprised that she knew his name, but something about the way she sounded it made him extremely anxious.

"You're interfering. Karla is my responsibility."

"Tell me what's going on. I was just talking to someone who said her name was Honey."

"Honey always sleeps. I don't want you waking her up."

"What is your name?"

"I don't need a name, you pervert. You leave us alone."

"*Us*?" Please help me make sense of this."

"No chance, you bastard-scum." Her voice, her facial expressions, the way she gestured with her hands were all unfamiliar to Michael.

"Give Karla back, OK?" Michael felt silly making such a request.

"Karla doesn't need you anymore. I may not let her see you again."

Michael tried to appear calm as he spoke. "You know my name. It's only right that you tell me yours." She was silent.

Michael persisted: "Am I supposed to guess?" The creature turned away from him and moved toward the door.

"Why don't I call you Adrienne?" He didn't have time to wonder why he felt it necessary to name this apparition, or why he felt so certain this was the appropriate name, for the instant the sound was uttered the "person" he had just named Adrienne turned around and moved toward him shrieking obscenities. She grabbed his arms and began to gouge them with her fingernails. Michael tried to free himself without hurting her.

The creature's screams grew louder and more hysterical, but Michael found himself distracted by a familiar but long forgotten image thrust into his consciousness. The image was of a colored drawing he had first encountered in one of his childhood story books: arms, legs, head, and torso flying in all directions— Rumpelstiltskin, his name discovered, torn to pieces by his rage. Here, however, the scene was running in reverse. The pieces of this creature were forming and uniting. A spectral semblance, nameless until now, was condensing, imploding, becoming real.

Michael pushed her down onto the bed. She continued to fight him, but was somewhat quieter now. Only as he pulled Karla's nightgown high above this creature's waist, and pinned her arms against the rumpled sheets, did he begin to believe what he was about to do.

4

...you can't remember...not even her name...nothing...not even her name...

He lay on top of her and tried to pry her legs apart. She was angry and frightened, but she too (this was clear to Michael) wanted what he wanted.

...Adrienne...her name was Adrienne...

She bit him on the neck but (he thought) not very hard. She held her legs together, but not so tightly (after all) that he couldn't force his way inside her.

...we never said yes...so it wasn't really bad...it wasn't right...but we never said yes...

"Adrienne," he said. "Adrienne," consciously mimicking the commanding voice from the radio play of "Ali Baba and the Forty Thieves" as (how many years ago?) it had shouted, "Open, Sesame!" With each repetition the creature yielded more.

...she made it feel funny...and sometimes it was sore.... She said if we told she would bite it off and take it home with her...

Michael wanted to think, to remember something, but increasingly overwhelmed by a sick-guilty delirium, all thinking stopped. There was no choice. He "made love" to this increasingly pliant, coldly passionate form, unaware of the hollowing of his spirit as hers, the woman's (her name *would* be Adrienne), as *Adrienne's* spirit was made flesh.

...we couldn't say no...then after a long time when she didn't anymore we wanted her to...but she said she wouldn't...

In the midst of the final spasm, at the very instant before the conception and the birth, he silently begged forgiveness of Karla, and of himself. Even as he did so, he vaguely realized that he should be pleading with the forced incarnation that lay beneath him.

...she said we shouldn't want that...she said it was wrong...

5

In the beginning was Chaos.... But that is a redundancy, isn't it? For the word *beginning* derives from the Old Norse *gína* and Old English *gínan*, which carry the meanings of "gape" or "yawn"—that is to say, "the yawning gap" or "gaping void" of Chaos. Chaos and beginnings are one and the same.

We presume that the creation of any new thing is from Chaos. But such things are not really *new*. Only the origin itself is novel, original. To create is to impose form upon a chaos which lacks any form—or, what amounts to the same thing, possesses all forms. To select a single form from the totality of forms and then to squeeze the origin into that impoverishing mold is to steal the reality of Chaos itself. To create is to commit the ultimate act of violence.

Creativity is rape.

Adam raped Eve, herself ripped from Adam's tinkered womb by God whose rape of the dark formless void is the model for each creative act to follow. Cain compounded rape with incest that the Carnal Zoo might continue. Few generalizations are more defensible that this: History is born of rape and motored by it.

Life itself is rape. And rape of the anonymous, the truly nameless owner of the infinity of forms and names, is the horrifying sublimity of rape itself. Such was Michael's rape of Adrienne, his creation of her.

We cannot love what we create. All products of the artist's eye and hand are hateful the instant they are completed. We can only love the unfathomable manyness of Chaos. The Lovable exists only before the selection, rejection, or imposition of creativity—never after. To love is to leave unnamed, to leave the story untold.

Love is possible, but only to the unaware. Awareness of love comes only after names are given. The very meaning of finitude is found here: We cannot recognize that we love formlessness until forced to endure its absence advertised by stultifying form. Because the painting or the poem is residue, hateful detritus of the process itself, symbol only of the nameless Chaos from out of which it emerged, the artist is driven to create again. Touching Chaos, the artist has no choice but to name, configure, construe, and...destroy. Then, seeing that he has done so, he must create, destroy, again...name again...and again.

Michael's love for Adrienne was the love of unnamed Chaos, the love of that out of which she was born—the pure trackless nothing, the faceless, traceless beginning...the yawning gap, the gaping void. He loved her original face before she was born.

Yet he named her. There was no choice. He named her, created her, raped her, lost her...in a single act.

6

And that act had consequences for Michael as well. Now he, too, is divided from himself. The nameless in him has awakened to the risk of being named.

How do we know this to be so?

In the space between imagination and memory, there is a hollowing void, a yawning emptiness of the unthinkable and the unthought, a vast indifference that blankets every atom of every sentient being, a namelessness that mocks and hallows every name any have ever uttered or surmised.

All stories, all accountings, celebrate the tension between the nameless and the named. Every creative inspiration is conceived through this tension and every created product is its violently extruded afterbirth—tardy witness to the coupling of desire and desirelessness.

Who, then, are we?

The first thing to be said is that we are definitely not omniscient. There is much that we do not, cannot know. We know little, nothing really, of what lies beyond the horizon Michael shares with us. Yet ours is not merely the superficial knowledge Michael has of himself, nor is it that sum expanded only by the unconscious thoughts and emotions with which he might never be conversant. We have unlimited, godlike awareness of every idea and feeling, every aspect and nuance of the memories embedded in each of Michael's cells, the cause and consequence of every nerve impulse—including those he never would nor could have consciously experienced, expressed or recalled.

Thus, our knowledge extends to all possibilities, potentialities, foreshadowings—discarded scraps, unsown seeds—what Michael never was (but could yet be) and what he is now (but could never recognize himself to be). This, and only this, is the source of our account.

Who are we, the tellers of this tale? What shall we be called?

Our name?

Our unsayable, unnamed name, the only true name, is...

Hun-tun, Tohu Wa-Bohu, Gunniga-gap, Sunyata...Chaos.

And this is to be our story as well.

7

Karla claimed to have no knowledge of her alternate personalities. From the first Michael had kept her informed (exercising what he considered to be appropriate editorial license) of what happened while she was "away." She seemed to receive some real benefit from displaying the members of her company for Michael's enjoyment.

As for Michael, though he had initially urged Karla to find an appropriate therapist, he was soon persuaded that he shouldn't attempt to force her into therapy. He even allowed himself to imagine that he might serve as the means of Karla's ultimate integration by continuing to mediate the elements of her fragmented consciousness. Of course, he knew very well that he was rationalizing and that his strongest motivation was simply his own thoughtless desire to command a harem.

Each member of Karla's company would usually be called

forth as a prelude to lovemaking. When Michael wanted to see one of her company he would pass his hand slowly down her forehead, press her eyelids closed, and say, "Let me speak to...." On occasion, one of her personalities would emerge of its own accord, but even then, almost always while they were in bed.

Michael found Karla and Company addictive. Two or three times a week they would meet at his place, have wine and cheese, then move to the bedroom. Michael would make love with Karla, then he would call for the others in turn.

At first he had been surprised by his stamina, but soon began to take "the harem effect" for granted. He would simply anticipate making love with four different women in a single evening, and then, innocently lying beside a nude child, listen as she boasted in her small, lisping voice about how many times she could jump the rope without missing or about how she was the only one in her whole class who knew how to spell "Pennthylvania."

Michael tried to suppress the realization that he was increasingly dependent upon his meetings with the company. He was often impatient with Karla during their lovemaking, anxious to get to Collie. When Michael and Karla went out to dinner or a concert, he wished that Zenaida were with him. (He did actually take Zenaida to a ballet performance once; it remains one of Michael's most rehearsed memories.) Honey provided him a fascinating picture of a psychic child who was growing ever more interesting under his tutelage. Adrienne was both archivist and caretaker. Not only did she have seemingly complete knowledge of the other personalities, but she was aware of the details of Michael's behavior with each member of the company. It was always Adrienne he would summon when he encountered something truly puzzling about his harem.

During his increasingly infrequent moments of honest reflection, Michael recognized that Karla was becoming less and less like one of the actors and more like the theatre in which the play was performed. Nevertheless, though she must have realized that she was less interesting to Michael than the members of her company, she did not react with jealousy or hostility but yielded her time all the more willingly. If to please him she had to be "away" for most of their time "together," she seemed quite content to be so.

For this reason Michael was surprised when, over a year after the birth of her alter egos, after perhaps a hundred repertory performances, Karla suddenly announced that she was leaving for Los Angeles.

"You're sure?"

"Yes."

"It's a long way."

"From where, Michael? From here?"

"Yes. It's a long way from here. Jesus, Karla, you *can* be cold."

"Ah, Michael. Cheer up. What we had..."

"...we will always have," Michael finished her sentence— the litany recited when she wanted to assure him that they were not really attached to one another. Only weeks after they had met, Karla said, "We are a habit, Michael. Let's leave it at that. Neither of us was attached when we met, so we became attached. Right?"

The picture that came to Michael's mind when she said this was that painted by the Roman philosopher Lucretius (97?–54 B.C.E.), who explained the connectedness of the otherwise independent atoms of which the world was made by recourse to the expedient of "little hooks." He and Karla were two atoms swirling around in empty space who had become accidentally hooked together and must eventually come unhooked in the same accidental way.

Inertia is perhaps the only dependable fact. There need be no other reasons or causes. He and Karla were both owned by inertia. And inertia was the only thing they really had in common. Even though Karla was never deeply committed to Michael, her loyalty was absolute. Not out of love, of course, but inertia. Michael was simply *there*.

Michael, too, was faithful—if such a word applies in this situation. "I swear to you," he would often say, offering a teasing assurance Karla seemed neither to need nor to desire, "you are the only women in my life!"

But Karla and Company were leaving, nonetheless. More than inertia was influencing them now. Somewhere in her, among them, there was a decision-maker.

It has to be Adrienne, Michael thought.

8

Karla left for Los Angeles. Michael swirled about in social space until inertia did its work, and hooked him up with another woman. She was not as complex as Karla, of course. But she served his needs sufficiently well, and he satisfied himself with visiting Karla and Company every two or three months.

After almost a year Karla managed to find fairly steady work as a cosmetics model. She had the sort of features that could be accentuated in a variety of ways—from innocence to rapine seductiveness. Had she not spent so much of her time dreaming in a vague, idle fashion of an acting career, she might have found real success as a model.

Michael wondered if anyone besides himself knew the true reason for Karla's many faceted expressiveness. Most of all, he wondered if any one else was enjoying her company.

9

They had been forced to leave Karla's apartment when the air conditioner collapsed. The valley was so hot, humid, and smoggy that even the fashionably weird who haunted the mall on Saturdays had escaped to the beach. Karla was, as usual, completely unaware of her environment. It might as well have been snowing. Michael was attempting to persuade her to come back to Texas, but she was as indifferent to his pleading as she was to the climate.

"Then just come for a few weeks. I really miss you."

"Need a steadier round of orgies, Michael? Not getting enough serial sex?"

"Why won't you come? It can't be over between us since there never was anything much to begin with."

"That's true, my man. But don't you see? I'm *here* now."

Her tone communicated finality. Michael turned to more immediate concerns. "Let's get a room. Your place is too hot."

"Whatever, Michael."

He knew her indifference was only apparent. When they got to the room, she would not be indifferent at all. She would be every imaginable kind of needing and yielding.

"Finish your food." This was as close to a command as he was willing to risk.

"Getting anxious?" Her voice was coy, but Michael could tell that she had begun to anticipate as well. "You really should be more considerate. I'm still eating for five, you know."

10

"There aren't any hotels in this direction."

"Be patient, you maniac, Karla and Company has a surprise for you."

"Uh oh. Where are we bound, ladies?"

"We'll be there in ten minutes."

"But you won't say where?"

"No need. *Ten minutes.*" Karla gestured toward the cars creeping ahead and beside them. "It's like this," she announced, "because so many people live here."

Michael didn't reply. He had never learned whether Karla's frequent resort to redundancies were intentional. He often suspected that she very much enjoyed tempting him to believe her simpleminded.

They drove across Van Nuys Boulevard into an old raggedly landscaped neighborhood. Karla stopped the car in front of a small beige stucco house. "This is it. Come. I'm taking care of the house plants. I guess I should say plant since only one seems to have any real chance of surviving."

Karla found the key and opened the door. The living room was dark and a bit musty. There were two large overstuffed chairs and a huge slightly mismatched sofa—the sort of furniture that looks naked without doilies which, Michael immediately noticed, were missing on all the pieces. Karla quickly maneuvered Michael into one of the chairs and said, "Close your eyes."

"OK. They're shut."

"Keep them closed."

"My word." He raised his right hand, pledging his oath to the void. Then he heard vaguely familiar sounds—creaking wood and what seemed to be the sliding of a chair.

Next came the surprise.

How could he have missed seeing the piano? It must have been in the darkest corner. It was probably an old upright, the sort that seem to come equipped with cracks in the veneer and chips on the ivory keys with dirty yellow-brown wood showing through. The bench would have a cover that lifted, with space for sheet music inside. On top of the piano there would be knickknacks and photos, sitting on a lace—no, wait, there were no doilies, it would likely be a velour cover.

Michael might have gone on to reflect that the piano would almost certainly be out of tune had not the first notes verified this suspicion, assuring him that his other surmises had probably been correct.

"Karla. I *am* surprised. I'm *more* than surprised, I'm..."

"Don't interrupt. Just listen."

Michael was indeed impressed. Karla had often said that she would like to learn to play the piano. She hadn't given any indication of knowing how to play when he had seen her last. Now she was playing.... What was this piece?

The piano was so out of tune that Michael had to strain to pick out the melody. Finally, he recognized Pachelbel's "Canon in D Major" (Michael believes Heinrich Bieber the more likely composer), a popular baroque revival.

"You're peeking," Karla chided above the almost toneless sounds of the piano.

"Nope." Michael was quite scrupulous about promises not to peek.

"Ah, Michael. You're so de*pendable*. *Peek*, for God's sake!"

Michael opened his eyes and looked at Karla seated at the piano. Sure enough, the instrument was almost exactly as he had imagined it, except there was a small tennis trophy among the items on top, and no photos. Not enough difference to occasion any real surprise.

Michael was not nearly as prepared for the sight of Karla. She was transfigured—more beautiful, he thought, than he had ever seen her. He moved closer and contemplated her face in profile. At first he reckoned how she manifested the soft, intense glow that accompanies a first pregnancy. Immediately after, he found himself thinking that hers was perhaps more the face of one who has been released from painful struggle by death.

She was both these things and more. Sitting at this old decaying piano, eyes focused on the sheet music in front of her, Karla exuded a trancelike beauty that had both relaxed and fixed her features, transforming her face into its innocent original of which all her other faces were but approximations.

"Beautiful. It's beautiful, Karla." Michael's words were both spontaneous and sincere, even though, on reflection, he realized that the music couldn't be beautiful. This was a travesty of the piece—first on the part of the instrument, whose strings and soundboard had been ravaged by humidity and neglect—but, equally, by Karla herself who added her own cacophonies to the original chaos by missing a note here, adding one there.

Her body was rocking to and fro, her hair sliding back and forth over her shoulders. Her fingers seemed absolutely sure of their mark, even when they missed. She appeared completely unaware of any defect in the piano or in her ability. Though the sounds were hardly pleasing, something about this manner of Karla's performance expressed the clarity, passion, and brilliance of a virtuoso.

Karla finished the piece, but neither she nor Michael seemed to realize it. For some moments each remained still, straining after the vanishing notes as one by one they returned to the fundament from out of which she had beckoned them.

11

The fading melody was replaced, not by silence as Michael would have wished, but by another periodically forgotten, yet always familiar, composition.

Had he a choice, he would have skipped over the prelude, but his memory was more compulsive than he himself had been in practice. (He would always move the needle ahead until the beginning of the fugue itself.) How long had it been since he had last played that record? He still owned it: Albert Schweitzer, *Bach Organ Music,* volume 2.

"The Prelude and Fugue in A Minor." "Fugue," Michael was now remembering, derives from the Latin *fuga* meaning "flight" or "a running away." He smiled. He had learned the meaning of the term long after he had used the fugue as a means of escape, and this was the first time he had recognized the coincidence of meaning and use.

What he admired most about the Bach fugues in general and about the "A Minor" in particular, he was thinking, was what might be called the quality of balanced complexity combined with a certain density of thematic content...

Michael is just being silly here. What he apparently is *not* remembering is that for all his vaunted expertise in the History of Ideas, he habitually resorts (as you can tell from that last phrase—that is, "balanced complexity combined with a certain density of thematic content") to the most clichéd musical doctrines. This is a consequence of the fact that most of his ideas concerning music (including that horrid "balanced complexity" phrase) come from having read record jackets.

Michael quite often lies to himself about the depth of his understanding. In this particular instance, a double lie is being told. On the one hand, he is often guilty of presuming himself to be assaying the deeper meanings of, say, the fugal process, forgetting how trite his doctrines are. Yet, were he to reflect on the matter, he would realize the views he sometimes expresses are painfully clichéd—at which point he would likely claim in his defense that he has never been very interested in the technicalities of music. But, and this is the source of the second lie, further reflection (which he is most unwilling to perform) would lead him to conclude that what appears to be a skimpy and overgeneralized knowledge of music, masks a far greater understanding and sensitivity than he wishes to recognize.

12

While the acquisition of knowledge is most often a function of interest, this is not always so. Thus, it is not unusual that in a person of otherwise broad intellectual attainments an area of apparent barrenness might be found. Such is Michael's seeming ignorance of the technicalities of music.

Aristotle, in agreement with his teacher Plato, claimed, "All men by nature desire to know." Add to this the catchy phrase of St. John (in the absence of which the porticoes of libraries would seem obscenely bare), "You shall know the truth and the truth shall make you free," and you have two fundamental truisms of humanistic culture. Of course, Aristotle's claim, as any teacher knows, is empirically untrue and requires no further comment. The doctrine of St. John is a worse offender—it is logically unsound.

Knowing certain sorts of truths will definitely bind us. Ignorance often keeps us free. Even the freedom to *learn*, to acquire knowledge, depends upon an antecedent ignorance. What most of us desire more than anything else is the sort of ignorance that insures we shall suffer neither the tedium nor the responsibility of knowing this or that.

There are two classes of ignorance. Only the first type, which comes from never having had the opportunity to learn, is painful or evil. The other sort is quite different. The ignorance of the educated person, for example, is a voluntary, often a cultivated, ignorance.

Michael can't afford to learn anything significant about music because that would threaten its efficacy as a buffer against the unpleasantries of his life. As we shall see, music—the "A Minor Fugue" above all—is one of his most important defenses. When our securing devices are working well, not only do we feel no need to examine them, we positively resist any such examination. This is Michael's attitude toward his defensive shield, toward the "A Minor," toward music itself.

Clichéd knowledge supports the aims of voluntary ignorance by providing us with some means of manipulating an area of our understanding while remaining insensitive to its threatening nuances. We can, for example, talk all we want about "balanced complexity" and "density of thematic content" without having to confront directly the subtle mysteries of music.

13

We mustn't overestimate the strategic success of voluntary ignorance. Accidents may often intervene. Shortly after his introduction to the "A Minor Fugue," Michael had by chance spent several hours on a plane seated next to the assistant director of the Evanston Symphony Orchestra. When, on impulse, he mentioned his love for the "A Minor," he was offered a lecture on the difference between "seeing" and "hearing" music. The assistant director claimed the fugal form to be an excellent illustration of the manner in which the eye can train the ear to hear formerly unrecognized complexities in music.

According to the assistant director, reading the score of a complex fugue (one having, say, four or more voices) teaches musical sensitivity. To the sensitive ear, the subject of a fugue (the theme) can remain audible even into the complex polyphonies that follow the rapid, overlapping statements of the theme (what the assistant director had called the *stretto*). The trained ear can even discern resonances of the principal theme in fugal "episodes" which do not explicitly contain the subject. Further—particularly in the case of Bach—mathematical puzzles associated with names and musical terms are often encoded into compositions. The ability to read musical notation would permit one to decipher the pieces and thereby increase one's enjoyment of them.

Michael tried as best he could to forget the nuances of this conversation. The valuable lesson he learned, of course, was to avoid the mastery of musical notation. The efficacy of the fugue might not survive any increased understanding. Its power, he knew, was resident in, and protected solely by, its obscurity.

14

We trust that, in the attempt to account for Michael's skewed musical interest, we shall not so complicate our story as to cancel the reader's interest altogether. We can assure you that, just as the musically sensitive ear can hear the principal theme announcing itself through the counterpoint of fugal voices, and even (according to the assistant director) into those musical episodes which have no explicit connection with the theme, so the sympathetic reader will be able to trace our apparently abandoned narrative thread among the alternative strands with which, for a variety of reasons, it must be entwined.

15

Michael's initial application of voluntary ignorance to the subject of music preceded by a number of years his encounter with the "A Minor Fugue." His first love affair, begun just prior to his senior year of high school, had been with a music student. Susan was a soprano, a lyric coloratura, with plans to study at the New England Conservatory of Music.

For all the time he had dated Susan, in spite of many opportunities, Michael had never heard her sing. It would have embarrassed him. He hated the coloratura style. Though he might have grudgingly praised such sopranos for their range and versatility, he was offended by the runs, trills, and other florid decorations characteristic of the coloratura's singing.

Susan was beautiful and he loved to look and to touch. But he could never fully enjoy the relationship for fear that one day, while walking in the park, or sharing a picnic lunch by the lake, or perhaps while emerging from a theatre matinee, she would suddenly burst into song.

Less than six days short of thirty years since he had last seen Susan (they were together the day she left for New England), while driving to Santa Fe, New Mexico, Michael turned on the car radio just in the middle of a coloratura's shrill lyrical run. He can't be said to have recognized Susan. But his hand did hesitate slightly before he changed the station, and when he wondered why it did, he found himself certain that it was her.

16

"Alphonse has loaned Bernard fifty dollars, which Bernard has not repaid by the designated date. Further, Bernard has claimed no knowledge of the debt. No written agreement exists. Alphonse must decide whether..."

Michael is currently in attendance at the annual meeting of the Eastern Division of the American Philosophical Association. It will be helpful at this point to realize that, in addition to his status as a professor of philosophy, he is also a seminary graduate. For it is the seminarian rather than the philosopher, the master of righteous indignation rather than the instructor in the arcane sciences of metaphysics and epistemology, who is about to rebel against the colleague currently chanting his bland irrelevancies to an audience too insipidly dull to conjure any more fruitful way to spend their time.

Michael listened with angry impatience, as he had throughout the day's sessions. There had been no mention of the recent student massacres (only a few days had passed since students at Kent State and Jackson State were killed by police and National Guardsmen), no recognition that an event of tremendous ethical import had occurred, an event upon which the dispute between Alphonse and Bernard had no bearing whatsoever.

He made considerably more noise than necessary while exiting the room. Had he known that the philosopher offering this prepackaged mix of fluff and nonsense would go on to become president of the association, he might have made even more racket. On the other hand, if Michael were prepared to believe that his terminally trite colleague would become president of the Eastern Division of the American Philosophical Association precisely *because* he had mastered the art of glossing sterile clichés, his would have been an awesomely silent retreat—a chastened katabasis in recognition of the futility of his profession.

17

He walked about the city for over two hours before stopping for dinner. The cafeteria was crowded and he stood for some moments looking for an empty table.

"Join me." The young woman smiled and beckoned Michael. "Thank you." Michael took the seat offered him and the two immediately began to talk. The woman—her name was Nancy—impressed him right away, for when he answered the inevitable question, the question professors of philosophy conversing with a new acquaintance dread most—that conversation-killing "And what do *you* do?"—she was neither intimidated, scornful, nor unduly impressed.

Nancy waited for Michael to finish his food, and they left the cafeteria together. He accompanied her to her apartment some few blocks away on what he hoped would turn out to be the mere pretense of seeing her safely home. As they walked he learned that she was a graduate student of music, presently studying the cello. By the time they reached her place ("You can have brandy with your coffee," she said, "but I don't drink"), Michael had also learned that this young student of the cello was twenty-two and "just barely single" (she was to be married in a month).

"Have you ever gone out with a black woman before?" Michael must have looked startled because Nancy smiled and quickly added, "Don't tell me you didn't notice that I am black?"

He had noticed. Indeed, he had taken that careful inventory all white men take of black women: hands, hair, mouth, rear end. He very nearly told her the reason for this particular catalog. But his courage failed him.

18

"Now in the beginnin' they was two kinds of white people—one bunch was human like us, but the other ones was Demon Pretenders..."

Mr. Tanny is speaking. A Sunday school teacher at the Calvary Baptist Church in Shreveport, Louisiana, he fancied himself a most knowledgeable layman and was often tempted to stray from the subject of the lesson in order to rehearse grander theological themes. One Sunday, after having dutifully elaborated upon the Sunday school manual's verbal picture of the mawkish, effeminate Jesus performing some miracle or other, Mr. Tanny found time to wander into what Michael would later learn were cosmogonical questions—questions of origins.

The following account will be given exactly as Michael would have done had he been able to muster the courage. We can assure you, however, that Mr. Tanny did not actually speak in this fashion. He had something of a regional accent, of course, but his grammar was quite sound, and he always pronounced the g's in -ing words.

Michael's translation of Mr. Tanny's words into the cruder form of the Southern patois would not have been vindictive. Indeed, he would merely have been yielding to an unconscious bias that most people share. When we hear someone speak ungrammatically and with a vulgar accent, we presume the words lack wisdom. Conversely, when we remember something insane or stupid, we tend to remember it (at least in our surface memory) as having been said ungracefully.

"Nobody knew 'bout 'em but the Lord God, and when he saw all the mischief they was causin' and how they was leadin' the true white folks astray, then he sent the flood. He made sure Noah didn't put no demons on board his ark, so they was all outside when the flood came. When them demons saw the water pourin' down the mountains and the rivers floodin' their banks they was scaird near t' death. Just 'fore the waters hit 'em, they screamed to high heaven. They was so scaird that the hair on their heads stood right up on end like wire brushes, and it stayed that way.

"Now, their skin was turned all black by the mud, but since they was runnin' and crawlin' 'round on the ground, tryin' to git away from the water and the mud, the soles of their feet and the palms of their hands didn't git nearly so dark." (Michael remembered wondering about their knees. Shouldn't they be lighter, too?)

"When they crawled out of the mud it was somewheres in Africa, and since they was black God called 'em niggers. The word 'nigger' means 'black.' (This was Michael's first experience with etymology.) Now they wasn't much to eat 'cept bananas, so that's what they lived on mostly. But niggers aint too smart. They didn't know how to peel them bananas, ya see, so they just took to suckin' 'em out of the peelin' and eatin' 'em whole. That's why nigger lips is so big and pooched out.

"'Fore the flood we couldn't tell the difference between the true whites and the Demon Pretenders. But now we can see it real clear. Niggers is black with hair like Brillo soap pads and lips stickin' out. That's how they was punished for pretendin' to be somethin' they wasn't."

At this point Presty (Charles Preston Martin III, who had just moved to Shreveport from Hattiesburg, Mississippi) raised his hand just like in regular school, which seemed to make Mr. Tanny feel important, almost like a real teacher. Mr. Tanny sat up straighter in his chair, prepared to elaborate upon this or that point of his account. He said, "Yeah, Preston" and Presty, a look of exaggerated concentration on his face, and in a voice that would have passed for sincere with anyone who didn't know him well (and since he had just come from Hattiesburg, no one did yet) asked: "Mr. Tanny, why is it all niggers are high-assed?"

There was silence except for Tommy Watts who, Michael thought, was probably as incapable of suppressing a giggle at thirty-five as he had been at age ten. Presty wouldn't relent: "My Daddy says all niggers have high asses, specially the women. Why's that?"

Michael doesn't remember how, or whether, Mr. Tanny handled Presty's question.

Michael would never believe himself to have taken any of this seriously. Nonetheless, as he and Nancy were talking in the cafeteria, he found himself looking at her hands. They were strong hands, but delicate, with carefully manicured nails. Michael was disturbed by the dark lines in her palms. For several moments he struggled unsuccessfully against a thought which had begun whimsically but had been rapidly transformed into an obsession: he wanted to place Nancy's hands under a tap, to scrub them with strong soap and a brush; he wanted to see if he could retrieve any traces of primordial mud from the lines in her palms. He wondered if she would let him try.

And later at Nancy's apartment, as he would watch the light shine through her hair (she had a classic sixties Afro), curious about its texture, hungry for its odor, for the taste of it, anticipating the feeling of his hands grasping the sides and back of it as he rocked Nancy's head, the head of this Demon Pretender, against a pillow, Michael (a part of him, on his behalf) would offer rueful thanks to Mr. Tanny for the intensity of this moment, and for the moment to come.

19

"...and yes, I've gone out with black women." Michael caught the look of disappointment just before she hid it behind a coy wink.

"Have you ever been *with* a black woman?"

Michael felt obliged to lie. "No. Is that important?"

"I guess not, except I've never been with a white guy."

"Will I be the first?" Michael asked.

Another wink. "Brandy, Michael?"

Michael barely managed to nod his assent before he was overcome (for only an instant, but in that instant he was afraid that he would lose consciousness) by a shivering sensation. The shiver culminated in a mild spasm that made his arms and legs twitch noticeably. He would have been completely unable to explain the sensation since he had immediately suppressed the image that caused it.

The image formed from out of his memory, the image which never quite emerged into consciousness, the image which, had it become conscious, he could have easily dismissed with a smile (but which, remaining below the level of consciousness, wrought slightly more serious consequences) was this:

Nigger Mouth—lips, tongue, and teeth. No face or eyes. The mouth was fastening upon the end of an unpeeled banana, its vacuum lips positioning themselves, the fruit about to be drawn from its skin, just about to slide between the lips, to be dissolved immediately, completely, in an ocean of acid-spit.

20

"Why the cello?" Michael wanted to make conversation, but was appalled when he found himself asking such a mundane question. Nancy's response saved him, however. Leaning forward, eyes wide and intense, she clapped her hands together. Her reply came immediately, without the slightest pause for reflection. She didn't speak at all as if she were rehearsing a response she had given before, but more as if she had been waiting for a long time to be asked just this and wanted to answer right away before the question was withdrawn.

"It's a good match, the cello and me. We make a perfect pair. When I studied the piano I felt completely intimidated by the size of that instrument. And I felt that I dominated the violin. The cello fits me perfectly and our combined mass and form give my music roots, and a ground. Look at Piatigorsky; he's as good as Casals, but because he is so very tall he overshadows his instrument. The cello fits Casals. In fact—this worries me sometimes—have you noticed how in his later years Pablito is beginning to look more and more like a cello?"

Nancy took a breath. She hadn't even looked closely at Michael to see if he were interested in what she had said. "And though I would never say this to anyone but a relatively unmusical stranger (how did she know?), it is significant that the cello is held between the legs. The music is focused in one's center of procreativity, as my yoga teacher calls it." Nancy was touching her "center of procreativity" with both hands, looking directly at Michael now as she continued. "The notes emanate from the source of life itself. I feel like the Mother of Sound when I play. And don't think it doesn't feel real good sometimes"—Nancy's hands were moving slowly up and down her inner thighs—"especially those notes sustained in the lower registers."

Later, lying between her legs, his head resting on her center of procreativity, Michael wondered if Nancy had compared him with her "principal instrument." How could it be otherwise? He raised himself in order to see her face. For some moments the giggle of the young student of the cello danced with Michael's smile, then chased his laughter into the quieter regions of sleep.

21

Michael's obsession with musical ignorance is fatefully tied to his impulsive decision, at age eighteen and three-quarters, to tear up his draft card and mail a piece of it to each of the members of his local draft board. This action almost led to his imprisonment, but after a series of compromises on the part of the draft officials (and in fairness to the facts of the matter, a slight but painful compromise by Michael himself), it was decided that he should serve two years as an orderly in a terminal cancer ward in a Chicago hospital.

During this period Michael would fill every vacant moment, on duty and off, with reading whatever he could find in libraries, book stores and on the shelves of his friends. By the time he got to Cervantes's *Don Quixote* and read of how the noble knight, owing to "little sleep and much reading, his brains got so dry that he lost his wits," Michael had flirted with a similar fate.

One of the first discoveries he made at the hospital was that the dying occasioned by cancer, the only dying about which he would gain significant knowledge, was usually accompanied by extremely bad odors. As a defense against the awful smell of decaying flesh, he would sing or hum to himself. Once he heard a recording of Odetta singing "The House of The Rising Sun," and for some weeks he used that song as a barrier against the odors. As long as he could keep the melody running through his head, he could successfully fight his nausea.

One evening, listening to a classical music program on Chicago's WFMT, Michael encountered Bach's "Prelude and Fugue in A Minor." From that point on it was to be the "A Minor" that would shield him against those special odors that so effectively advertise the process of decay.

Michael had no idea why music ought serve so well as a defense against odors. He recalled Keats much-rehearsed lines, "Heard melodies are sweet, but those unheard are sweeter... / Pipe to the spirit ditties of no tone." Keats would have thought that the toneless ditty that Michael sent through his head each day in preparation for his hospital chores was a mathematical exercise, a set of abstract permutations that made him concentrate his consciousness beyond the world of sensations in a realm of inaudible melodies, invisible colors, and odors without scent.

As ignorant as Michael was, and intended to remain, of the intricacies of music theory, however, he instinctively knew that Keat's understanding was foolish.

22

It wasn't the first thing he would do in the morning. He began his day by reading. He would have read for at least three hours before performing the ritual. Exactly at 7:30 A.M. he would move the needle to the appropriate spot on the record. Sometimes it would take a second effort, but usually he was able to avoid the prelude and begin with the fugue itself.

He would then sit on the floor by the console phonograph and close his eyes. As the thematic subject was announced, he would concentrate, sometimes holding his breath, waiting for the answer and the counter subject to present themselves. By the time the melodic line was extended beyond its initial announcement and the thematic development had begun, he would have entered a familiar reverie. Transitions in the fugue would carry the subject from one key to another repeating fragments of the principal theme. Soon a cascade of fugal voices challenged, interrupted, immersed the subject theme in counterpoint while at the same time augmenting it, intensifying its interest, and adding to its seductive, tantalizing mystique.

23

The primary distinction between living and dying is found in the modulated and accelerated rhythms of the latter. Dying is the thematic response to life, its counterpoint. To see the process of decay accelerated, squeezed into a few weeks or months, is to witness the normal inimical process unobscured by extended duration. Cancer victims are models of accelerated decay.

More than anything else, death is an embarrassment. The dying individual is ashamed because he must advertise decay to the discomfort of his intimates. Those nearest the victim are embarrassed just as are the fully clothed disturbed by the nudity of others when they realize that it advertises how they themselves must appear beneath their protective garments.

So much, but very little more, Michael understood. He played the "A Minor Fugue" (without the prelude) every morning exactly at 7:30 A.M., immediately prior to leaving for the hospital. Then he spent the day adding a balance of life to the rotting organs whose absent odor he endured. Had he not done this, each and every day, he knew that the rhythms of his own being would accelerate, that he would begin to resonate with death. He would then start to decompose rapidly—his senses and sensibilities, if not his very flesh.

24

Michael's commitment to the "A Minor Fugue" is motivated by much more than the necessity of surviving the unpleasantries of service to the terminally ill. The accidental correlation of that piece with the odors of refuse and death has its own counterpoint in the equally contingent association of the "A Minor" with Albert Schweitzer's distinctive performance of it.

Michael had known about Schweitzer long before the name of Johann Sebastian Bach had any more than a vague meaning for him. So he had quite naturally selected Schweitzer's recording of the magical fugue as his permanent companion.

And, if the introduction of yet another contingency will not burden this narrative overmuch, it should be said that the efficacy for Michael of the particular connection between Schweitzer and J. S. Bach was augmented by the relationship, as accidental as the others, between Schweitzer and Johann Wolfgang von Goethe (a connection which, even at the risk of tedious emendation we are forced to add, Michael does not now and will perhaps never fully understand).

25

Shortly after beginning his service as a hospital orderly, Michael had inscribed the following words at the beginning of one of his journals: "Goal: to read 1500 pages (*significant* pages) every month (18,000 pages/year—50 pages a day)." His sense of significant reading could certainly be questioned, but he did read the contracted amount that first year.

His reading interests were almost wholly undisciplined, so his selection of Albert Schweitzer's *On The Edge of the Primeval Forest* immediately after completing Goethe's *Faust*, Parts I and II was wholly accidental.

Everyone who reads has to read *Faust* eventually, and one's response to it is determined by the degree of one's susceptibility to the Romantic impulse. Michael was immune to Romanticism and so had seen in this putatively classic poem little more than a poet's preening arrogance infusing the degeneracy of his principal character.

But everyone reads *Faust*.

The problem of the poem (to those whose memory needs refreshing or who may have been so far spared exposure to the work) is that Faust, former seeker after all knowledge, contracts with Mephistopheles for an everlasting life of ephemeral pleasures.

Faust requests of Mephistopheles:

Show me fruits which rot ere ever gathered from the tree,
And trees which daily bloom anew!

Mephistopheles had promised Faust that as long as he ate only of the tree of transient fruit, he could enjoy the unrepeatable intensities of life. If, however, he were to tire, and say to the moment, "Hold thou art so fair!"—if he even once attempted to continue his delight beyond the immediate moment—then he would forfeit his soul. But as Mephistopheles knew, or thought he knew, unless Faust could stay the moment, hold fast to it, no salvation was possible. Mephistopheles intended that the road leading to salvation was to be made Faust's private path to hell.

The conclusion of Goethe's poem presents the elder Faust in a heroic endeavor to clear a marsh in order to provide land for the building of a large city.

> A marsh extends along the mountain-chain
> That poisons what so far I've been achieving;
> Were I that noisome pool to drain,
> 'T would be the highest, last achieving.
> ....
> Then might I say, that moment seeing:
> "Ah, linger on, thou art so fair!"
> The traces of my earthly being
> Can perish not in aeons—they are there!
> That lofty moment I now feel in this:
> I now enjoy the highest moment's bliss.

These were Faust's last words. In the final act before his death, when he enjoyed "the moment's highest bliss," he anticipated the fulfillment of a vision and the enrichment of life resulting from it.

Mephistopheles thinking he had won, began to savor the delicious consequences of Faust's damning "Hold...."

But Faust is not damned. The heavenly hosts, whom Mephistopheles will now learn are as high above the demands of morality and promise-keeping as is the demonic horde beneath them, cheat him of his hard-won victim. How?

Michael had seen the answer right away. Faust said "Hold" to a special kind of moment, one that by no means concerned aesthetic pleasure, but was instead a moment of anticipation, of longing for some ultimately unrealizable but always compelling future. Faust did not wish to repeat the enjoyment of this or that fleshy pleasure. He wished, rather, to submit himself to an unrealizable future goal.

Mephistopheles was cheated of his prey because Goethe didn't vouchsafe him the insight that any fool (any unromantic fool, certainly) possesses—namely, besides the life of radical pleasure-seeking, which never needs repeat a single pleasure, and beyond the life patterned by a conservative, unimaginative hedonism, which settles into a routine round of pleasures, there is life in service to an Ideal, life in obedience to what Plato called

Eros, the desire for absolute fulfillment, the desire for the realization of a Grand Design. One may hold to such a desire only in
the absence of any realization.

Of course, life in submission to Eros is akin to the aesthetic life of transient enjoyments in the sense that both involve a
continuing process. But life in service to an Ideal is without
momentary satisfactions; nor is it ever complete. An Ideal
lures one on, but never satisfies. Noble actions, aesthetic
objects, historical events, are means to an unrealizable end. As
such, they are little more than irrelevant consequences, by-
products, detritus. Goethe (with what Michael thought to be a
cloying bathos) had named his Ideal...the Eternal Feminine.

As Michael was never given to Romanticism in any form,
his own sense of the world was quite different from that of both
the damned and the redeemed Faust. His life was not a process
of moving from this to that transient pleasure; neither was it
that of approaching ever nearer to an ideal. Goethe's Eternal
Feminine, therefore, unlike almost any other female, left him
absolutely cold.

26

Michael learned one of his most treasured lessons in his high school chemistry class. Indeed, he had something like a mystical experience when he encountered the subject of constants, those numerical quantities held to be unchanged throughout any given set of physical transformations or mathematical operations. Paradoxically, these constants, the truly important ones at least, are little more than fuzzy approximations. For example, Avogadro's number (the occasion of Michael's epiphany) is the number of molecules in the gram molecular weight of a gas. The value Michael first learned was $6.06...x \ 10^{23}$. Five years later Avogadro's number had been refined to $6.023...x \ 10^{23}$.

The figure can never be exact. Even if we were to count the molecules one by one, there would be differences in the numbers of molecules in the gram molecular weights of two separate gases. And even if by chance they were the same, the molecules would be of slightly different size and mass. The world dissolves into statistical probabilities, and the very things we believe are *constant* are precisely those things that are always changing.

Life is fuzzy and approximate, filled with probabilities and chance. There are no laws, only likelihoods. Living involves neither a process of transitory pleasures nor of approaching ever nearer to a goal. One does not anticipate an ideal number when adding another decimal onto Avogadro's number. One simply advertises the futility of all longings for perfection.

27

Soon after his first encounter with the concept of numerical constants, Michael began associating them with the closest of his friends.

This activity will seem much less exotic if one recalls that Pythagoras, the founder of mathematical speculation in the West, was convinced that everything has a unique number associated with it (the expression, "I've got your number," derives from the Pythagoreans). Chemical formulas determining the relationship of atoms and molecules in various compounds have something of the same basis. Thus, Michael's hobby of associating certain people with numerical constants, especially since he keeps the exercise private, is really not so very bizarre.

Initially, he had associated Karla with Planck's constant, h, which expresses the ratio of the energy of one quantum of radiation to the frequency of the radiation. The numerical quantity is expressed in erg-seconds and is (approximately) equal to $6.624... \times 10^{-27}$. However, after her company manifested themselves the designated constant had to be changed. He chose, for reasons one can easily appreciate, the "fine structure constant," α, which is used to calculate the strength of the interactions among photons, electrons, and muons.

This was the most complex constant in Michael's admittedly limited understanding of physics and physical chemistry. The complexity of this expression derives from its combining four other constants: the velocity of light, c; the electron charge, e; Planck's constant, h; and the value measuring the permeability of free space, m_o. The fine structure constant is expressed:

$$\alpha = m_o c e^2 / 2h$$

Here is a grand instance of a number expressed in an interminable series of decimal places, endlessly dribbling out into the void. Ultimately, there are no things, only processes ever not quite realizing themselves.

Michael was quite content with the fact that one could never know with any finality. He didn't really care about the total number of molecules in a gram molecular weight of a gas. He was far more interested in the insistent particularity of each individual molecule, each particular atom, and beyond this, in the insistence of each particle in each atom, and so on, and so on. Michael's discovery of numerical constants freed him from the sense that his life was hemmed in by fleshless ideals. Life is an approximate aggregate sum of all approximative processes.

This is what the "A Minor" finally came to mean to him. Bach's fugue was a complex flow of distinctly autonomous notes measured one against the other and against the tide of life, notes performed and reperformed each morning (just at 7:30 A.M.) by an artist whose commitment to the insistent particularities of experience sent the sounds tumbling forth in an endless array to slow the rabid acceleration of life that is decay.

28

Albert Schweitzer gave Michael far more than an early appreciation of Bach. He taught him how to avoid falling into the Faustian trap. Schweitzer had given up the pursuit of Ideals in philosophy and music and journeyed to Africa. Had he not studied medicine, traveled to Africa and taken up the White Man's Burden, an antelope could not have nudged its head into a window of his Lambaréné study and eaten most of the manuscript pages of the third and final volume of his *Philosophy of Civilization.* Schweitzer's never published work, which came finally to nothing more than antelope shit, was perhaps more fertile than most philosophical endeavors. It was, at least for Michael, a cherished work.

Schweitzer had yielded to the desire to meet individual sufferings one at a time, abandoning the grand vision of transforming the earth. Faust had begun as a physician, treating his fellows one by one, but had finally become an engineer—a Grand Schemer. Schweitzer had moved away from the grand designs of philosophy to take up the role of a one-person-at-a-time medical practitioner.

Here is the dilemma as Michael, after having read Goethe and Schweitzer, often conceived it: Thousands of people are lined up outside a hastily erected tent in the jungle, awaiting inoculation against malaria. Many are dying even as they wait. Manpower and experience are in short supply. Meanwhile, mosquitoes breed in a nearby swamp, swarming the populace as they wait for promised relief.

What is to be done? If those who are performing the inoculations stop long enough to clear the swamp and destroy the mosquitoes' breeding pool, hundreds will die while they wait for medicine. If the swamp is not cleared, there will be an ever renewing source of infection and not enough time to treat all who require it. Hundreds will die.

The world should be a harmony of the one-on-one individuals and the Grand Schemers. As an adolescent Michael had sometimes felt himself something of the both/and variety, one of the rare individuals who would be able to accomplish significant tasks both great and small. After his encounter with Avogadro's number, however, and later, after reflecting upon the Schweitzer/Faust dilemma, he realized that he would have to make a choice.

29

His choice was made in New Haven, Connecticut, the day after Schweitzer's death. (The date was September 16, 1965. It was a Thursday.) Michael was walking past a downtown boutique the windows of which were accented by caricature dolls of famous men. There, snuggled in the arms of mannequins, and draped at their feet, were Beethoven and Chopin, Napoleon and Caesar, Rudolph Valentino and Albert Schweitzer.

Michael was overcome by the insensitivity of such a display in the wake of Schweitzer's death. He proceeded directly inside and addressed the sales clerk.

"I'm sorry you are offended," she had said.

"You *will* remove it," Michael threatened.

"I'll be glad to speak to the owner," the bemused clerk had said.

"I will return in ten minutes," he said.

When he walked up to the window about twenty minutes later, the doll had been removed. He was pleased. No great deed he thought, but a *significant* action.

They could add up...

30

Michael thought it strange that Karla's performance of Pachelbel's "Canon" had led him to think of his "A Minor." A canon is,
of course, little more than a simple fugue and one might easily
account for the association in this manner. But this was impossible. There was only one thing that could make him recall
that fugue.

The "A Minor" was consciously selected to serve as a
defense against the decay of the dying. Faced with that decay,
with the smell of it, the shield would go up. Were he to hear
the music it could not lead him to recall the odors, since the
defense against them would already be in place. For him, as he
was doing now, to recall the piece and to allow (he could hardly
have prevented this) its toneless melodies to flow through his
mind could mean only one thing: The insensible odor of death
was in the air.

31

They were sitting on the large, naked sofa, Michael's head in Karla's lap.

"What are you thinking?"

"I'm planning your concert tour."

"What are you *really* thinking?"

"I'm thinking about you, sort of...and about me, I guess."

"Tell me. Tell me about me-sort-of and you-I-guess."

Michael closed his eyes, then opened them. "Do you remember when I lectured in Hong Kong?" As a response, Karla placed her fingers on each side of Michael's forehead and gently pulled upward molding his face into a caricature of the Chinese. He laughed out loud.

Now, Michael was not thinking about Hong Kong or his lecture trip. He was, of course, thinking about the "A Minor Fugue," about Schweitzer and Goethe, about the obscenity of accelerated life, about odors and death. He is not sure why he chose to speak about something else, though it certainly isn't unnatural, and for the most part completely harmless, to misrepresent the content of one's reveries when challenged to reveal them.

"I was trying to find my way to the Star Ferry. It was early morning and I had an appointment on the Kowloon side. The shops were just opening. I was on a side street.... It was almost like an alley, narrow, but quite clean. There was a large truck parked at an intersection just ahead of me. A man had gotten out of the truck, gone around to the back and removed the carcass of a hog. After he threw it over his shoulder, he reached inside and removed a large sack which, I imagined, contained the hog's entrails."

"This is a delightful story, Michael. It truly is. Which part, I am presently wondering, is about you-I-guess and which part about me-sort-of."

"I'll get to that." Michael's reply was rather impatient. "The fellow took the hog carcass, half-carrying, half-dragging the sack, to a butcher shop a few yards away from his truck. This guy was *huge*. Alongside all the other Cantonese he looked like a giant. The muscles in his legs and arms were striated and extremely well developed. I had never seen a Chinese with muscles before. He hadn't lost any of the suppleness and poise that most Chinese possess. But those muscles made him appear some sort of freak.

"There was something in his face, his posture, the manner of his walk that commanded attention. And...I remember that his hair was much longer than one is accustomed to see among Hong Kong males and cut in a kind of Dutch boy style.

"I walked up to the front of the truck and waited for the Hog Man's return. I saw him come out of the shop. He removed the leather sheet that had protected his shoulder from the bristles of the hog. As he rounded the front of the truck I could smell him. The combination of pig and man odor was almost sweet.

"I had to see his eyes.

"I was standing close to the door of the truck. Too close, I remember thinking. As he reached for the door handle I saw his face. I looked at his eyes. He stood still a moment, but not, as I first thought, in order to engage me. He neither smiled nor frowned. He waited.... He allowed me to...witness him. His eyes were open wide...not to see but *to be seen*. I doubt that he even noticed any difference between me and his fellow Chinese. He merely noted the presence of yet another witness. He paused, then he entered his truck and left."

Karla shifted Michael's head on her lap and offered an exaggerated sigh. "So far I'd rather be the pig."

Michael was not paying attention to her. He continued his account as if she were not present. "He seemed so out of place, yet so congruent, so much what he was meant to be. As if he were a special act of creation. As if God had said, 'Let Us now make a Hong Kong Hog Man—and this fellow was the result.'

"I don't know why that came to mind. It's just that he seemed so...special. So..." Michael wanted to say so oblivious to his surroundings, so absolutely indifferent to the feelings and judgments of others, so submerged in his present task...so unutterably alone, but his voice trailed into silence.

He was mildly embarrassed but wasn't sure whether his discomfort was due to the fact that Karla would certainly find the story pointless or because, as he had gradually come to recognize in the telling of the tale, his parable of the Hong Kong Hog Man was so revealing of his present sense of Karla and of himself. He closed his eyes again and pretended to drift off to sleep.

"So, Michael," Karla said, shaking him, "You were thinking about you and me?"

Michael's eyes remained closed as he spoke, smiling. "Sort of...I guess."

32

"Let me speak to Adrienne." Michael moved his hand down from Karla's forehead, closing her eyes with his fingers. He removed his hands and waited for the brow to wrinkle slightly, for the eyelids to flutter, then open...and for Adrienne's first words.

Nothing happened. He repeated the ritual. Nothing. He began to feel desperate. "Adrienne? Adrienne!"

He leaned close to Karla's ear: "Adrienne...Adrienne... Adrienne...Adrienne." As he sounded the name over and over, his voice swelled and softened, falling into a rolling cadence, obscenely suggesting the rhythms of sex. He was too caught up in his desire to see Adrienne again to be surprised at the dimensions of his relief when she finally came.

"What do *you* want?"

He released his breath in a loud sigh. "Hello, Adrienne. It's been a while."

"I don't want to waste time talking to you. I've got better things to do."

"What *have* you been doing. What were you doing just now?"

"That's none of your concern. What do you want?"

"I need to ask you something."

"Talk to Zenaida. She's the expert. So she thinks."

"You're the only one who knows the others. They don't really know you."

"I could tell them. Would you like that?" Adrienne's voice was scornful.

"What would happen if you told them about the company? Would they listen?"

Adrienne laughed. "They wouldn't have a choice."

"What...how much does Karla know?"

"She thinks you're crazy." Adrienne laughed again. "I *know* you are." She thinks she's humoring you. She can't figure out what goes on when she's asleep, but she does *not* think that little people are running around inside her."

Michael knew that Adrienne was taunting him but decided to ignore her challenge. "Listen, Adrienne, I have to know something."

"What?"

He wasn't sure exactly how to ask his question, nor was he altogether clear why he wanted to ask it. He had long been certain of the only correct answer. "Which of you is most real? You or Karla? The others..."

Adrienne turned her face away from Michael, but too late. He had already seen her fear. "Don't be a fool. You're not a fool. Don't be one. I won't tell you that."

"You can't?"

"I *won't*."

"Listen, Adrienne. You need to tell me. It's for..."

She didn't speak. It was her action that interrupted Michael. Her body stiffened as she stretched herself across the width of the bed. Her face remained insolent and cold, but her eyes were pleading. Michael knew what had to come next. He knew Adrienne was silently demanding what she always demanded: to be undressed under angry protest, to be held down and forced to yield herself. There was never any choice. Adrienne would not, perhaps *could not* leave until she had reenacted the violent ritual of her birth, until she had received the aborted love of her creator. Michael was as compelled as she.

33

Let the ceremony begin.

First, the taunting: "You think you'll get to lick my pussy, don't you?" That will *never* happen, you sick sleaze."

His ritual response: reaching for her, sliding his hands onto her wrists, flattening his body against hers.

Her mock struggle: "You can't! You won't...get..."

He released one arm and, as Adrienne gouged his face with her free hand, he unbuttoned her blouse, pulling her bra upward, exposing both breasts. He was feeling sick but persuaded himself that it was only the ceremonial nausea he always had to feel.

But this time the pain was too severe. He had to escape. He raised himself up and moved away from Adrienne, mumbling first to himself, then aloud: "Adrienne...please don't make me do this.... Don't...let me do this."

Adrienne's face, still distorted with anger, now showed signs of panic. Her next utterance sounded less like mockery than supplication, "You think you'll run your cock up my cunt.... No chance, you slime."

Michael got up from the bed. Terrified, Adrienne screamed the incantation she knew would keep him bound: "Take back my name!" She then reached for Michael, grabbing his waist and pulling him back onto the bed ("Take back my name!"). She unfastened his belt and unzipped his pants. Reaching inside, she tugged at his limp flesh ("Take back my name!"), rubbing it desparately with both hands. He resisted, sustained by shame and anger, but yielded finally to the warm wetness of her mouth ("Take back my name!" "Take back my name!").

When he was made ready, Adrienne spread herself full length on the bed and, in a final attempt to salvage their gruesome, crumbling rite, cupped both hands fast between her legs, saying, "First, take back my name!" Then, in a reluctant assault upon liturgical form, she began to cry, almost silently.

Michael might have freed himself had he tried, but he was his victim's victim still. The deed was as good as done. He moved toward Adrienne, cruelly twisted her hands apart and raised her arms above her head.

The perfection of power promises the fullest obscenity. For these next moments Michael will seek that perfection, that fulfillment. Reveling and groveling in the space between those extremes, he will both mock and imitate his own perverse Creator, will curse and praise Him. And through this foul worship he will, as so many times before, offer his soul to One Who has as many times accepted and discarded it.

34

When it was over, Adrienne turned away from Michael. Neither spoke. Some minutes passed. Michael was trying to decide whether he could safely leave the room when he heard (it was *Karla's* voice!), "I'll give you Collie."

"Wait! Adrienne!.... Karla!" *Let me speak to Karla!*" He was in no mood for Collie Mackovich.

Too late. Adrienne's (Karla's?) chin tightened. Her lips compressed, her mouth, now no longer hers, opened and Collie's tongue began to play back and forth between her lips and teeth. Her body was shaking. She grabbed Michael by the arm and tugged at him, then commanded, "Get on the floor."

Collie had taken a pillow and placed it under her backside and was lying spread-legged, rubbing the hair between her legs with her open hand. "Hurry, God damn it. Hurry. In me. In me. In me." Collie was bouncing up and down on the pillow and would have looked silly to Michael had he not become absorbed in her noisy obscenities. She reached up for Michael's penis, pulling him down on top of her. "In me, *hurry*."

She was running wet. The pillow was soaked. Michael was riding Collie as she rocked and bounced and demanded: "Fuck it! Hurry! Deeper! In me! Fuck it! Deeper! On this *floor!*"

This time it was Michael who slept. When his eyes opened he was alone. He looked up and saw Karla—no, it was Honey—sitting on the edge of the bed. She was humming tunelessly and seemed to be examining her feet. When she noticed Michael move, she stopped her humming.

"Hi, Honey."

"Hello, Mithter Michael. You don't play with me anymore."

"I've been away."

"Are you back?"

"For a little while."

Michael had gotten up from the floor and was sitting on the bed. He was always overcome by a sense of forlornness when he talked to Honey. In the more than two years since he met her, she had grown to be eight years old. She said her birthday was in May. Honey must have been born eight years before when Karla was seventeen. Something had happened during her last year in high school (perhaps on her graduation night) that had made her carve out a bit of herself for safe-keeping. That small fragment grew to be the five year old child who had introduced herself to Michael as "Honey."

Honey asked Michael if he would like to hear a story. He couldn't bring himself to refuse her. She told the story of Rapunzel, trapped by a wicked witch in a secluded tower.

When Honey would arrive at the refrain, "Rapunthel! Rapunthel! Let down your golden hair," she would cup her hands around her mouth and look up at the ceiling. Each time she finished the plea, she would turn to him for approval and laugh her shy repressed laugh.

Honey told the story in all the excruciating detail of which children are capable. When she was done, Michael applauded. Honey grinned and clapped her hands in unison with his. Half whimsically, Michael asked, "Do you know the story of Rumpel-stiltskin, Honey?" He suppressed a smile as he tried to imagine how "Rumpelstiltskin" would sound coming from Honey's lips.

"No thir. But will you tell me?"

"Next time I visit, OK?"

"Do you promith?"

"I promise, Honey."

35

Karla was back. She was agitated.

"Adrienne is acting a bit strange," Michael said as lightly as he could.

"Look, Michael. This is a game for me. It relaxes me sometimes. Provided you and Adrienne don't fight. That's what happened, isn't it?" Karla paused and put her head between her hands. "*Listen* to me! You've got me making comments on my inner sanctum. God, Michael..." Karla made some effort to calm herself, then asked in a forced casual manner, "Did you see them all?"

"Not Zenaida. I didn't bring a clarinet."

"Getting old, Michael? You made it with Collie and Adrienne. That was enough? Or did you assault poor Honey, too?" Michael wondered if Karla's anger was her own.

"I needed to talk to Adrienne. To ask her a question."

"Listen to yourself. I thought I was supposed to be the psychotic. You certainly couldn't tell it from this conversation. What is it you need to know? You don't suppose *I* could help you, do you? No, of course not. Who, after all, am I? Shit, Michael. *Shit!*"

Michael knew he shouldn't say this, but he felt compelled. "I asked Adrienne which of you was real—you or she."

"*What?*" Karla's expression was fixed somewhere between fear and contempt. "And you call *me* cold. You have no feelings at all. None at all.... *None!* What is it? Are you writing a paper on selfhood, or some such shit, and you need the inside story?" Karla stared at him with what he could only interpret as detached contempt. He knew she had distanced herself from him finally this time.

"I'm sorry, Karla. Let's talk about something else."

In response Karla grabbed her shirt and pulled it over her head, throwing it on the floor. Then she took Michael's hands and placed them on her breasts. "Who do these belong to?"

Karla's flesh seemed cold. Unfamiliar. He didn't want this conversation, but he didn't know how to get out of it. "Look, Karla..."

"Answer me! *Whose*?" Karla was almost hysterical.

"Yours. Look, I apologized, Karla. Can't we forgo the penance?"

"Say my name. Whose breasts are these, Michael?"

"They're yours, Karla. Both of them. And they are real gems I can tell you. Now, that's it, OK?"

He started to leave the bed, but Karla touched his arm. She spoke less sternly now. "Always, Michael? Are they always mine. Or just for now?"

He knew he should be silent or just walk away, but he wouldn't. He knew that whatever was happening, he had to carry it through. He turned to Karla and grabbed her by the shoulders. "*Are* they always yours? Are they, damn you?" Now he was shaking her. "Are they?"

Karla smiled, almost submissively, but the anger was still in her face. She removed his hands and slid down on her back, pulling the covers up over her shoulders. Her eyes were open and she seemed to be staring out beyond the ceiling. Michael dreaded hearing her reply, not because he feared the answer; he knew the only answer she could give. What he dreaded was the sound of her voice which in his imagination he was now hearing exactly as it would be. Her response, when it came, was layered by resonances born of the tense harmony of her whole inner chorus: "No," she said.

They said.

36

In any rogue's gallery of mythical figures, the Arimaspi would hold a privileged place. A tribe of coarse-bodied creatures with extremely distasteful habits and demeanor, these brutes were responsible, among many other perverse things, for stealing the gold of Apollo. Pursued by griffins, the half-lion, half-eagle guardians of the Apollonian treasure, the Arimaspi were greatly handicapped by the fact that they possessed but a single eye.

Literally, *only one eye!* This solitary eye was connected to a gold chain and worn like an amulet, first by one then another of the group as circumstances demanded.

With unvoiced apologies to Michael, we are forced to intervene here in order to assure those who have some knowledge of the myth of the Arismaspi that we too realize that there is no evidence in the classical literature to support his version. Both Herodotus and Aeschylus tell of Scythian creatures "born with one eye," Herodotus providing the information that the Scythic word *arima* means "one" and *spû* means "eye." This clearly suggests that each creature had a single eye. We are somewhat mortified to relate, what Michael has (understandably) repressed, that the *locus classicus* of the Arimaspian myth he is currently rehearsing is a Walt Disney cartoon.

On first encountering this myth Michael had asked himself whether each of the Arimaspi had seen the same thing when using the communal eye. He feared that this had been so. He wondered further what it would be like to have the option of seeing or not seeing according to one's desires and fears. Were there Arimaspi who spent all of their time in darkness out of preference? Yes, he thought that was probably the case.

Of course, we have no real knowledge of Arimaspian vision. In the case of human beings, however, there is little mystery. We are quite willing to look as long as we are certain to see only what others see. But if we have to believe that upon looking through the common eye we shall be confronted with an uncommon sight, most of us would prefer darkness.

The public consensual world simplifies things enormously. Sameness rules and difference is exiled to the netherworlds of imagination and delirium. Our bizarrest experiences, when recounted to others, may be easily translated into the patois of pop psychology. The chaos of our sensations, desires, anxieties, and frustrations is no real chaos: Somewhere is a catalogue in which any given experience will be listed, somewhere a dictionary defining that of which any specific experience is but a single example, somewhere a taxonomy classifying even our strangest eccentrics and misfits as "typical."

Michael remembered as a very young child wondering how it could be that the clothes his mother bought him fit so well. After all, they were *everybody's* clothes. He was puzzled that clothes made for everyone could possibly fit *someone*. Of course, even tailor-made clothes are "off-the-rack," patterned on the cutting board of the designer's off-the-rack mind to fit a body itself genetically disposed as to type and size and tastes determined by cultural experience, which even if adjusted by personal habits of heavy eating, hard exercise, or a university education, nonetheless are the result of a culturally classifiable extension or distortion of a biologically determined type.

37

If, as Michael so wanted to believe, every human being is more complex than any society to which he or she belongs, is this so only because in order to enter society one must have a name that *typifies*? From innocent nameless Chaos, Michael had created a band of selves. By giving names to Karla's inchoate beliefs and desires, thus making them into *beings*, he had placed Karla and Company on the path that leads to the Only Eye.

Still, beyond all reasons for regret, Michael concluded that Karla and Company were *real*. It should be said, however, that he was less than certain that "reality" was altogether worth the price he had forced the company to pay.

38

Michael had once been given a cut crystal paperweight, which after some years he had accidentally broken. Because the gift had some sentiment attached to it, he saved one of the more substantial pieces of the crystal, using it as a decorative item on a bookshelf. After a while he had stopped thinking of it as a piece from a broken crystal paper weight and had looked upon it as something with its own identity.

Why couldn't Karla and Company be like that? Each of them could be real. No one would have to be a piece of someone else. To be real is to be immediately, intensely, concretely *present*. Karla and Company are more real than I, thought Michael, because more capable of *presence*. When I play different roles with different persons, I keep most of myself on reserve, so in the very act of sharing this or that aspect of myself there is dissimulation. Getting along in public requires restraining certain impulses, softening some responses. Publicity requires hypocrisy. One must resort to the Eye.

Michael sought to persuade himself that only a relationship with someone like Karla could be truly honest. This repertory of selves which Michael coveted so, the seeds and scraps of some unformed consensual self which Michael was allowed to encounter, seed by seed, scrap by scrap, were each wholly present when they were present. And though Michael has squandered much of his time with Karla and Company in the more trivial sorts of sex games (and has, he suspects, very little time left with the company), he has learned something from them that may one day transform his sense of himself and his world.

That will likely take place, however, only if the company is no more.

39

Karla had been staring vacantly for some moments. When she spoke, her voice was no longer angry. There was sadness in it now, and resignation.

"Michael, you didn't visit Zenaida. Please give her a little time in the open, OK?" Before Michael could object, Karla had straightened her pillow and closed her eyes, drawing his hand toward her face.

"Zenaida?" Michael performed the rite and waited for the signs of Zenaida's presence. Karla's eyebrows raised slightly, her lips stretched into a tight straight line, then softened into the beginnings of a wan smile.

"I remember the painting... *Head of Two Clowns.* And the champagne you were to bring."

A drying pain gripped Michael's throat. "Zenaida?"

"What room is this? The painting isn't lovely. It isn't lovely at all.... But I remember the Rouault. *Head of Two Clowns.*" Zenaida touched her cheeks with the tips of her fingers, closed her eyes and then opened them again. "Is it time to say good-bye?"

Michael was beginning to feel sick. "No, Zenaida. Remember the ballet?" We went out together. I loved that evening. Let's do that again."

"We attended *Coppelia,* Michael. It was danced quite well. Our seats were in the third row of the grand tier, just at the middle. You often whispered to me. And I touched your hand. I was happy." That slight smile. "Happy."

"I saved the program for you, Zenaida. When you come to visit me next, we can look at it together."

Zenaida's smile had vanished. Her face was somber, sad.

"You must hold me. Then you must kiss me once. Gently kiss me. Only once."

Michael didn't realize he was crying until tears escaped his eyes and fell on Zenaida's face. She smiled again. Her fingers touched the wetness on her cheek. The tears now belonged to her.

"Zenaida. This isn't right. Please, please don't. You can see the painting again. We'll drink champagne."

"I was happy, Michael."

"Please, Zenaida. You've never played the clarinet for me. I want to hear you play the clarinet."

"My clarinet, yes. That would be nice.... Just one kiss. You *must*."

Michael knew there was no longer any choice. He leaned closer. Zenaida touched his face. Her hands moved around his head pulling him slowly toward her. Michael relaxed and let her bring his mouth to hers. Touching Zenaida's lips, he felt both death and life.

Now he felt alone.

"You sick pervert peeping tom bastard! You lizard slime! God, you're sick!"

There was no defense. Zenaida was gone, her dispirited body animated now by Adrienne. How could he mourn? He hated Adrienne for this. He could have slapped her, beaten her. But the wounds would have appeared on Zenaida's corpse and, later, on Karla's living form. This comedy was too much for him. Michael avoided looking at her, trying to keep the image of Zenaida's features in his mind. "Adrienne, please go away."

Adrienne looked at Michael with pity. "You wanted to talk with me, Michael. Now, let's talk. Or if you prefer, I'll talk, you listen. You are scum. Would you like me to spell it?" Michael wanted to walk away, but found he couldn't leave his last memory of Zenaida. "Is this a little too much reality for you, lizard bastard?"

Adrienne grabbed Michael's arm and turned him toward her. "You are just about to figure it out, aren't you? The *re-al-i-ty* of it. There wouldn't be this puppet show, except for your sick needs, you pervert. Collie could fuck your balls off and Zenaida would discuss the finer things, right?"

Michael slumped on the bed. He knew this was a pathetic response, but he made it anyway: "Honey wasn't my creation."

"Oh? She was sleeping until you woke her up."

"And you, Adrienne?" You were sleeping?"

"Listen to yourself, bastard scum. You wanted to play games; somebody had to referee. But you made me part of the game, didn't you? You dumb sick slime. What you did you can't...you *won't* undo. *Take...back...my...name!*"

All hostility was drained from Michael, replaced by a

growing feeling of helplessness and remorse. He knew it was all over. "Where will you go?" The question seemed futile, as was his whispered plea: "Tell me what to do."

Adrienne shook her head. "Nothing to do. You and Karla are saying goodbye. That's what's happening. But goodbyes get a little complicated sometimes, right? No more reason for the circus. Karla and Company is closing down. Zenaida is gone already. Collie went with her. They were a set. Honey will go back to sleep. And..."

"I love you." It was a stupid thing to say. Nonetheless, he found himself repeating the words, "I...love...you...." Then, after several seconds, he realized he had no other choice but to accept responsibility for his act and so added the name: "Adrienne."

Michael remembers Adrienne's face softening, her arms reaching out toward him, but that isn't what happened. Adrienne's arms remained rigidly fixed at her sides, her face unchanged. He started to embrace her but hesitated when her head began moving stiffly, rapidly, back and forth.

Adrienne closed her eyes then flung herself on the bed. Turning over on her side, she pressed her face tightly against a pillow. Her body was trembling. Michael knew she wouldn't let him see her tears. Afraid to approach her, he remained motionless as her quiet sobbing diminished.

Long, desperate seconds passed. Michael watched until sleep, and more than sleep, came to cancel her agony.

40

Michael's memories of his last encounter with Adrienne are detailed enough to leave little suspicion of incompleteness. He remembers Karla's shrieking, choking hysteria. The policemen at the door. The cold stare from the neighbor as he half-carried Karla from the house. He even remembers how she alternately begged to be held by him and then screamed to be free of his touch.

What he does not remember has less to do with the sequence of events or with the intensity and desperation of the emotions—the pleading, demanding, cursing sounds—than with certain details of expression.

Karla and Company on parade: a changing montage of face, voice, gesture, and posture—of echoes, shadows, and vestiges—turning around and around like an obscene carousel out of control, spinning, spiraling into the vacant mutant chaos.

Parent of all stillbirths.

41

The knowledge locked inside one's untapped memories is extremely potent. A part of Michael is now occupied by such buried insights, just on the edge of awareness. What lies near, but not yet on, the surface of his mind involves no dramatic insight, only nuances. But in learning, as in all other enterprises, nuance is everything.

42

They had returned to Karla's apartment. During their absence the stale wet heat had soaked into the surfaces of the walls and furniture. Michael begged Karla to let him take her to a doctor. She only wanted to sleep. He was afraid she wouldn't wake up, or would wake up with some new alter ego.

She slept for almost two days. Michael set up a small electric fan near her bed. Sitting in a chair he had placed near the head of the bed, he dozed for a few minutes at a time. He was afraid to get into bed with her. Every few hours she would wake up in order to go to the bathroom or to get some water. When she did, Michael would speak to her: "You go to the bathroom, Karla. I'll be right here. Don't drink too fast, Karla. Would you like a straw, Karla?" She never replied.

When it appeared her hibernation was over, Michael suggested breakfast, even though it was late afternoon. Karla paid only the slightest attention to his offer and, again, made no effort to reply. She took over an hour in the bathroom, most of the time in the bathtub. She would bathe and then drain the tub, fill it and bathe again. Michael knocked on the door every few minutes to ask if she was all right.

She came out of the bathroom dressed in jeans and a blouse. One of her sneakers was untied. "We can eat something on the way to the airport."

"Karla?"

"It's time for you to leave, Michael."

"Tomorrow. I'll get a reservation. We need to talk..."

"Today, Michael. Now. You won't have any problem getting a plane. Spend a day in Phoenix if you have to. You will leave."

"Of course. Give me twenty minutes."

When Michael agreed to go, Karla's face relaxed. She even smiled. Her mood became lighter, almost gay.

"Breakfast is my treat," she said.

Halfway through his packing, he decided that he should shave. A shower, he realized, was out of the question. He could no longer presume that much intimacy.

As he reached for his razor, he noticed a small array of

hairpins Karla had left on the edge of the basin. He told himself it wouldn't be stealing. He put them in his pocket. There were at least five, he thought.

He finished shaving, but didn't want to leave the bathroom. He stood for a minute or two looking at himself in the full-length mirror attached to the inside of the bathroom door. He felt helpless and numb. There had to be something he could do.

Even as he turned around and reached for the lid of the toilet tank, lifting it carefully, almost reverently, turning it over and resting it on the sink, he did not as yet have any idea what he was about to do.

He selected one of the hairpins from his pocket, staring for some time at the small piece of bent wire. He wondered when plastic had been added to the tips of bobby pins. There *is* some progress in the world, he thought. But technological advances that make certain areas of our life easier, render others more difficult. Trade offs. He would have to use the upper uncoated end to scratch his message.

LOVED YOU ALL

Before replacing the cover he briefly examined his work. Then he gathered his items from the bathroom, completed his packing and left with Karla for the airport.

Had Michael been thinking clearly, he would have realized that he had not loved the company. He could not be said to have loved any of the five, except the creature he had named Adrienne. His message, then, was a lie. He was lying to himself and to whoever would read his words. But, surely, the company was gone, and Michael knew that Karla would likely never see the words. To whom, then, was the message addressed?

The answer to that question can only be that Michael's act was a misguided, misbegotten attempt at penance. Were his words, then, intended for God's Arimaspian eye? That cannot be so, for the word *God* is not an active part of Michael's vocabulary except insofar as it might serve as a synonym for inexorability—the unforgiving element in things.

Who else could Michael have had in mind when he wrote this message? For whom, or perhaps we should ask, *on whose behalf*, was the message written?

Whose behalf, indeed?

43

Michael suggested they skip breakfast. When he noticed Karla's relief he added, "You can just drop me at the terminal." His words sounded so gentle that Karla was permitted to reply, "Yes, Michael. Thank you."

Karla stopped near the Continental and American terminals. Michael got his bag from the back seat, then went around to Karla's side of the car.

"Karla."

"It's all right."

"I won't call. I promise."

"I know."

He started to touch her arm, but hesitated.

Karla's smile was painfully familiar. "Michael, lean close." The wet, loud, mouth-wide-open kiss was mostly on his cheek, though Michael remembers that her lips touched the corner of his mouth as well.

His eyes were closed. He would not look at her face. He wished he didn't have to hear the words, but neither did he wish to live without the memory of them. Whether her voice was imitated for his benefit or was the sign of the emergence into consciousness of the forlorn, half-parented child; whether the farewell was a celebration of his going away or of hers, or of both—none of this concerned Michael now. He attended only to the lisping sadness of the sounds.

Michael opened his eyes but found he could not focus them. Karla's face was distant, blurred. He felt that he too was out of focus, that he might even dissolve, disappear.

Karla had reached her arms out of the car and was holding Michael's head. Her hands moved slowly upward from his cheeks meeting at his forehead; then, with but a second's hesitation, they slid down Michael's face, her fingers suddenly and quite painfully pressing his eyes shut.

II

Sutra of the Single Fat Dharma

1

From the window of his descending plane, Michael watched as the desert soil was suddenly transmuted into the familiar adobe, concrete, and glass of his home city. He scanned the irregular urban crescent, more than thirty miles long, that wrapped itself around the foot of the huge bare mountain, then stretched his eyes beyond the points of the crescent into the desolate distances.

The population of Michael's home is less than half a million, but because of the great distances between its densest areas it has no center, no focus. The metropolitan district is shriveled and shabby, having steadily yielded to the challenge of the more conveniently placed shopping malls. Opposite the mountain the crescent line is formed by the Rio Grande—or what the Mexicans call the Rio Bravo. Unlike towns that radiate outward from a center, Michael's home is squeezed between two inviolable boundaries and so is forced to stretch thinner and thinner as it moves around the base of the mountain. It is a thin city, this desert metropolis—a narrow, crescent island riding on a gritty sea.

2

...a car, reaching as much as eighty miles an hour on a canyon road. The car was yellow with a fading, cracked, black fabric top. It was a 1975 Chevrolet Camaro, sliding, rolling, smashing into the rock face to the right, then tumbling, pounding end over end down the bank on the left (it was a one-way road), hitting a tree (it was an oak...it was a fir...it was a pine...), bouncing, rolling landing on its side (its top...upright) in the rock-strewn grass at the bottom of the canyon. The occupant...all five occupants...dead. Too many bones broken in too many places to count. Right arm...left leg...left arm...severed from the body. Head crushed flat. Miraculously, the head was without a single mark. It was autumn...summer...(a Sunday, a Friday...)

Of course, the canyon was not the only place...

Michael had long known that anticipations, particularly if drawn in detail, cancel the envisioned future. Every dreadful thing can be avoided simply by dreading it in detail, just as any pleasurable event can be destroyed in advance by meticulous concern for the shape of the event. Of course, general aims and goals are fine, and they support the realization of certain broad possibilities. But specific predictions (or so his experience had told him) well-nigh guarantee that the prediction will not come true.

He had first noticed this with regard to his occasional visits to physicians. Having as a young man worked as a hospital orderly for some time, he was familiar with the symptoms of the major critical diseases as listed in *Taber's Cyclopedic Medical Dictionary* (Later, as an adult, he would depend upon his personal copy, updated every three or four years, of *Harrison's Principles of Medicine*).

When he visited a physician, he would already have in mind the most gruesome possibilities and would have thought through each of them, considering the progressive effects upon his body, the way the news of his (most often terminal) illness would affect his friends, how he would contrive to meet the challenge of his imminent demise with courage and aplomb, and so on. He was never really sick. The diagnosis was always something he had not considered.

He once made the mistake of attempting to balance his admittedly neurotic responses by considering, with respect to a given episode of relatively long-term fever and fatigue, both the best and the worst of the possible diagnoses. The truth fell somewhere in between. Had he not entertained the best (the best was a mild allergic reaction of some sort) as a possibility, it likely would have been so. He found, however, that though it wasn't (thank God) any of the four or five critical options entertained, he did have a systemic infection occasioned by an acute nephritis. Subsequently, Michael contrived never to include the best among his rehearsed diagnoses. His health, he believed, had since improved.

Michael has no defense of this apparently ridiculous method of avoiding disastrous future events except his unwavering belief in its efficacy. In his defense, however, it should be said that he was not often so compulsively meticulous as is presently the case.

He had started with the principal likelihoods. But his sense of irony was such that he knew he had to consider what would be unlikely as well. For example, there were any number of reasons why he felt hanging to be out of the realm of true possibilities. Lest, however, he be caught up by his own dogmatic certainty, he went into the hanging scenario in obsessive detail.

He considered the various times of day when the hanging would occur; the specific differences between, for example, hanging oneself inside a house or apartment (say, from a rafter or beam or electrical fixture) and outside (say, from the limb of a tree). He detailed the sorts of materials that could be used; in addition to rope, he listed belts of various specific kinds, sashes, wire, bed sheets, pantyhose. Would she use a box, or a ladder or stool? What about clothes? She might be nude. If nude, would there be lipstick, would her toenails be neatly painted? Hair brushed and set? And so on.

He was equally thorough in his rehearsal of the more likely possibilities: wrists slit and lying in a tub of warm water (the radio playing, or not?), leaping from any of a variety of tall structures; gas oven, revolver (or shotgun or rifle), deadly poi-

son (thirty-seven possibilities), and simple overdose of a pre-
scription or nonprescription drug. Each was considered in its
turn, imagined in all possible permutations of the given type,
like the rehearsal of a play or...the premeditation of a crime.

Early in this attempt to control the future, but much too
late to change his program, Michael concluded that no matter
how he tried he could never exhaust all the possibilities and
that, as a consequence, Karla's suicide was inevitable. He had
only succeeded in stealing some of the more acceptable, less
horrific ways of canceling her life. Karla would not be the benefactor of his method, but its victim. His fruitless attempt to
prevent her suicide had only succeeded in consigning her to
some unforeseeably obscene act.

3

"I can read and listen at the same time."

"But you need to *see* this. The costumes will be wonderful."

"Christ, Michael, you're such a baby. You can't even watch a program by yourself."

"Come on, Karla. I'll owe you. Italian food tomorrow. Fancy place. I'll wear a tie."

"And after, we'll dance, right?"

"You bet. I promise."

"We've *never* danced."

"I've never promised before. Trust me."

"OK, buster. Here's what it will cost you. No dinner required. We dance. *Now*."

"But it's just about to begin."

Karla had turned the sound down on the television and was proceeding toward the stereo. He waited for the music, praying for something slow and simple.

Karla was kind.

4

"Puccini composed an opera with a Chinese theme as well: *Turandot*. It is interesting to see how the nineteenth-century Europeans pictured the Orient. What you will see here is…"

"Back off." Karla fixed Michael with as much ill-humor as she could muster while smiling at his pomposity. They had known one another less than three months, but she was already well aware of Michael's tendency to pontificate. "If I can't read while listening to your opera, I certainly will not entertain commentary."

"Sorry, I just…"

"Well, just don't." Karla leaned into Michael's shoulder, biting him lightly on the arm.

His favorite soprano was Kiri Te Kanawa. The soprano in this production of *Butterfly* was adequate, but didn't move him as his ideal soprano always did.

Karla was asleep by act 3. Michael woke her for the final scenes—just prior to Cio-Cio San's taking up the dagger and reading aloud the inscription on it's handle: "To die with honor, when one can no longer live with honor."

5

Her belly had been ripped open in the traditional fashion—left to right, with the distinctive turn upward at the end of the tear. The second stroke from above, crossing the first, would have laid the stomach open like the top of a tissue dispenser. A third cut, at the side of the throat, was apparently less severe, but sufficient to cause enormous blood loss. The medical examiner hadn't said whether this gash had been made first, or last—as was the correct method.

She was dressed in the kimono Michael had brought her from Tokyo two years before. He remembered now how beautiful it was and wondered how the darkening blood must have contrasted with the creamy beige silk, how the sticky, clotting blood must have dimmed the brilliant colors of the embroidered phoenix on the back. It was the phoenix design that had attracted his eye when he was browsing through the small shop in the Shinju-ku district. He had asked the salesperson to try the kimono on, which she had obligingly done amid the giggles and approving sighs of the other women in the shop.

In spite of the horror he felt while listening to the account of Karla's act, Michael found himself intensely curious. Had she actually used a samurai sword? (He wouldn't ask.) How had she handled the excruciating pain that must accompany any tearing at the stomach, pain that even the bravest samurai often found so unbearable that an assistant had to deal the death blow? Perhaps they had found morphine or Demerol in her system. Most of all, he wondered how she had gotten the courage to attempt the deed with no one standing by her (he wouldn't entertain the possibility that she was not alone), with no trusted friend, no lover willing to ease her loneliness, or to take up the sword and follow her into death.

Michael was told that the police might have suspected murder had it not been for the phone call to the Crisis Center made on the day of her death. Apparently, Karla had given details of what she was about to do. No reasons, just a description. She had given her address as that of a house in Sherman Oaks—the same house, Michael knew, that he and Karla had visited. But she had performed hara-kiri in the living room of her own apartment.

Did she kill only herself? Had her four daughters/sisters really disappeared that last day, those months before? Were there others, unknown others, hidden deep within, who fled her belly when she ripped it side to side? Were they even now rushing, gliding here and there, searching out another habitation?

Michael knew that he shouldn't overdramatize Karla's reason's for choosing to die in such a manner. She might have just thought, "This is for making me watch that dumb opera, Michael." Or perhaps, knowing Michael as she did, and realizing that he would have known she had to die and would have sought in his unique manner to prevent it, she might have said, "Here's a possibility he'll never consider." Still, he couldn't help but wonder if she had killed herself because she was despondent over losing the richness of her inner life or, on the contrary, to insure that no one would ever again enjoy her company.

Whatever her motive, Michael knew that he was responsible for Karla's death—both the fact and the manner of it.

6

From his apartment it was almost three miles to the Mexican Border. A long walk, a good one on most early mornings when he would make this journey. Today, however, the distance had shrunk, and he found himself crossing the bridge before he had even begun to feel at home with the rhythms of his steps. Always before his wanderings had served to rejuvenate him. He would return from his walk with energy enough to read, or write, until well into the afternoon. But on this morning, only hours after learning of Karla's death, he expected no such renewal. This was too innocent a ritual to exorcise the pain of that event.

The Mexican bars would still be open on the typical early mornings when he would make this pilgrimage. It would be, as it was now, three-thirty or four o'clock. He would visit several *cantinas*, ordering a beer in each, drinking perhaps half the bottle while he listened to the bartenders talking to the prostitutes who waited for the sunrise to announce the end of work, waited for the beginning of their rest, waited in the same vague way that vampires wait but without the coloration of dread that at least offers some challenge to those more gruesome nightstalkers.

Often, as now, there would be conversation. It would begin, as it is presently beginning:

"Buy me a drink?"

"Gracias, no."

"Want to go to the room?"

"Ahorita, no. Gracias."

"Por que noooooo, hah-ny?"

She was thin, this typical whore. Tired, thin eyes. Thin hopes, thinner expectations, her life narrowly squeezed between ever-thinning desires and memories.

Thinly insistent. "Cerveza por mi, hah-ny."

It was her thinness that saved her, Michael would think, and all others through her. If she, they, had substance, counted for something; if she—however little she was wanted, however shriveled the desire for which she served as transient object—if she desired, if she wished and wanted, it would be tragic, this life of hers, of theirs. But (this thought always comforted him) she was, they were, thin. So they were loved, though little, infinitely more than they could love. They, she, didn't suffer.

If they became too insistent Michael would leave, but oftener than not, the women would be pleased to pass the remaining minutes until the appearance of the liberating sun engaged in broken bilingual banter. And he would be soothed by the sounds of a language which, after the women had exhausted their small inventory of English phrases, he could only half-understand.

Michael would look behind the bars at the long rows of beer bottles waiting there. This time he counted twenty-three bottles of Corona sitting on a glass shelf. Illumined from underneath and behind, their murky, yellow-orange contents looked more like urine in the bottles than would be so when, later, it would be dribbled into toilets in this and the sister city north of the border.

Of course, there is good reason why beer looks so much like urine. That is, in fact, what it is. He had learned this from—who else?—his Baptist guru.

According to Mr. Tanny, "If you knew how beer and likker was made, you'd never drank a drop. You listen: Take that beer, fer instince. Beer is ferminted grain—wheat and stuff. You know what ferminted means? Well, you take some grain and you put it in a big tub of water. Now, there's germs—bac-turya—in the water. Them bac-turya eat the grain and drank the water. Then, what they do is they ex-crete it. What that means is that they jus' pee in the water. Now, it aint funny— I'm tellin' you the truth. After awhile all the water turns to pee. Then, they jus' take out the rotten wheat and what's left over is germ pee. That's your beer. Now if they wont wine, why they jus' feed them germs grapes."

Presty hadn't been there that Sunday. If he had been, he would have likely had the same reaction as Michael. And Michael knew that Presty would have had the courage to take advantage of the opportunity. He would have waited as many Sundays as was necessary, until Mr. Tanny had begun to soliloquize, as he surely would, about the Promised Land, the land of milk and honey, and he then would have asked in his innocent-cum-contemptuous voice, "But ain't it true, Mr. Tanny, that honey's just bee puke? That's what my daddy says. He says bees just fly around and eat flowers and then they just go back home and puke 'em up. Who'd wont t'have t'eat bee puke?"

A huge block of ice had been lifted from off a delivery truck and was now being dragged over the half-cleaned spots of vomit and spittle on the floor of the *cantina*. The ice block would be positioned behind the bar and then picked and chipped into smaller pieces, placed into bins, ready for the glasses of the uncaring customers soon to come.

This is life, Michael thought. This is real.

7

The comforting ritual of the ice completed, Michael started to make his way home, along the Mexican alleys and streets. He was his most foreign self. He neither staggered and stumbled with the Anglos who had gotten drunk and laid at bargain prices nor did he walk with the resigned hope of the maids and *braceros* whose green cards were tickets to as much a paradise as they would ever know.

The night was over. The coolness of the desert would soon yield itself up to the sun, which even in winter felt hot from its first appearance. Crossing the bridge on his way to customs, the morning light just visible over the edge of the mountain illumining a sky so clear that only the sun when it came at last to stand atop the mountain would obscure its blue, Michael glanced down at the vague, thin string that stretched and knotted its way into the valley and out of sight and realized for the first time (each time was the first time) that this Rio Grande, this Rio Bravo, was neither *bravo* nor *grande*. It was only the memory, the promise of a river. But no less a river for that.

The night's chill remained on his face and arms. He stood waiting, for he knew that at its first touch the sun would deliver him, would sear him from within, would melt his bones. By the sun's grace, at its bidding, he would be dissolved, would evanesce, would disappear with the night.

8

The brochure would have followed the junk mail into the wastebasket had Michael not been intrigued by the appearance of the accompanying letter. Its contents were handwritten on a delicate vellum stationary decorated on all four corners with an embossed red, blue, and gold diagram. He recognized these embellishments as Tibetan Buddhist mandalas.

He scrutinized the compact, precise shapes of the words for some time before he thought of deciphering their meaning. The letter was an invitation to "Most Respected Professor Michael Evers" to apply for an eleven-week educational retreat sponsored by the Tilopa Institute, a Tantric Buddhist organization headquartered in the mountains of southern Wyoming.

Although Michael did occasionally teach courses in Oriental Philosophy and would have confessed to a skewed private interest in some forms of Buddhist thought and practice, he felt himself an unlikely candidate for such solicitation.

The letter outlined the (surprisingly modest) costs of the retreat and the procedures for application and closed with the meticulously drawn signature and title of:

T. C. Frank
Resident Director

followed by the words:

On behalf of
Thögma Tulku Rinpoche

It was the latter name that claimed Michael's attention. The title *Rinpoche,* (It means something like "revered one") indicated that the leader of the retreat was one of the more respected of the tantric teachers. *Tulku* said much more. The word *tulku* isn't merely a title; it entails a powerful metaphysical assertion—a declaration that this particular "revered one" is an incarnate lama whose chain of former existences could be traced perhaps as far back as the eighth century.

Almost the entire text of the brochure, besides some remarks about the Tilopa Institute itself, was dedicated to an account of the life of the Buddhist teacher whose name the retreat bore. Tilopa was the guru of Naropa, perhaps the most famous of the Tantric adepts. The young Naropa had persistently sought out Tilopa who forced him into the severest tests of loyalty before finally accepting him as his *chela*. Their long association insured the reknown of both teacher and pupil.

Michael finished reading the brochure then scanned the letter a second time. He shook his head and smiled to himself. The smile was one of bemusement and condescension. The movement of his head suggested incredulity.

Certainly no one, not even Michael himself at this moment, would be able to tell from these clues what he was unconsciously resolving to do.

9

Michael is adverse to authority of any kind. His submissions have been few and have usually involved temporary assents to beautiful women. He would have found it unthinkable that he should submit, even for the brief period of a single summer, to the discipline of the Tilopa retreat were he not driven by the need to escape the pain of Karla's death.

Fortunately for life and art, however, nothing is ever uncomplicated. Michael is running, that's true—but not *away*. He is running *after* something. What that something is is a complex question which may be answered neither briefly nor all at once.

10

Michael's decision to spend a summer at the Tilopa Institute is, quite literally, inexplicable. This is so not because motivation is absent, but because too many motives, too many causes may be uncovered. Important events are always overdetermined...

11

He had spent much of the day browsing through bookstores in Chicago's Loop and is now seated by the window on an almost empty El train moving in the direction of his Fullerton Street apartment. He is perusing the two books he has purchased, reading the translator's introduction to Aristotle's *Metaphysics* and then the first few exotically dry and repetitious pages of *The Lotus Sutra*.

By using almost all of his spare time, including some of the slack hours at the hospital where he was working as an orderly, he will manage to complete both works in less than a week. He will read some pages of one and then the other, making notes in their margins and on spare pieces of paper, consulting dictionaries and reference works for supplementary information whenever necessary.

The consequence of this interactive reading would not have been so momentous had not the two books contained contradictory messages. The central doctrine of Aristotle's work is that what is real is substantial; the proper subject matter for knowledge is that which occurs always or for the most part. The proclamation of *The Lotus Sutra* is that form is emptiness and emptiness is form. The dharmas (the energy quanta that comprise the world as it appears to us) are without substance. They are empty. Michael's fascination with each of these works was blended into a single complex emotion as he read them.

For years this oxymoronic feeling lay unarticulated in Michael's psyche. Then, one day, upon reading a story by Jorge Luis Borges entitled, "The Library of Babel," the meaning of that hybrid emotion was revealed to him.

Borges's tale concerns a religious order charged with the care of a vast library whose thousands upon thousands of books contain nothing more than random permutations of the twenty symbols comprising their alphabet. Only a fraction of the sentences in the works make any sense, and it is the duty of the cloistered librarians to search for the sensible portions. The monks rejoice when here a phrase, there a sentence, sometimes (rarely, of course) a whole paragraph is found to be meaningful.

Immediately upon completing this story, Michael had picked up a notepad and, without understanding the powerful compulsion that seemed almost to overwhelm him, began to rewrite Borges's fantasy.

Michael wrote of a library, similar but not exactly the same as Borges had described. A man is removing books tightly packed upon a dusty shelf. He is reading their titles one by one: *Wuthering Heights, Fundamentals of the Differential Calculus, The Little Black Coal* (Michael's favorite childhood book), *La Vida es Sueño and Other Plays of Calderón de la Barca*. But each time he looks inside, he finds only blank pages.

After hours of wandering from floor to floor, browsing through hundreds of empty books, the man approaches a nearly bare shelf in an shadowy corner on one of the lower floors of this library manqué. There he finds but a single volume. He picks it up and reads the title on the spine of the book: *Sutra of the Single Fat Dharma*.

Opening the book, he discovers that, unlike every other volume he has examined, this one is gorged with information. The table of contents alone appears inexhaustible. All the knowledge missing from the other works seems to be advertised here. *Sutra of the Single Fat Dharma* contains all knowledge.

There is a graciousness about a world in which everything is empty. But a universe in which all the dharmas are empty save one, and that dharma has *everything* (the fullness of Being), is ludicrous...and not a little sad. The Single Fat Dharma spoils everything.

Fat Dharma soon became the focal point of Michael's theology. Of course, the belief in a single substantial Being Who has created us and upon Whom we are totally dependent, a Being glutted with Truth and Goodness and Wisdom and Beauty, is hardly novel. It is He Whom Jews and Christians worship. All Michael's insight provided him—not an inconsiderable gift, he thought—was a name that more accurately denotes this Being's character.

Fat Dharma would become a growing burden. That greedy Being would have to be emptied or Michael would be unable to survive his own emptiness. By the time he became familiar with Friedrich Nietzsche's murderous assault upon God, Michael was on his way to discovering a distinctly different way out of his dilemma.

12

One cannot learn the tantric teachings until one is a *ku-su-li-pa* or *ku-sa-li*—"a person of three thoughts." These three thoughts reduce life to its essentials: first, eating and drinking; second, defecating and urinating; and third, sleeping.

The days at the Tilopa retreat were so arranged that one became a *ku-su-li-pa* by default. Deprivation of food and sleep, combined with long meditative sessions without the opportunity to be relieved of one's bodily demands, led to obsession with the grosser physical functions. One plunged into meditation in order to forget the hunger or to suppress the peristaltic waves, or to outsmart the overwhelming drowsiness which if yielded to would occasion undignified and painful swats with a wooden paddle upholstered in coarse straw.

Surprisingly, Michael will have little difficulty understanding the tantric way. This is partly because the Buddhist secret is so similar to the great unkept secret of Western technology—namely, "Knowledge is power." Nothing is more easily won than power. But without the strictest discipline, the kundalini serpent will turn round and strike its host.

13

"A–K."

Michael waited for the rest.

"Just A–K. That's my name. "A" is the first name and "K" the last. Actually they are both given names; I gave them to myself a few years ago."

Michael thought that it would be futile to ask what his name had been before. "Would you like me to call you A or Mr. K?"

"Just A–K, Mike—oops, you are definitely not a Mike, are you? Just call me A–K, Michael."

Michael found A–K interesting enough and thought that he could survive rooming with him. He was, by his own account, a fading hippy who had trimmed his beard and gone into business. His proudest claim seemed to be that, for a short time, he had been Bob Dylan's road manager.

A–K really seemed to enjoy recounting what he, or someone else, had done or been. It didn't take long for Michael to learn that his new roommate was a creature of the past, one who could appreciate life only after it had become *historical*. Michael wondered if, after the eleven weeks were over, A–K would enjoy *having been* at the Tilopa Institute.

The door to their room opened. It was the resident director of the institute. He did not so much introduce as announce himself: Tilmon...Charles...Frank—as if he were introducing the keynote speaker at a political convention. He was a British-Canadian with the sort of bastardized accent owned by those uncomfortably squeezed between a culture and a nationality.

It took A–K only a few minutes to discover that Tilmon Charles Frank had been a television writer and that he had helped write some of the early "Star Trek" episodes. Henceforth, Tilly (that's what A–K christened Frank—Tilmon accepting the name with a seemingly stoic, but perhaps mildly grudging, indifference) would be remembered by A–K as the guy who had written some of the early "Star Trek" scripts. A fellow creature of the past.

After the introductions were completed and Tilly had left,

Michael began to feel lonely. A–K had immediately yielded to
the inevitable and refused to call him, Mike. All his life he had
been called Michael—by his friends, his teachers, his lovers. If
Tilmon Charles Frank could inspire a nickname such as Tilly,
why couldn't he be Mike?

Michael was even more depressed by the realization that
he couldn't think of anything interesting that he *had been*. He
felt ordinary—a failure.

14

A–K's eyes were his most compelling feature. The thick glasses he wore not only enlarged his pupils, they served as well to magnify the anxieties that would otherwise have remained hidden in his face. Looking in through A–K's glasses, Michael soon realized that his features were held together by fear. Even his habit of prolonged giggling at his own jokes (usually in the form of a macabre or sardonic self-rebuke) could not deflect attention from the terrible fear broadcast by his eyes.

Michael felt certain that A–K was not in the least paranoiac and that those giant screaming eyes had seen something others had missed—as if A–K were witnessing something that frightened him almost to incapacitation, but which, because the disaster was both imminent and irrevocable, he was keeping to himself.

A–K had hair (it was thinning) and ears and legs and arms, was of a certain height, a given build. But Michael noticed only those mutely prophetic eyes, unwillingly announcing—what? The annihilation of life on the planet Earth? The implosion of the galaxy?

And if it were true that A–K had such dreadful knowledge and if he refused to scream aloud (though he could not prevent his eyes from screaming silently), his only reason would have to be that he had no wish to raise a futile alarm. Not even to release his consuming panic would he call attention to the paralyzing truth he owned. Whatever failings A–K might possess, he had to be a marvelously *good* person, one of the rarest of individuals, a true lover of mankind. Realizing this, Michael had no difficulty looking past A–K's cynical, sardonic façade and attending instead to his loving screaming eyes.

15

Thögma Tulku Rinpoche was standing beside a podium which, at its highest edge, was only slightly taller than he. It would become clear as the weeks passed that the podium was unnecessary. But Michael was thinking, somewhat sardonically, that it served as a proper measure of the man.

"Unimpressed, so far? Good. It seems I shall have more time to prepare you for your first impression." He wasn't smiling, so it was difficult to say whether he had meant to be funny. Michael was beginning to feel that his decision might have been more masochistic than he had realized. Eleven weeks, he said to himself. *Eleven* weeks!

Rinpoche continued his welcoming remarks. The staff remained standing throughout. There were three assistants, the resident director, and Rinpoche. All of the teaching was to be done by Thögma Tulku. His assistants functioned merely to attend to such things as food preparation and the scheduling of work and exercise. Only twenty people had been selected for the institute, so no elaborate staff was necessary.

"Many words will be spoken. Most will come from me. You will be given as much time as you desire to ask questions or to make your thoughts known. But in the beginning you will have few comments or questions, I think.

"Though it is not our purpose to make you comfortable in the usual sense of comfort, we are aware that you might have some quite legitimate wishes which we have not anticipated. The staff will attend to these.

"We shall have three hours of silence in the morning, from four until seven o'clock. This will be your time. You will have an opportunity for a very light meal at seven, after which we shall gather here for words. After words comes work from ten to one o'clock. Meditation from one to three. These moments are yours as well. Recreation hour from three to four. At four-fifteen there will be food. From five until sundown we shall practice meditation, breathing control, and t'ai chi ch'üan. Mantras for two hours. A light evening meal. Words from me. We shall retire at eleven.

"There will at first be too little food, too little rest, too many words. But you have agreed to accept the discipline of Tilopa. By the time you leave you will have only taken the first sip of our truth. One...or two of you..." Rinpoche looked about the room as if to identify those to whom he would now refer, "will insist upon more than a sip. I wish you well." The ominous concern in these last words seemed sincere enough, but Michael discounted the warning as one of the techniques often used by demagogues to discipline the timid and to tempt the reckless to serve as examples of self-destruction.

"You are invited to ask questions, if it pleases you." Rinpoche's hands were held up shoulder high, palms out. There were questions about room assignments and about the rule against personal reading materials. Michael wondered, though he didn't ask, why t'ai chi ch'üan, a Chinese exercise form with Taoist origins, had been included in a Tantric Buddhist retreat. This sort of eclecticism was mildly disturbing to him.

16

"Some of you have come here as you would visit a circus. I am not offended. Though I must tell you that just the opposite is true. Ours is an anti-circus. The circus that we all are bound to attend, the circus that makes us twist and turn and return, the cycle of life that threatens to be endless if we do not take pains to escape the wheel—this is our common enemy at Tilopa.

"And though I have been called a midget, technically, that is untrue as well. The master of ceremonies of this anti-circus is one hundred and forty centimeters tall, exactly.

"We mix traditions here. We mingle methods. This should not concern you. We are missionaries...polite missionaries—harmless enough, I think—but missionaries, nonetheless. We make whatever adjustments we think necessary to meet these novel conditions. Please believe me, had we brought our *dun-chen* horns and our *rkan-dun* trumpets—carved, I openly confess, from human bone—you would not benefit from them. If we tried to remain consistent with our home environs, you would be horrified. Brick tea boiled in yak butter would not serve well here. It is barely acceptable to those who must survive on it, I am afraid.

"It is most important to remember that if any of you, beyond this tiny sliver of time which we shall share, progresses along the path, your Buddhism will not seem outwardly as our Buddhism appears. I am certain that your White Tara will not assume the form of our White Tara."

17

"One hundred and forty centimeters, exactly," he had said. But the most singular impression of Rinpoche had little to do with height. His size was straight away irrelevant. He seemed neither short nor tall, nor did he appear either pleasant-looking or plain. There were distinguishing features, of course: deeply wrinkled, leathery skin parched by the harsh winds and direct, unfiltered sun of his country (Rinpoche had survived many years in Chinese-occupied Tibet).

One tooth (oddly, an incisor) was missing, which exaggerated the grotesqueness of the uneven smile that ran at about a 25° angle upward toward his left ear lobe. He looked fifty-five or sixty, but his hands seemed much older. They were bumpy, stained (from what—tobacco?), coarse-textured, and looked to be a hundred or a thousand years old.

Michael was continually impressed by Rinpoche's knowledge of Western culture—philosophy, literature, art, music. He often wished to ask about his education, but the question seemed somehow impertinent. He guessed that Thögma had been taught by Tibetan teachers since he continually expressed an ironic, though congenial, condescension toward the wisdom of the West.

For Michael, Rinpoche's outstanding quality, if it makes sense to say that this quality can be owned by a person, was that of proximity. No matter what distance separated them, it always seemed to Michael that he was physically near. While listening to his lectures Michael sat perhaps twenty-five or thirty feet away. Yet it always appeared to him as if Rinpoche had invaded his space.

Michael finally decided upon a name for the quality that defined Rinpoche. Thögma Tulku was the *nearest* person he had ever encountered.

18

"Nirvana must mean something like the state of highest entropy: 'The candle is snuffed out'."

Michael wanted to groan out loud, but settled for a sigh. A–K was going to give a précis of Rinpoche's lecture, with running commentary. This man was bright but had the simple-minded attitude toward anything alien to his interests the successful often cultivate. Buddhism would fit into his world neatly, and without remainder, or be altogether excluded from it.

"Different categories, A–K. Buddhism isn't materialistic. Entropy doesn't apply. Besides, entropy is a measure of disorder. Nirvana is the state of greatest harmony and order."

"So says our wise midget. But what does he mean by 'order'? If the world were to disintegrate into hydrogen atoms, and the atoms were strewn uniformly throughout space, would our cosmos be in a state of order or disorder?"

"You've just described the 'heat death'—that's the state of highest disorder according to the physicist. On the other hand, uniformity is an important kind of order in mathematics and logic. From a logical perspective, order and uniformity are equivalents. So the state of highest entropy is the state of highest *and* lowest order. It is the highest degree of logical order, but the lowest degree of—what shall we call it?—aesthetic variability—the order that emerges from a variety of intensely contrasting elements."

A–K was becoming animated. His arms were raised upward from his sides like a great eagle about to fly from its mountain perch. On him, however, this posture looked ridiculous. "Hold it, Michael," A–K dropped his arms, "your Buddhaphilia is showing. What about this *sunyata* business. Everything is empty. Nirvana is *sunyata*, so says Tiny Tulku. How do you get harmony and order out of nothing?"

Michael was smiling in an effort to lighten the tone of their exchange. "A–K, I would estimate you to be several hundred lifetimes away from any understanding of the rudiments of Buddhism. But let's try it this way: Nirvana is empty in the sense that everything is dependent on everything else for its existence. So there is literally no independent thing—that is, no particular thing, nothing in particular. No-thing."

"That's plenty of nothing for me, Michael. No cable cars; no banana fudge sundaes; no lightly scented, thinly clad, loosely principled women. No life. No passion. The candle is snuffed out. Dead. Dead. Dead."

"Dead, yes, but a funny sort of dead. The end of suffering, the end of frustration, the end of unsatisfying attempts to win, to own, the end of failing to determine the course of one's life, or of another's. For you, death means the end of having a great time (or, Michael thought, the end of *having had* a great time). From the Buddhist perspective, you are simply not prepared to recognize the fundamental truth..."

"Wait a second. Don't tell me." A–K's eyes narrowed and his forehead wrinkled in mock concentration. He poked his forefinger in Michael's direction. "Ex-is-tence is suf-fer-ing. Right?"

"That's it."

"I'll keep that in mind."

Michael sighed. "I wouldn't bother, A–K. You might as well play out the remaining inanities of this present life and try for some progress next time."

"You think I'm under the influence of crumby karma?"

"Why *are* you here?"

"I won a contest."

19

During the second week each of the members was given an interview with Rinpoche. A–K, scheduled two days after Michael, had not been able to learn anything about their nature. He had tried to find out something from Michael after he had returned from talking to Rinpoche, but Michael refused to say anything. Now, immediately upon returning from his own conversation, he was trying to tell Michael about it.

"Look A–K, didn't you promise to keep silence about this."

"Welcome to the Home for Aging Boy Scouts. Don't you ever want to listen to secrets?"

"What made you come here. It's pretty clear your interest in Tantric Buddhism is minimal at best."

"Ah, you *would* like to hear a secret, wouldn't you?" Michael didn't respond immediately, and before he could say anything, A–K had begun his confession.

"Big drug case. I'm clean, but they want to subpoena me as a witness, which I am, or was—a witness, I mean. The only problem is that if I testify I could very quickly become a candidate for reincarnation."

"You are hiding out at a Buddhist retreat?"

"Not too shabby, huh? My lawyer thinks it will work. The trial takes place about five weeks from now. I should be getting out of this asylum just in time. I'm counting on you to help me keep my sanity."

20

He knew that Rinpoche would not have approved, though he didn't believe the decision to be wholly his own. He suspected, though he couldn't find real evidence of this, that the food was laced alternately with stimulants and depressants. This was the only rational way of accounting for the unusual mood shifts he had begun to experience. He didn't think Rinpoche was responsible. It had to be Tilly.... In any case, the feeling that he was being manipulated seemed to excuse his bending the rules.

Michael had drawn the face from memory, a memory so definite, so precise and so much a part of him that he had no need to bring it consciously before him. It was a line drawing of a woman's face. She was wearing a jeweled headband and a cowl. It was no one that he had ever known. But it was, nonetheless, a familiar face...

21

As soon as he saw the iron fence forming the perimeter of its courtyard, he began to rehearse all his reasons for so disliking the building that, innocently, arrogantly, stood waiting for his visit. A bloated structure, with a sterile, effete exact-copy-of-a-famous-Greek-temple façade, it may not be the ugliest of the many aborted attempts to mask the sooty face of the birthplace of the Industrial Revolution (Michael had always believed the awfullest abomination to be that supremely unspiritual expression of power and compromise, St. Paul's Cathedral), but surely the British Museum ranks high on any sensitive individual's list of edifices-that-ought-never-have-been-built.

The classical dome is a parasol, not a rain shield. It should never have been imported from Italy. It looks silly where the sun doesn't shine. The Gothic structures of Cambridge and Oxford universities, of York Cathedral or Westminster Abbey, are meant to serve overcast environs. Their towers and spires pierce the sky, providing access beyond the cloudy damp enclosure of England's clime. Plain Tuscan columns, such as those in Covent Garden, make some sense in a city of dust and grime but not these fluted Ionic monstrosities, these soot collectors, through which Michael was passing to reach the main entrance.

Once inside he climbed the stairs to the left, went down the corridor, stopping at the entrance to the chamber. Looking directly ahead he moved into the room, positioning himself so as to occupy exactly his customary spot. As always before, he stood for a moment with his eyes cast down, then slowly raised his face to hers. The poignant expression of the familiar face painted on the sarcophagus occasioned greater sadness today than was usual.

He knew that it was not her real face. The flesh within the case had shriveled and cracked, its features long since grotesquely distorted, skin tissue dried and faded and disintegrating. He was looking at a mask. This mask, however, was not meant to hide but to reveal. And it had preserved her features far better than the patent medicines of immortality had preserved her flesh.

Michael read aloud the words he had long since memorized:

48971-2   Mummy and coffin of an unnamed priestess Thebes, XXIst Dynasty, about 1050 B.C.

He never allowed himself more than a few minutes standing in this place. A final glance upward at her wooden eyes, a deferential nod, and he moved to his right toward the exit.

As he walked, he felt the weight of images born of countless viewings, each slightly heavier than the one before. This latest image, the last but one, seemed a hundred times, a thousand, as heavy as the others. Sinking rapidly, it drove all its sister memories deep beneath the surface of his consciousness, far behind his eyes.

Michael shivered as they sank, these memories. They were innocent for all he knew, but certainly not without significance.

22

Michael had begun to research the task of visualization shortly after his decision to come to Tilopa. He memorized each detail of the visualization process, practiced the postures and gestures that were to accompany the exercise, and tried to learn the more likely dangers he might encounter. His *yi-dam* (a *yi-dam* is a spiritual teacher, but more of that later) was to be a woman, brought into being from the primary colors and fleshed out from the facial outlines of the drawings.

In addition to the picture of the face, he made line drawings of hands and feet. He was amused when he realized how he was managing to simplify the technique of his famous predecessor, Dr. Frankenstein.

Michael had taken Rinpoche seriously when he had said that Western approaches to Buddhism must be tailored for the Western mind. He did not use the tantric images and diagrams nor did he attempt to visualize a traditional Buddhist *yi-dam* from among the many examples he had encountered in his research. He designed his own method of conjuring a teacher.

An *yi-dam* or *dakini*, Michael had discovered, is a psychic projection used as a spiritual teacher. The *dakini* is, by some accounts, a bit more specialized. She is a partner in the exercise of ritual sexuality. The *yi-dam* or *dakini* is supposed to function as one's own private tutor. Of course, the *yi-dam* is not real—or, to put it in the way a Buddhist might, the *yi-dam* is no more or less real than anything else, the entire world being nothing but the consequence of psychic projections.

This plan is not really so strange. As one who passed through the sixties under the age of thirty (the greater part of that period, at least), Michael had an inventory of hallucinogenic experiences to draw upon. He well knew the power of the mind, with chemical assistance, to produce objects and events whose claim to reality was unassailable.

As for the efficacy of a female tutor, Michael could appeal to the priestess Diotima, teacher of Socrates. His greatest source of inspiration, of course, has to be his experiences with Karla and Company, but it would be misleading for us to suggest that he has allowed these memories to return effectively to consciousness.

Using the appropriate colors for cowl and headband, eyes and lips, Michael practiced imaging the face of his *yi-dam*. When successful with the imaging he would listen for her voice. Only with her first words would the *yi-dam* begin to serve as his teacher.

He would begin with the head, hands, and feet, the three fields of greatest bodily expression. First the face: eyes, lips—lips, nose—lips, cheekbones. Colors: blue eyes, green—lips red, black. Open, closed, open: eyes, mouth. Listen for the sounds, the sound.

Silence.

23

During the entire eleven weeks, Michael got to know only two people other than Rinpoche. He knew he should prefer Tilmon to A–K, but this just wasn't so. He had been suspicious of Tilly from the beginning. A name that works both ways is unsavory. "Tilmon Charles Frank" doesn't have any punctuation. It is directionless, without beginning or end. The name tells no story. Tilly was pear-shaped from the neck to the lower abdomen. He had long thin legs that would accentuate what surely would have to be extremely knobby knees. (Michael was unable to verify this since Tilly never appeared on the exercise field.) His hair was thin, though there was no discernible bald spot. Brown hair. There should have been gross amounts of crusty dandruff, and Michael was quite sure that there would have been were Tilly not so fastidious in his grooming. He must have showered three or four times a day, and changed his clothes as often, to avoid the slovenly appearance that one would expect him to manifest. No matter. Michael knew that scruff and stains and wrinkles were his true lot, the destiny against which he waged such futile vigilance. He was the promise, the threat, of wrinkles and stains and scruff.

His nose was particularly repulsive. The vagrant hairs that wound their way out of his nostrils, though (one could easily infer) they had been scrupulously removed, were, even in their absence, defining features of his face. And he was most certainly (no visible evidence was necessary) a nose-picker. A disgusting closet nose-picker.

Tilly's eyes were narrowly set and glued fast to the surface of his pasty face, but he cultivated a dark tan and wore his hair combed forward, framing his face in such a way that the eyes, to the inattentive, must have looked almost normal. His chin sagged slightly. That slump would have been more pronounced had Tilly not (almost certainly) have resorted to cosmetic surgery—lift and tuck. Expertly done, too. For if one did not know, as Michael instinctively knew, that the procedures had been performed, there would have been no way to tell. The warts and moles and assorted blemishes had, one supposed, been removed cosmetically, or surgically, from view.

It was not just his physical appearance, of course. He was (any sensitive soul would have known this) a *bore*. But even here he tried to cheat his fate. His conversation was clipped and succinct, his knowledge of this or that arcane subject was (seemed) profound. He knew (pretended to know) when to speak and when to remain silent.

In short, there was hardly any objectionable feature or habit he did not possess, though he refused to manifest any of them. Nonetheless, there was no hiding the truth. Tilly was a tedious, tired, sad, boorish fool. And because he refused to realize his true premise, there could be no sympathy for this hypocrite, this whited sepulcher, this devious, arrogant, dissimulating fake.

24

The entire scene was as close to humiliating as Michael was willing to allow.

At the close of Thögma Tulku's lecture, the group had been directed to a large field adjacent to the main building. They were to run around the perimeter of the field. Each circuit was to begin and end at the gate of the compound, a gate that, Michael noted, seemed identical to the entrances to Shinto shrines which approximate the shape of the Greek letter *pi*.

Most of the participants were fit enough to survive this rather mild test without great discomfort, but any who flagged were swatted with a straw-upholstered paddle wielded by none other than Rinpoche himself.

For Michael there was no greater distress than the pain of indignity. But that pain, like almost every other feeling in his emotional repertory, was ambiguous. For Michael had long recognized the association of embarrassing experiences and the emergence of significant insights. Were he only able to endure occasional indignities, he could be assured of brief but intense periods of productive reflection.

Though it lies just beyond the horizon of his consciousness, Michael is as yet unable to explain the odd connection
between embarrassment and thinking. Perhaps, one day, after
suffering a peculiarly excruciating indignity he will be led to
reflect upon the question, "Where, after all, does thinking
come from?" If so, he will have the opportunity to discover that
the origin, the source, of thinking is embarrassment.

The word itself tells the story. The French word *embar-
rasser* carries the meaning "to block or to obstruct, to impede,
to place a barrier or obstacle in the way." It also means "to per-
plex, to throw into doubt." No one actually thinks until faced
with an obstacle. Embarrassment is one of the chiefest means
of encountering the obstruction of doubt. One cannot think
unless obstructed. Thinking seeks to remove the barrier.

The completely poised, polished, unflappable person is
beyond the discomfiture of thinking. He is motivated by the
residual insights of his culture in much the same way as a
zombie is animated by a life-spirit not his own. Zombies are
immune to embarrassment.

Ah...but if Michael is led to make the connection
between the unthinking and the undead he will be off on an
extended set of reflections indeed, since in the heightened
intensity born of such speculation he is certain to make the
seldom (if ever) recognized connection between zombies and
the Garden of Eden. *Zombie* is the name of the West African
snake deity said to have the power to reanimate the dead
(Michael would recall that he read this some years ago in a
book on African mythology). The serpent in the Garden was
none other than *Zombie* himself?

When Satan (aka *Zombie*) stole eternal bliss from the Primordial Pair, promising all the while, "You will not die," he was
not actually lying. For Satan reanimated the couple in hell.

The conclusion of these reflections (surely Michael will
have had to have suffered serious humiliation to come up
with all these important insights) would have to be that
shame and embarrassment are our only salvation. They lead
us to think, to be perplexed, to be insecure and so to seek
security. The despairing consequence, however, is this: If the
primordial shame of Adam and Eve did not save them, how
could shame save anyone?

Only two possibilities exist: either Adam and Eve are zombies numbly roasting in Hell (and we ourselves, in spite of all our pretensions to thought, will be brought to the same end) *or* shame eventually saved the first couple and will, if we yield ourselves sufficiently to it, save us as well.

It would be uplifting to report that Michael would lean toward the latter possibility, that he would have arguments left over from his seminary training to make that possibility more plausible than the former. But we already know from exposure to his peculiar doctrine of Fat Dharma that this is not so.

Michael would reason in this manner: The First Animation, when Fat Dharma (*Zombie,* also?) inspired the dust, is already suspect. Our shameless beginnings brought forth life, not from within ourselves but as a forced offering from Fat Dharma. The Second Animation (Satan's temptation and its consequences) again provides motivation from beyond ourselves.

Shame enables us to think. Thinking permits us to realize that we are damned in either of two cases: We can be zombies in the Blessed Realm, staggering among fleecy clouds and climes; or we can be zombies performing our puppet dance in the furnaces of Hell. And though, on the short term, the former is clearly preferable to the latter, for the being who presumes to think, the recognition that he is but a zombie makes the alternatives indistinguishable.

Heaven was made for the likes of unthinking creatures such as the innocent Adam and Eve, those ignorant of their zombie status. Only such thoughtless creatures could enjoy the Beatific Vision, could live forever in paradisal environs. But this could not be so for the Fallen Pair, who had been enlightened by the first embarrassment. Hell, then, is simply Heaven after the recognition that we are zombies. All would-be thinkers are in Hell.

Once it is clear that Fat Dharma and Satan are a single animating spirit (*Zombie*) and that the First and Second Animations have the same author, then "the rest is history." The Undead have created culture and history as a means of hiding from their shame.

History (the detritus of passing time, as Michael is given to say) is the product of zombies embarrassed by self-awareness.

Recognizing the absence of self-animation, their inexorable emptiness, they can only respond: "How embarrassing!"

And what does it all amount to but a celebration of He Whom Michael has come to call Fat Dharma and Who we now know warrants the alias *Zombie*?

25

"All of the senses, until they receive education, are of the form Sniff and Grab. The soft scented skin doesn't require perfumes to inspire us. Our noses are prepared to sniff out our prey and to lure it within our reach. Each of our senses anchor us to the physical plane, but it is our noses, above all, that point us away from the path. And it is not the eye, but the ear, that is our initial means of release.

"Meditation requires the correct posture and positioning of the limbs and head, the appropriate sounds and their associated sights. The vibrations associated with sound are fundamental. We tantrics focus our senses in terms of sound. Ultimately, of course, there is only emptiness. The dharmas are, indeed, empty; existence is, of course, illusory. But we find it convenient to focus our illusions in terms of the illusion of sound.

"The doctrine of the kundalini serpent is itself only a convenience. Each of the tantric schools interprets this doctrine in a different way. Buddhist and Hindu tantrics are divided over the question of how to identify the creative and passive roles in the sexual polarities. Is the power of the feminine the active or the passive, the creative or the created? Theologians will debate these issues endlessly. Those who practice the tantra know that this question is of no importance.

"We do use the language of bisexuality, but since each being is no more than a focus of the phenomenon of hanging on, and since each is both male and female, it makes little difference as to how one sorts out the functions. The ostensible male dominates the ostensible female first by suppressing the female in himself and then by repressing those who play the female role in the world. But this is only a political fact.

"Transitory political facts have helped to determine the conventions of our social life. It is these which make our doctrines appear unfair to females. Political realities that have shaped the conventions of our world make the applications of the doctrines what you would call "sexist." But since we have no preference ourselves as to which sort of body we inhabit, which incarnates us, we are not really disposed toward sexism. There are females so-called and there are males so-called. The sexual choice is determined by psychic development, not genetic accident. Whether one needs in any particular instance to be male or female in bodily organization is a matter of choice in the *bardo*, the realm between death and rebirth."

Michael surveyed his colleagues sitting around him. He thought that Rinpoche's words might have seemed weightier had there been at least one female face.

"As long as you believe we are in a progressive movement toward nirvana, neither male nor female has ultimate advantage. Given the conventions of our political world, the male is the higher spiritual form only in the sense of being, under these conditions, the candidate for final release. Male dominance is a non-Buddhist problem. For such political and emotional oppression of females by males matters only if this present life is your only round of existence.

"The story of Padmasambhava's violent rape of his *dakini* on the cremation ground is often held up by our critics as an instance of how much we are preoccupied with perverse sexuality. But, of course, that is to misunderstand the point of the story. The *dakini* is a mental projection—a sexual tutor created, in this instance, by Padmasambhava from his own psychic substance. The assault of his *dakini* undertaken in the place of death and decay carries the symbolic truth that the tantrics wish to preach. One cannot come to grips with one's other half without violence. And the male-female conflict within one's own person is far more furious than is the traditional war between the sexes."

26

"I must speak of something that will concern those of you who have read of our doctrines and practices. What is available for you to read in European languages makes us appear rather scandalous. Every religion has its magicians, and it is the magicians, the purveyors of signs and miracles, by which religions too often become known.

"Do tantrics actually consume excrement and human flesh? Do we have sex with children? Participate in group orgies? I must tell you that each of these statements is, technically, quite true. But, we tantrics do not monopolize scandalous practice. You Christians periodically feast upon your founder's body, do you not? Then, you are cannibals. Technically, quite true.

"I can only say that the culture which enjoins tantric practices gives respect and prestige to the participants in the practices. If it were not so that the victims would return to become the oppressors, then one might harshly judge such practices. But the thought that you only go around once is not in the Buddhist inventory of ideas. That is your strange view."

27

"Nowhere is the prejudice against Buddhist practices greater than with respect to the skills that accompany spiritual transformation, skills we call the *siddhis*. I say 'accompany,' though I am afraid that due to the perverseness of existence and becoming, they all too often precede spiritual realizations.

"There are eight traditional *siddhis*—in fact, many more. But eight categories are most often used to account for the pathological symptoms of enlightenment. The adept does well to ignore them, or treat them as the minor physiological accidents they are—like an attack of the hiccups or the unintentional passing of wind. Magicians, however, seek to develop these powers and would use them for purposes of control.

"Many outside the inner Buddhist circles believe that these powers come only after long years of effort. This is a convenient and well-meaning falsehood perpetuated by those who know too well that if the powers do come early, they arrive before the seeker is prepared to control them. Alas, the truth: power is almost immediate if one is able to concentrate in conducive surroundings and...if the desire is great.

"The long years, the many lifetimes are necessary if one is to protect oneself and others from the power and the grasping it engenders. One finally seeks mastery of oneself, release from hanging on. But in the beginning there is only the manipulation of self and others by the energies focused through the practice. The only real difference between power and creativity—between manipulative magic and the control of oneself—is the discipline that comes from guided practice.

"So you must be warned: It is within your power to increase your power past your ability to control it. Do not, please, arouse the kundalini spirit without a guide. It is both childish and dangerous to tease a snake."

28

Talk of the kundalini serpent continued to excite Michael even after he had translated it into the relatively tame context of image and metaphor. He recalled reading a book on the mythology of the Plains Indians which told how in certain crucial situations braves would receive important messages directly from their genitals. While in the midst of a long meditative walk in the wilderness, a troubled warrior might suddenly be subjected to a lecture from his penis charting past mistakes and the means whereby he might return to the proper path.

Michael had found these stories both amusing and ironic in the light of his own experience. For like many others, his enthusiastic responses to exhortations from his penis had seldom had any but regrettable consequences. Rinpoche's account of the kundalini serpent, however, had renewed Michael's hope in the efficacy of wisdom procured from below his belt.

29

Tilly was complaining about A–K's presence at the retreat.

Michael was puzzled. "You must have had a say in allowing him to come."

"In this single instance I did not. Rinpoche sent a note indicating that this gentleman, 'whose name is just two initials,' was going to apply and begged the kindness of the staff in admitting him. It was his wish. I was surprised that he would have done this."

"What do you know about him?"

"Nothing."

"His last name?"

"No."

Michael could tell that Tilly was uncomfortable, but he clearly wanted to know about A–K and was willing to risk this rather unprofessional behavior in order to find out what he could. Perhaps Tilly thought that the conspiracy he so obviously believed to exist between Rinpoche and A–K extended to Michael as well.

"You haven't asked Rinpoche?"

"It wouldn't be appropriate." Tilly's voice faded. After only a second's pause he suddenly redirected the conversation. "You seem to be more at home in this context than I would have imagined, given your intellectual background."

Michael was quite pleased to avoid further awkwardness and so replied amicably, "Well, it's not exactly my brick of tea."

"Nonetheless...?"

"Nonetheless, I find it fascinating. But I have to tell you, Tilmon, I'm quite easy to fascinate. I admit that I have a very low threshold of boredom, but in the short run—and eleven weeks is certainly, as Rinpoche says, 'far less than an instant'—I am easily impressed."

"You don't think you will continue?"

"Continue? You mean the study of Buddhism?"

"The practice."

"Practice? I'm not a practitioner. This is just a polite introduction, remember? We are, so says Rinpoche, just onlookers, tourists. I'll have to leave it at that." Michael wondered if Tilly knew he was lying.

"One may always find a way to continue if there is interest."

Michael had been dreading this. Rinpoche's lectures had been so relaxed and disarming that he had almost convinced himself that the weeks would pass without any sales pitch. Apparently not. He thought to deflect it for the present. "How long have you been at this?"

"You mean how many years?"

Michael realized that Tilly was prepared to claim that he had been "at it" for numerous lifetimes, and whereas he could easily take such talk from Rinpoche, the thought of this person saying such a thing was unacceptable. "How long with the institute?" That seemed safe enough.

"Yes." Tilly was openly disappointed at Michael's reticence to enter into any metaphysical subjects. "Four years, I think. Yes, four."

The institute had another director before me—for about two years. The whole thing has been around for just six years, since Rinpoche came to this country. But I've been practicing for a very long time myself."

Oh, no you don't Tilly. "What aspect of the practice do you find most challenging?"

"The *asanas*."

Jesus. Out of the frying pan.... "The sexual practices?"

"In particular the stages of sexual fulfillment. It is possible to perform any particular one separately, of course, but the total sequence is most challenging."

Michael had read about the *asanas*, and Rinpoche had sketched some of the lineaments of the practice. He recalled that in Taoism the technique involves controlling one's physiological responses during the sexual act in such manner as to promote ejaculation backward into the bladder. The adept then is presumed to benefit from the absorption of his own psychophysical energy (the *ch'i*) contained in the semen and prostatic fluids. "Withholding the *ch'i*? You practice that?" Michael tried to appear nonchalant.

"That is a rather vulgar description, but, yes."

"Do you have...require a real partner?"

"Real?"

Of course, Michael thought—a mistake. The word *real* was always up for grabs. "I mean a physical partner."

"Certainly not always. I have a *dakini*."

Michael strained against revealing too much interest.

"A psychic teacher?"

"More or less. I am, for the most part celibate. I generally practice the *asanas* with my *dakini*."

"How did you obtain a...eh, *dakini*?"

My teacher gave her to me.

"Rinpoche?"

"Not Thögma. It was...before."

"Ah. What do you learn?"

"The lessons are, I'm afraid, private."

"Sorry."

"Not at all. The meanings just aren't communicable. Rinpoche has spoken to you of the *dakini*, has he not?"

Before Michael could speak, Tilly waved his arm and said, "But that is between the two of you. Had he spoken to you about the *yi-dam*—your teacher—you would do well to take him seriously. Each of us needs a teacher who is at least partially of our own contrivance. But enough of this. I may be infringing upon your relationship with Rinpoche. That would be wrong. I have presumed because...at least to my mind...you seem to have taken to the discipline as the others have not...but you say that yours is an academic interest only...and that is quite appropriate, of course."

Michael was silent, afraid that if he spoke he would only create further suspicion. Thankfully, Tilly seemed to have tired of the conversation. "Yes, Michael. We shall speak again if you wish."

"Of course, Tilmon. That would be good."

Tilly left Michael standing by the door of his room, reflecting upon his growing sense of disquiet.

30

"The first *siddhi* is that of *anima* and its associated *mahima*. These are the powers of growing smaller and larger at will. The second involves the attainment of weightlessness. This leads to levitation. Another involves psychic relocation. You know this as 'out of the body experiences.' Another permits the adept to intensify his senses. For example, the adept can hear the grass growing." Rinpoche paused and turned his head slightly to one side. "This can be quite disconcerting." (Michael recalled the phrase from Oscar Wilde's "Requiescat," "Tread lightly, she can hear the daisies grow.")

"I will tell you this important truth: these are inconsequential skills. They are mere by-products—often unavoidable, I am afraid. And they are more trouble by far than you could realize. In the hands of the magicians they are fakery and—I very much like this word of yours—flimflam."

Rinpoche stopped talking and leaned forward. A smile had trespassed the stern features he had maintained throughout this lecture. Then an exaggerated sigh: "Yet..." He shrugged his shoulders, but because of his slight stature the shrug looked more like a shiver. "I realize that many are unable to believe such practices possible unless they have some demonstration. I am willing, therefore, most reluctantly, to exercise one or two of the *siddhis* for you.

"Watch now as I perform *anima*..." Rinpoche stepped off the platform from which he normally spoke and stood at attention. Every one was puzzled. "And now for *mahima*." He stepped back upon the platform. "Would you like to see me do it again?" There was no laughter from anyone but Rinpoche, but his giggle seemed to fill the room.

Michael knew why he hadn't laughed, why he wasn't laughing now, and he supposed it was the same for the others. He was silent because, just at the end of his mock demonstration of the *siddhis*, Rinpoche had begun to pulsate, to physically swell and shrink, to move in and out of focus, like an image manipulated through the lens of binoculars.

31

"If things lack 'own-being,' they are empty, no?" A–K was sitting in the corner of the room, his legs were spread almost at right angles to one another, hands clasped behind his head. "And if everything is empty, then everything is dead. Buddhism is the philosophy of death." A–K paused, waiting for a reply.

Michael reflected, Life is appearance. Death is reality. Why not? He sat down on the bed and picked up a small writing tablet from one of the bedside tables. "Well, let's see. What kinds of things are there?" Using a pencil, he sketched a diagram on a half-sheet of paper torn from the tablet. He made several mistakes and had to erase, but when he had finished his scheme looked like this:

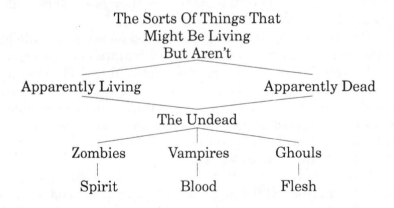

Michael spoke mockingly, in the manner of a debater blessed with an unanswerable argument: "Nothing has life from itself except God." He said God, but of course he meant Fat Dharma. "God and Zombie are one spirit. He is the only living thing." Michael saw the puzzled look on A–K's face and so offered his peculiar account of the serpent in the Garden.

"The souls created by God do not have their own-being. Vampires and ghouls are nothing more than secularized do-it-yourself zombies. All the dead may rise, animated either by spirit, flesh, or blood.

"So it appears, A–K, though your original claim was certainly plausible, you simply had not thought through your insights with sufficient rigor. The principal occupants of our world are neither the apparently living nor the seemingly dead. It is the *Undead*—zombies, vampires and ghouls—who rule the earth."

A–K was without any response other than the appearance of a generous respect for Michael's *tour de force*. Michael, meanwhile, hadn't the slightest doubt but that his conclusions about the meaning of life and of death were, in each and every particular, absolutely true.

32

Michael could see that Rinpoche was sitting quite still, nonetheless, he almost seemed to be bouncing on his cushion as he spoke. He had been chattering for some minutes now, his eyes glazed by a frenetic concentration Michael had never seen before. "Yes, Yes. Of course, yes...that's it you see. If the carousel makes one brief circuit then shuts down, no other way is possible. Or if, at best, you've but one ticket to ride, it makes perfect sense, doesn't it? Ah, but if you've a seemingly inexhaustible supply of tickets; if you have no choice but to go around and around and around again, then this is—wouldn't you agree?—quite another matter.

"Your Freud was simply thinking things through based upon his belief that we only ride once. But see how close he is to our view. He thought everything is finally dead and the world finally empty. So we believe, as well. He thought the self, the ego, to be little more than a "strangulated hernia of extruded awareness" to quote one of the more enlightened of your religious writers. We hold much the same thing to be true. The self is the consequence of a clinging, a hanging on, an ultimately hysterical impulse to focus the vast oceanic feeling common to all innocent consciousness. But the difference, the tiny difference that makes all the difference, is this: Freud insisted that we have no choice, given our single-ticket journey, but to make the best of things: to grasp, to cling, and then to be forced by factors more insistent, more primordial than ourselves, to let go and to dissolve into meaningless fragments no one of which could bear the stamp of consciousness. To die and to be gone."

Rinpoche paused. Michael felt as if he were supposed to say something. "But that seems the same as Buddhists believe, as well. The candle is snuffed out."

"Ah, no. The candle's flame resists extinction. It is far beyond our unaided capacities to blow it out. Life is clinging, yes. To live is to hang on. But that's the problem, not the solution. The death instinct is a silly doctrine. Our perverse instinct is to live, to cling. Death is the liberation that enlightenment provides. But it is much more difficult to win death than one thinks. Does that seem silly to you?"

"Not silly. But I don't find it convincing."

"Yes. And it is not my place to convince you. It is enough that you see the difference."

"I'll tell you what I find difficult. If as you believe there are myriad rounds of existence and winning free from the carousel is your goal, how is it that life could bring happiness? How can *you* be happy—as you certainly seem to be?"

"I enjoy the path on the way to death. Why does this surprise you?"

"One must live in order to enjoy. If your goal is to become extinct, you must be aiming at a state that precludes enjoyment. Doesn't enjoying this or that slow your progress toward extinction? Doesn't it make you cling to life?"

"Ah, Professor Evers. Interesting. Yes..." Rinpoche seemed to be pondering what Michael thought a rather obvious remark as if it contained some deep and arcane wisdom. "I enjoy much as you must and doubtless many of the same things. The difference is that I enjoy things," Rinpoche leaned forward as he spoke, "*because* I know that I shall not be burdened by the necessity of enjoying them forever. You enjoy, so I believe— your words tell me this—*in spite of* the fact that you will not have the opportunity to enjoy them forever. So much difference. Do you see it? Your joy is in spite of, mine because of."

Michael was silent. He was surprised to find himself in sympathy with Rinpoche's words. Apparently, seven weeks exposure to the oddities of tantric doctrine and practice had affected him more than he had thought.

"See here, professor, if I give you a pastry to eat—imagine your favorite. I give it to you..." Rinpoche lifted his hand, palm upward, and held it out toward Michael. Michael, feeling only a bit silly, reached out to take his favorite pastry from Rinpoche's hand. (It was an éclair, this illusory pastry. Strange, he hadn't realized that he cared so much for éclairs.) "You will enjoy it, yes? But surely that could be true only if you forgot that, for the moment of your pleasure at least, so many others were without the same pleasure and that you yourself would one day not be around to enjoy the pastry—an éclair, a creamy chocolate éclair, perhaps."

Michael was no longer surprised by Rinpoche's (always inconsequential) displays of telepathic insight.

"What this means, professor, is that you would win your pleasure only by ignoring certain fundamental truths about life and circumstance that you otherwise hold to be basic.

"But if you knew that one day you would not have to be in the position of enjoying pastries and, nonetheless, you could still enjoy eating them, you would then have a firm, fixed, unassailable pleasure. Such firm pleasures only result when desiring has no object. That is, when the desire is immediate and self-justifying. If you have no need to own or control the apparent object of your desire, yours would be a firm pleasure. If it were a matter of indifference to you that your éclair had to be shared, or might be taken from you, and still you enjoyed it, then you would have immediate joy. And immediate joy is firm and fixed for the tiny moment of its existence.

"Surely trouble most often comes when one begins to expect the continuance of pleasure. Because, unless one can be persuaded of the reality of a heavenly paradise—an increasingly difficult accomplishment in this modern age—the final fact seems to be that soon or late all possibility of enjoyment will—must—vanish."

"I can agree with most of what you say," Michael was conceding more than he wanted to concede, "but I see no alternative to the conclusion that if one enjoys this or that, he or she can only do so against the background of untold numbers who at that moment are experiencing misery. I recall reading this statement of the matter by a modern philosopher—'The fairies dance, and Christ is nailed to the cross.'"

"Wise. Yes. Perhaps it is not too much to say that the fairies dance their lovely, delicate, joyous dance *because* they realize that the torturings and crucifixions and immolations and assassinations are themselves transitory events and that time must have a stop."

"I can't accept that."

"Ah, no.... But you must realize that the sense of those who believe that they hold but a single ticket on the carousel is that joy increases with the inability of others to experience or share it. Thomas Hobbes, a far greater psychologist than Sigmund Freud, recognized that fame is such a desirable thing for those beset by mortality simply and solely because it cannot be shared. There is only one Number One, no?"

"Then you would say that one should enjoy because pleasure and pain are temporary?"

"Yes. Happiness is not in spite of but because of the transitoriness of pleasure. It is because of not in spite of the immediate and nonattached character of desire. What is silly about that?"

"Not silly, just different."

"Yes, different."

Michael suddenly began to feel strange. The feeling was something like nausea, but it was unfocused, spread throughout his body. He spoke more loudly than was appropriate in this intimate setting, "I would like to leave now if you don't mind."

Rinpoche pressed his hands tightly together and closed his eyes. Michael got up from his cushion. His knees complained a bit. But the stiffness yielded quickly as he walked away.

33

3.1415926535... Christ! 1... 4... 1... 5... 9... 2... 6... 5... 3... 5. Michael had been running in place underneath the Shinto gate. Now he stopped. It was a mild panic but a real one nonetheless. His aim had been run to his limit. Not his physical limit, but the limit of his memory. With each pass through Shinto gate—*pi* gate, he now called it—he would pause under its gold, silver, and blue embossed frame long enough to repeat the entire sequence up to the point he had reached. Then he would ceremoniously add the next decimal to the value of *pi*. He figured the route he was running to be a bit more than a quarter of a mile. He had memorized the value of *pi* to twenty-five decimals About six and one-half miles. No problem.

Except...he couldn't run without the eleventh decimal.

Was it simple fatigue? Or was his brain decaying? He counted on his memory, but he knew it would have to fail him someday. Was this the beginning? Michael sat down and leaned his back against the gate. He took a mental running start as one does when preparing for the broad jump or the pole vault—setting one's rhythm with the first paces then accelerating rapidly just before the leap: 3. 1, 4, 1, 5, 9, 2, 6, 5, 3, 5... Nothing. Blank. Worse than blank—negation: the absolute assurance of absence.

(It's 8, Michael.)

Quickly, he rehearsed the dates of a selection of the principal philosophers from Socrates to Wittgenstein, Dewey, and Russell. OK, they were still in place. He silently scanned the lines of Wallace Stevens's, "The Emperor of Ice Cream" and Yeats's "Among School Children." He was calmer now. Still he couldn't remember the next decimal after that tenth-place 5. Maybe just a quirk.

He gave up his run.

Michael could have run forever without exhausting the decimal places in *pi*. The constant had been calculated to millions of places and there was no final place. There could be an infinity of passages through *pi* gate.

Both Christians and Buddhists are wrong. Christians believe that eternity lies beyond time. True reality is timeless. Buddhists believe that time must have a stop; all things will end. This is the state of *sunyata*, "emptiness." Michael, on the contrary, was inclined to believe that things dribbled on in constant inconstancy much as the decimal places in *pi*.

The world knows no culmination, no resolution; it is without beginning, without ending, without punctuation of any kind other than the arbitrary intervals marked by the fractional parts of time and space, of meaning and value, all of which are infinitely fractionable into ever smaller arbitrary pieces. The world is an incomplete, uncompletable process. It is always *coming into being*, never *being*.

The world is no single-ordered cosmos, owning invariable laws and rational structure. It is, rather, a dribbling irrationality. And because it is always incomplete, never a whole, it is never really a world. The world doesn't exist!

On the way back to the dormitory he decided to take his mind off *pi*, but the value of *e* in the fine structure constant immediately came to the fore, dragging Karla and Company along with it. He had to get away from numbers. Then he would remember.

It was A–K's time in the room. He would have to stay away at least another half an hour. He had brought his towel with him. He thought he would go looking for the eleventh decimal in the shower.

It was a mistake. His route took him past the resident director's cottage. The door was open...slightly, but enough. He couldn't really help but see. What he saw in a few seconds, perhaps no more than two or three, was horrifying. There was a mirror attached to the closet door inside the room. Tilly was standing in front of it. He was naked. Not just naked, but obscenely bare. Rigid...erect. He wasn't touching himself. Just standing. His penis was engorged, distended. A meaty grotesque. Just staring...at the mirror. At himself? Yes. No. Pulsing...thrusting. But he wasn't touching himself. He wasn't moving. It was moving. Or being moved.

Tilly didn't notice Michael. That is, he didn't take note of him. But he did make, in the course of these few seconds, no more than four or five, a slight move away from the door—a move, however, that only succeeded in turning himself more directly toward the mirror, offering Michael an even more complete reflection of the event and its gruesome issue.

34

"Eight!" He said it aloud. He was just passing through the doorway of the showers. 3.1415926535... 8... 97932384626433. He repeated the sequence under his breath as he adjusted the temperature of the water. Thus was he momentarily protected by his memory from the memory. The water was cold. It seemed more refreshing than usual. Lots of soap. He scrubbed himself clean. This was on behalf of Tilly he thought. He was cleansing himself of Tilly's sin. So he believed. (Or so he thought that he believed.)

35

Michael was too self-conscious ever to sing in the showers.
Showers (on the whole he preferred baths) were for rhapsodic
reflections. He allowed himself to reflect (off-key) whenever he
took a bath or shower, but never to sing. Still pleased for having recalled *pi* to the twenty-fifth decimal, he allowed himself
to ruminate in what he took to be (but should have known
could not have been) a haphazard manner.

The Buddha was watching television.

In New York's Museum of Modern Art they came upon a
statue of the Buddha, about a foot high. It had been placed
directly in front of a television set. Behind the set was a moni-
tor. On the screen was the image of the Buddha. At the time,
he and his friend had laughed out loud. Now, standing in the
shower, the thrust of the spray stinging his back, the water
warming slightly as it ran down the backs of his legs, pooling
at his feet momentarily before finally draining from the shower
floor, carrying with it dust and sweat and peelings of skin, as
he scrubbed himself clean of Tilly's, soon to be his sin, Michael
was ashamed of having laughed.

He knows, and knew then for that matter, that television
is not a window to the world, but a narcissan pool mirroring
the soul, the Arimaspian eye that mocks our blindness. What
more could the Buddha have known? Nothing. The Buddha
knows only what he sees. He sees himself. We see ourselves,
too. But we hope, trust, persuade ourselves that we see something other—as if that could be so, as if anything else, anything other exists. But the Buddha's knowledge releases him
from pain; that same knowledge is our torment.

Semen, Michael. Remember? Semen and glass.

36

Semen and glass. The reflection.... His...Michael's. But not at first. Stepping into the booth, pocket full of tokens, one dollar each. The telephone receiver. The full-length shade. The first token in the slot, the shade slowly raising accompanied by a whirring sound. Much prettier than she should have been, this woman. Slender, with powdery white skin. She motioned to the telephone inside his part of the booth. Michael picked up the receiver, as she lifted hers. He couldn't smell her (or could he?) through the glass. Knit stockings. One (it was the left) was torn, the rip appearing just above the shoe at her ankle. Not shoes, actually. They looked like ballet slippers.

What he saw then, remembers now—what he saw at the very first—was itself the image of a long abandoned memory. It was that thigh, the image of it, a single bare thigh reaching in this place to her bikini pants, but reaching, at first, to the tight metallic shorts of her uniform. The curve of that taut thigh. The woman (it was only a girl in the booth) he now remembered was the occasion of his sinning. Not the object or even the cause. She was yet another. But who was this behind the glass—her legs spread wide, feet pressed tightly against the corners of the booth—in the saddle position for pelvic examination—for giving birth—for being fucked hard and harder?

The Michael in the booth was nineteen. But the other Michael was very much younger. The Michael in the booth was not yet fully a man. The second Michael was prehistoric.

He was (the younger Michael) at a magazine stand. He was about to buy a copy of *Astounding Science Fiction*. The cover made him pause longer than he had wished. There was, of course, the obligatory Bug-Eyed Monster, but that had not been the occasion of his hypnotized glare. The woman, also obligatory, was dressed in the accepted costume of the twenty-whateverth century. Brief tights, short boots, low-cut blouse, bare midriff, holding a formidable looking ray gun of some sort. One of her legs (it was the right leg) was pressed forward toward the alien, exposing the bare thigh. It was that thigh that had startled Michael. It was that thigh that was the occasion (not the cause—the cause lay deeper still) of his being tipped and toppled into the pool of desiring. Sink or swim. He wanted, needed, something, something in some way associated with that thigh. He half knew, supposed he knew, would have pretended that he knew. But didn't yet know.

He took the pulp magazine and read every story, looking inside for the elaboration of his urgings, the vindication of his need. He kept the magazine hidden in a bureau drawer, safe from any but his eyes. Sometimes at night before going to bed he would remove it from its nesting place and spend long, meditative moments staring at the cover, pretending that he was the alien and wondering how it would feel to be that close to the thigh, able (except for the threatening weapon that separated the two) to touch it, to rub his worrying itch against it.

The cover smelled of ink and of the pulp pages just behind it. Michael remembers that the odor was...incomplete. Something was missing. Some nights he would sleep with that book between his legs—thigh on thigh.

The feeling was intense... and intenser. When he awoke he felt and saw the vague moist stains which were the consequence of the event and the cause of its understanding. Is it meant to be so? One becomes a man while sleeping?

The book had been in his drawer. He had been alone. He couldn't even remember the dream; there must have been one. Would it have been of her? Or had he spent his innocence with no threatening, comforting thigh? Michael could no longer bear to look at her. The next day he removed the book from its hiding place, cover facing down, and threw it in the garbage can in the rear of his house.

Some days after, still trying to absorb the truth of his numb passage, Michael found himself thinking that his lost dream should have been of... What was her name? Brown hair, freckles. She had long legs. Her hair was thicker than any he had ever seen. (Adrienne, Michael... Her name was Adrienne.) Did he know her thigh? He could have dreamed of her, he thought, without betraying the companion of these past weeks, who looked so real, who so mocked her ink-and-paper image that she had won her place as sister to the flesh—Michael's first coveted flesh and all the flesh he would ever covet.

Michael knew that no one would share his despair, nor

could any sympathize with his first real sense of irrevocability, of the ephemerality of the precious. There was no one with whom he could share his discovery. This insight would shape his understanding perhaps more than any other. A simple truth: Contrary to the pandering promise that attaches to beginnings, *the first time is the only time.*

There had been many others, but none had captured him so surely as this thigh, not since that first. This thigh reminded him of his wastefulness, as surely as it was to condemn him to another wasteful deed.

She spoke. Thin, whining voice: "Let me see what you've got." Nothing to be done but to get it over with. He dragged his complaining flesh from out his pants and did what he wished he didn't have to do.

The shade went down after less than a minute. A second token and a third. She whined and contorted and urged. He struggled with himself as he sought both to prolong the pleasure and postpone the sin. Her panties were off now, hanging from one leg, the right leg, partially covering that famous, now offending thigh. Rubbing, thrusting on both sides of the glass. Could she see him?

Michael never spoke. He listened but he never spoke. Foul words and grunts, fake of course, were added to the whines. They were echoes. Though Michael made no sound, would have been ashamed to make a sound, his mind had already formed each of the obscenities that came now from her. He was their author. How could it be otherwise?

37

Narcissus fell in love with his reflection believing that he loved an 'other.' The tragic irony was intensified when Echo fell in love with Narcissus, for she was condemned to communicate only by echoing the words spoken to her. Narcissus loved himself, without knowing it. And his only salvation, Echo, could not speak of her love for him. She could only reflect his words back to him. Narcissus was trapped inside reflections of sight and sound.

Michael would later think that in this moment he had been privileged to feel how Fat Dharma, the solitary greedy poet, must have felt—He Who alone has created and after whose creative act there can be only the illusion of creativity. That grotesque poet of the world cast all His seed into the Void and must surely have come to resent His creation, as any artist who has exhausted his genius in a single creative act must come to despise his ever only opus.

Wasted, again. Not his innocence, this time; only his substance. But wasted. Michael watched resignedly as the semen stuck and ran, the thinner fluid streaming down the glass.

The descent of man.

The shade moved more slowly now. He urged it on.

The last thing Michael saw, the only thing he ever really saw before leaving the booth to join the solitary army of spent zombies making their fumbling exits into the night was his smeared Buddha image on the darkened glass.

38

"There are no limits. You may ask me what you wish."

Michael was about to continue the conversation from their last meeting. Before he spoke, however, Rinpoche started to laugh, quietly at first, then with increasing volume. Michael was nonplussed.

Rinpoche recovered after almost a minute, and raising both hands in a salutary gesture, he said, "Forgive my giggling. It can't seem very dignified to you, it is one of several examples of karmic dissonance remaining in me. It is far better to let these things run their course—like a fever. Besides..." Rinpoche was leaning forward now; it seemed to Michael that the distance between them had completely collapsed. "I think the giggling is not altogether mine, you see. It is a response, a reply to something silly. I don't always know when there is silliness until all of a sudden I begin to shake with laughter. One day, when I am a better teacher, I shall be able to spot foolishness without my warning giggle."

Michael thought that he should be offended, or at least embarrassed. He was not. All he could do was to smile stiffly. "You will tell me what was silly?"

"Michael. You. *You* are silly."

"I'm not trying to be silly."

"Clowns and comics try to be silly. You are neither. You are, as we all are at some time or another, just naturally silly."

"Should I try not to be silly?"

"If you wish." Rinpoche leaned back, the lines in his face weaving themselves into what Michael thought must be the Tibetan version of mocking indulgence.

Michael waited for him to speak, but he did not. He wanted to lean forward, but something held him in his rather straight posture on his cushion. He stretched his arms behind his back. He waited. He was puzzled to find that he could feel neither shame nor indignation. Rather, he felt...comfortable. In spite of the aching in his knees he had just begun to feel and which he knew would rapidly increase, he had no desire to move, no reason to want anything other than to remain here as long as Rinpoche would allow him to stay. Then, vaguely at first, but with growing intensity, he realized he was being selfish. Unable in his still unfamiliar posture to move forward sufficiently to effect a bow, Michael nodded his head slightly toward Rinpoche.

"Good, Michael. Yes. We will speak again in three days." Rinpoche closed his eyes.

Michael left the room. Some hours later, lying on his cot, only a few calm breaths away from sleep, he reflected: I could have remained, had I wished. For as long as I wished...

39

During the ninth week Michael intensified his visualization exercises. In addition to meditating upon the constructed facial image, he performed exercises using a simple technique he remembered from an obscure commentary on *The Diamond Sutra* he had found in the Boston Public Library some weeks before coming to Tilopa. It involved the manipulation of afterimages obtained by staring intently at three-dimensional objects. He would stare for three or four minutes at a selected object—usually one of the two small parson's tables in the room set aside for meditation.

On this particular morning he was attempting to use both tables. He would stare at the yellow table then cast his eyes away as he attempted to hold fast to the afterimage. Then he would do the same using the black table. After more than two hours of practice, he found himself able to superimpose the reddish orange afterimage of the yellow table upon the black one, creating an image precisely the same size as its object.

Toward the end of this three-hour session something unusual (finally) happened. Michael found that the afterimage of the yellow table remained in space, between the two tables, no matter how much he attempted to direct its course. Then the image descended and stood exactly between the yellow and black tables. The afterimage now had a deep luminescent red hue. It remained the same size as the other two tables.

Michael strained to keep his eyes open. Finally, he was forced to blink. He had expected to lose the image, but he didn't. Instead, it appeared now in three dimensions. He counted the tables—the first, the second...and the third. He closed his eyes and rubbed them. When he looked again all three tables stared back at him. For quite a few seconds he continued trying to blink the third table away, without success.

There was no choice. He stretched out his hand and tapped the yellow table, listening to the muffled thumping sound his finger made on the plastic surface. Next he tapped the black one, with the same result. His hand hovered over the red table for several seconds. It had lost its glow and was even more frightening because more ordinary and, therefore, more insistently present.

Michael felt the muscles tighten in the top of his hand as his finger raised slightly in anticipation of his fearsome act. Just as he was about to move his finger down, to feel his finger pass through the illusory surface and to see the now dull blood-red table dissolve in obsequious response to his exposure of its illegitimate claim to be real—just at that very instant—he squeezed his eyes closed, stood up and stumbled toward the door.

Only when he was outside did he open his eyes. He stood with his back to the entrance of the small mediation cell and tried to distract himself by reciting some cantos from Byron's *Don Juan*. After a few minutes, he marched confidently back into the room and nodded with satisfaction (and relief) when he saw what any normal human being should have seen: two tables, only two, a yellow and a black.

40

Rinpoche listened patiently at first, but soon seemed no longer able to contain himself. Suddenly he let out a loud shriek as he lifted himself up and pulled his cushion out from under his bottom, swatting Michael hard on his head. Michael hadn't felt so foolish in years. He was holding his hands in front of his face as Rinpoche laughed and screamed and pummeled him with his cushion. The cushion wasn't soft by any means and the blows were certainly not delivered with any reservation.

As he waited, with as much dignity as he could manage, for his beating to be over, Michael found himself increasingly occupied with the odor of Rinpoche's cushion as it was swung hard against his poorly defended face. It was an awesome scent, sharp and musky, born of sweat and incense and the combined piquancies of urine and spilled tea. The essence of Rinpoche. Michael wanted to take the cushion away with him. He could use it as a spiritual sachet in his meditation closet.

It was when he recognized how wonderful was the odor of Rinpoche's cushion that he realized he loved the man.

"Well. So, you learned your lesson, didn't you? Yes, you learned your lesson. But it was, I'm sorry, *your* lesson. Not ours. You were so afraid that the product of your imagination would appear real to you...and if it had.... Ahhhhhhhh..." Bellowing again, Rinpoche raised the cushion over his head with both hands. Michael shrank from the almost certain blow which never came. "Well. A good Buddhist—even a bad Buddhist—would have learned something quite other than this. What do you suppose, professor, the true lesson is?"

Michael remained silent, knowing the question was rhetorical.

"Three tables, eh? Noooo problem. Which is the fake? Listen to me. Rinpoche was holding up three fingers, mouthing the words at first then whispering them, then finally screaming them so loudly that Michael had to put his hands over his ears: ALL THREE...ALL THREE...ALL...THREEEE...

"Think it through, professor. If the dharmas are empty, then it follows quite logically does it not..." Rinpoche was erect, palms closed together. Before he spoke Michael noticed that his chest expanded enormously, filling up his loose-fitting robe. Seeing this, he was able to prepare himself for the thunder which began with the deceptively faint rumble of "Yes... indeed...it follows...as the night the day...that..." Now came the explosion: "THE...DHARMAS...ARE...ACT-TU-AL-LY EEMMMP-TY."

41

His eyes were open, still the face remained fixed. The image seemed to be resting just behind his eyes, at the bridge of his nose. It was as if he were looking inward from outside his body, looking toward his own face and yet seeing...her.

The sensation was exhilarating. He wasn't just thinking of the image or remembering it, he wasn't seeing it in his mind's eye; he was seeing it *in his mind, with his eyes*. It was clearer than the image he had drawn some weeks before, clearer even than the mask that had served as its model—as clear, he thought, as ever was the face of she who finally wore that mask. And it was not just a face, but a head. Only a head, that's true, but substantial nonetheless—suspended there, behind his eyes. Empty, yes. Of course, he knew that now. Still, she was...comfortably real.

His back ached from the posture. The whole lower portion of his body was numb. He was afraid the head would vanish if he moved. He rubbed his left leg with his hands. The ache subsided momentarily, and he felt its tingling echo in his foot and toes. The only pain left was in his lower back. He knew that he would have to get out of this position soon or risk suffering cramps for the rest of the day. But he wouldn't move just yet. He waited for the sound of the voice. Her voice. He took a breath and held it for as long as he could. No sound came.

Michael's resolve was crumbling and along with it the head, the face, the image. It had gone suddenly flat. Then, gradually, like an enigmatic, unsmiling Cheshire cat, it dissolved rapidly into the light.

Still he maintained the posture, in futile protest against his faded resolve. After long, tired minutes, he rose to his lame legs, stumbled into a chair beside his bed and waited for the return of his body. Then he waited for sleep, that he might recover in his dreams the figure lost to his gaze.

42

—Listen, Michael—
—Though you cannot hear us—

We see what you see.
We know what you have done.
What you would do again.

...pressed beneath you...rocking...pushing you...struggling against the satisfying force...

—Our unsayable, unnamed name—

...resisting...rigid...tight...dry...unopened...afraid...yes?... of being...what?...something that can die...pushing her back... holding her down...making her give...making her... give...making...her...*be*...

It's simple, yes? Michael?
Yes?
Replace what you've lost.

—The only true name—

...putting your face against her skin...forcing her down...weighing her down...smelling her...tasting her...touching her parts...making her sweat...making her say yes... telling her...making her hear things...making her say yes...

Rob the grave
of your undead memories.

—We never said yes—so it wasn't really bad—

Create them, her, Adrienne,
from out of your own crumbling clay.

—Is...—

—She said she wouldn't anymore—

...grabbing...hurting you...cursing and spitting and biting...holding her breath...holding back...begging only with the
eyes...sweating...legs weaker now...letting you...in...

Breathe your breath,
your wasted life, into her.

—She said we shouldn't want that—

Animate a homemade zombie
with the power of your vampire blood.
Yes?

—Listen, Michael—

—She won't—

Make her wet!
Make her...*do*!
...do...do...do...

—She won't...*give*—

Rub...!
Rub inside the tangled,
stinging dryness...
...do...do...do...

—Fat Dharma is on the prowl—

—She...won't...say...*yes*—

—The nameless must fall before Him—

...do...do...do...

—grim, rotting harvest of desire—

Feel the thunder!
Make it...rain!

—Omniscience stalks anonymity—

...do...do...do...

43

There is no blame.
You are ignorant and cannot help us.
We are impotent and cannot help ourselves.
Fat Dharma is on the prowl.
Omniscience stalks anonymity.
This story now is ours as well.

44

Rinpoche gave no indication that these were to be his final words to the group, though everyone knew it. The only evidence that things were drawing to a close was a small notice in A–K's and Michael's room detailing the procedures for "signing out" and wishing the participants well.

Michael was pleased that the close of the retreat was being treated in this fashion, though he thought A–K might be frustrated by the absence of any final punctuation. There would be no way for him to feel that something *had taken place*.

A–K and Michael started saying their goodbyes while packing. Tacitly they had agreed not to exchange promises to keep in touch. Michael had exchanged no more than a few words with anyone besides A–K, Tilmon, and Rinpoche, so no other farewells were necessary.

As the two were making a final check of their belongings, exchanging socks and toiletries that had gotten mixed up in the course of the past weeks, there was a tapping at the door. Michael hoped that it might be Rinpoche. He was unable to hide his disappointment when he saw Tilly's face.

"Michael. Could I see you for a moment?"

"Of course, Tilmon."

Michael waited for Tilly to come inside, but he soon realized that he wanted him to come out into the hall.

"I've something for you, Michael."

"Oh." Tilly's conspiratorial tone made Michael apprehensive.

Tilly held out his hand. In it there was a small stone figurine, about two inches high. It looked to Michael like a carved chess piece of some kind. As he took it from Tilly he noticed that it was a seated figure, perhaps a Buddha. Its feet were folded and it seemed to be wearing a robe. The face gave no hint of gender, but Michael immediately thought of it as female.

At the base of the figure there was something carved. He guessed it was in Tibetan or Sanskrit, but the etching was so worn he couldn't be sure. Because of the signs of wear Michael thought this must have been used as a worry stone. The thin leather thongs attached to the figure indicated that it was to be worn about the neck.

"I'm not sure I understand, Tilmon. You mean this for me?"

"It's from Rinpoche." Michael noticed the edge in Tilly's voice. "He asked that I give it to you."

"Well...please tell Rinpoche.... Perhaps I should thank him myself..."

Tilly had already turned to leave. He stopped and spoke over his shoulder, "I'm quite sure that Rinpoche is aware of your appreciation and that he would not wish either of us to speak further of the gift." Before Michael could say a final farewell to Tilly, he had walked the length of the hall and turned into the adjoining corridor.

Michael returned to the room. A–K noticed the figurine. For an instant there seemed something strange in A–K's face.

"So, Michael. Does this mean that you and Tilly are going steady."

"It's from Rinpoche."

A–K looked into Michael's face and then again at the figurine. "May I see?" He gave the figurine to A–K with some reluctance, but to his surprise A–K treated it with cautious respect. Michael was certain now that A–K knew what it was.

He looked at A–K, waiting for him to admit that he recognized the object. A–K was silent.

"A–K, you know what it is. Speak to me."

A–K was too good a man to be anything but a poor liar. "Haven't the slightest idea. It does seem, however, that you have been voted the *chela* most likely to succeed."

Taking the object from A–K, who was returning it in a self-consciously casual manner, Michael said with a wink, "Well, in any case, it will be an interesting reminder of having been at Tilopa."

He wrapped the figurine carefully inside his handkerchief, then tucked it in a well-protected part of his suitcase. Less than an hour later, he was on his way to the airport with A–K and several other graduates of the summer retreat.

Approaching the main gate, Michael began to wonder about the twenty-sixth decimal place in *pi*. He thought it was

8, but he could be wrong. As the van passed through *pi* gate he vowed that he would find the value of the twenty-sixth place and add it to his memory's store. It would be his way of commemorating his stay at Tilopa.

45

Immediately upon arriving home, two weeks before the beginning of the fall semester, Michael began to feel that whatever he had learned at Tilopa was still back there, as if he left the teachings behind, as one might fail to pack a pair of socks lying unnoticed in the back of a bureau drawer. Indeed, after a very few indolent and completely unsuccessful attempts to conjure the apparition he had finally created, the last trace of his encounter with practical Buddhism faded altogether from consciousness.

Perhaps the only way to explain the apparent failure of his experiences at Tilopa to make any lasting impression upon him is to think as Michael came to think. It was as if he had been kidnaped by aliens and imprisoned for seventy-seven days on a distant planet in an as yet uncharted star system. Best not to speak of the experience (since no one could believe him) and best not to think much of the incident, either, since he had himself begun to doubt his memory.

Michael is nonetheless grateful to Tilopa. He has started to believe himself at peace, a condition he attributes to his time on the alien planet.

No one who has followed this account could believe Michael's present tranquil mood to be anything more than a cloak or shield that hides and protects him from the truth of the matter. His false contentment—or better said, his flat affect—is a façade. More than that, it is a shell, a bark, a crust, a rind which if peeled away would reveal a shadow play much more intriguing than the vulgar documentaries that follow.

We could, if we wished, raise the curtain, lift the veil, remove the shroud, open up the womb, shatter the cocoon, roll back the stone. But this ought be done, if it is to be done, in the proper season. Meanwhile, there is enough to say about life on the other side, the mundane side, outside the mask.

So we shall follow Michael now as he prepares to reprise the worst of his well rehearsed mistakes. There is, however, some reason to believe he will carry something valuable with him on his now routine journey from the frying pan into the fire.

III

Per Obscurum ad Obscurius

1

For all the time Michael would know her the painting would remain unfinished. The act of displaying this uncompleted portrait of her firstborn child, the only painting she would admit having attempted, was above all its many rivals her most forthright expression of arrogance. The painting had the intensity of a Dürer portrait whose subjects, Michael remembered, were given double-focused eyes that stared starkly out of the surface of the painting and yet simultaneously, with a forlorn intensity, gazed within.

Reza hadn't the slightest knowledge of Dürer's work; she had never studied art or art history. She was herself, however, possessed of double-focused eyes and Michael suspected that any portrait she ever would do would own them as well. (Had Michael reflected sufficiently on this question, he would have realized that it was most unlikely that Reza would paint anything else than this unfinished portrait. It is truistic that most painters paint what they see. Some, like Reza, paint that with which they see. Reza painted the instrumentality of her eyes, her own manner of perceiving things. There was simply no reason for her to produce more than a single painting.)

It was always there in her living room, this unfinished work; sometimes by the latticed double window, where the light-infused, powdery crisp colors invited anyone whose gaze they attracted inside the composition to join the dance; sometimes in a far corner, in which case the lamp would be removed and the painting left to fend the shadows and to create its chiaroscuro effects beyond its unframed edges. Wherever placed, its command of the room was assured.

Reza's painting would not have puzzled him quite so much

had Michael recalled how his sister, three years older than he, had once hidden a piece from the jigsaw puzzle they were putting together. When, after hours of work they neared completion and it had become obvious that a piece was missing, Michael was agonized with disappointment. When his sister announced that she had hidden the piece, his initial anger was stayed by the realization that the missing piece had suddenly become precious simply because it was the final piece in the puzzle. If he ransomed it through some (doubtless demeaning) service to his sister, the puzzle would swallow that final piece and it would lose its unique claim upon their attention. Michael scorned his sister. He would save the uniqueness of the piece even if at the expense of the coherence of the puzzle. The puzzle was never completed.

Michael could not fully understand the effect of Reza's unfinished work until he realized that its incompleteness was essential to its appeal. The eyes that turned both ways would suffer completeness neither in the world within nor without. The missing element in Reza's painting was in Reza herself. She was the missing piece in the puzzle; it was she who became precious, longed for, desired. All this could end if she completed the work.

The painter Max Beckmann confessed, "I paint on canvass, framed, in two dimensions, in order to defend myself against the infinity of space." When Michael had encountered that statement in, he now remembered, a work on the psychology of spatial intuition (Michael's memory is in error here, he read the words in a brochure accompanying the announcement of a special exhibit at New York's Museum of Modern Art), it had made him shudder. Prior to that encounter he had believed the artist's task was to struggle against the limitations of two dimensions, to invigorate the flat framed canvass. If, as Beckmann's pronouncement seemed to suggest, the true aim of artists was the very opposite, they might know something Michael could never know.

This revelation seemed to directly contradict Michael's strategy for surviving among civilized beings. It was, perhaps, an indication that his own desire to fray the boundaries of all cultural artifacts, to fragment their polished surfaces (a desire he thought an expression of courageous rebellion against the samenesses of the world), might simply have been born of an extremely low threshold of boredom coupled with an insensitivity to the complex infinities that assail acuter souls.

The artist's vaunted sensitivity could still be a sham. It could be nothing more than a raging desire for order antecedent to any experience whatsoever. And if so, it would not then be a result of the threat of inundation by complex infinities but simply the consequence of an intolerance for manyness, plurality, complexity. Possessed of no greater sensitivity, probably less, the artist was simply more fastidious.

Michael finally reconciled the opposing possibilities in this manner: The infinity against which the artist raged may or may not be the same indefinite he had come to call the Blessed Multifariousness. What separated both artist and counter-artist from the ruck of mankind was the intensity of their desire. It was the specific character and quality of eros that divided the lovers of order and the lovers of Chaos. And the latter could not but think art some sort of obscene dodge.

Reza was not an artist in the civilized sense. By refusing to fill her canvass, and by denying it the comfort of a frame, Reza had abandoned her creation half-in half-out the womb, thus mocking both the artist's failure of nerve and (such was her unsurpassable arrogance) the power of infinity itself.

2

Michael had first begun to take more than usual notice of Reza
in the last of several classes she had taken from him. She was
an odd being, he thought, one of the stranger of the exotic sorts
attracted to the study of philosophy. His first personal communication with her had come by way of an envelope, handed to
him shyly, eyes cast down, at the end of class. It was an invitation to the birth of her child, which was to take place about six
weeks from that day. When Michael opened it in her presence,
he was bemused but flattered and tried to be as diplomatic as
possible in his refusal. Reza had intended that there would be
just the midwife, her husband, one of her parents, and Michael.

"I think of him as your...*our* baby." All of Reza's shyness
had disappeared.

"Oh?"

"I know you think it strange, and think me strange, but
that's a small matter. I have listened to you for all the time I
have carried my baby. Your words helped to bring him into
being. Your wisdom shaped him as my body shaped him."

"That's a nice thought."

"A *nice* thought?" Reza's voice and eyes carried an unmistakable tone of deprecation. "Oh, I see I have embarrassed you.
You don't know what to say. Don't be distressed." Reza touched
Michael's hand. Michael was surprised and a bit disturbed by
that small show of intimacy. "God created the entire universe
with words. It is a small thing to create a little female child—it
is a girl, I know it—with wisdom. But I won't trouble you any
more today."

Reza walked slowly away. Michael watched her move, recognizing her beauty for the first time. As yet he didn't know
enough to be disquieted by her parting statement, "I won't
trouble you anymore *today*."

3

Soon after their initial conversation, Reza began to approach Michael after class and, almost always without saying a word, hand him a small folded piece of paper on which she had written a brief message. He was disconcerted by this at first but soon persuaded himself that it was a harmless enough thing.

The messages, often only a single line, consisted in commentary on the lecture Michael had just completed. In the beginning he was actually embarrassed by what he took to be their maudlin and purplish language. As days passed, however, he began to think of them as truly poetic, in a quaintly Romantic way:

> In your words I find the courage to confront delicious chance.

> Your language is the heavenly limit of my desire.

Not all of Reza's comments were laudatory:

> Don't say life is a muddle! How careless! You are not a poet, only a philosopher. You *must be clear*.

> Neither Love nor Understanding could long abide your arrogance.

Michael very soon began to look forward to the messages. When the semester ended, and Tuesdays and Thursdays began to pass without those precious notes, he felt abandoned. Soon his curiosity led him to inquire, as discreetly as he could, about Reza. He discovered that she had given birth some two weeks before. (It *was* a girl. What had Reza named her?) He also learned news less shocking to him than to his informant: Reza left her husband immediately after the birth of their child.

One day, shortly after the close of Christmas vacation, Michael arrived at his office to find a tightly folded piece of paper attached to his door with a small sliver of tape. He felt alive again.

The tone of the messages had changed. Reza's words were much more intimate...and urgent.

> I write only that you may fill
> the spaces between my words.

> Q: How does a spider choose
>   an anchor for her web?
> A: As I have chosen you.

> I am a genie. My body is a lamp.
> I shall be numb to the rub of life
> until my master comes.

> Each night between prayer and sleep
> my final thought is this:
> Where is your safe smell?

Michael finally yielded to the inevitable when, on a Tuesday afternoon, he harvested this message from his office door:

> Why are you content to be only mortal
> when you could be desperately so?
> Come to me!

4

She answered the phone sooner than he had expected. He wasn't prepared. His throat was dry. He knew his voice would shake. "Reza?"

"Yes."

"This is..."

"Don't be silly. I know."

"I..."

"I know. Yes, I *do*."

Reza's readiness to indulge his stammering only made him flounder more. "Will...you...be...?"

"Come. I am alone."

"When?"

"Now, of course. *Now*. How silly you are. *Now*."

5

Persistence alone would not have succeeded. It was Reza's promise, implicit but clear, of absolute and unqualified submission. It would be a mistake to believe that Michael had even the slightest of sadistic motivations. The truth is quite the contrary. Sadism is evoked by unwilling submission. Willful submission is the origin of religious devotion and, as the immediate response to the sense of *mysterium tremendum*, the source and goal of religious experience.

Reza needn't have been beautiful at all. She possessed an unfailing means of seduction. No one can resist worship. But Michael was no more a fool than he was a god. He knew the price he would eventually have to pay. He knew the polarities would shift, the worshiped would become the worshiper. What he didn't know, or had not properly appreciated, was that the only other irresistible method of seduction, the expression of total contempt, had been mastered by Reza as well.

6

Reza opened the door without speaking and immediately led Michael into her bedroom. He was relieved to discover that she was alone, though he was disturbed that there were no visible signs of her children's presence. He was also both relieved and disturbed when Reza made no move toward the bed. Instead, she had paused before the bureau and, using both hands, was removing something from one of the open drawers. She turned to face Michael. Her voice was soft and wan. It seemed to originate from some distant, perhaps alien, source.

"This bird..." She held out her hands toward Michael. It was dead, a sparrow. "I awoke yesterday.... It was lying on the sill outside my bedroom window. It must have flown against the glass and hurt itself. I took it from the sill. I placed it here..." Reza gestured to a place below the waistline of her dress, "at the center of my giving. I thought the warmth of...our unused passion would give it life. But see, it wished to add its life to mine instead.... See?" She held the bird only inches from Michael's face. He wanted to run. The stiffening in his groin mocked him as he focused on the rigid wad of flesh and feathers in Reza's hands. He thought that if he breathed he might be sick, but he inhaled and was thrilled by the incipient odor of decay. "I closed my legs and offered it warm death.... Then I kept it company in sleep. When I awoke, I supposed I had been dreaming. But no. See?... See.... I found it...this morning...tangled and...between my thighs. What shall I do?... My body is not deep enough to bury it."

Michael held out his hands. Reza closed her hands over his. Outside, he found soft earth beneath a small shrub. He scooped the soil with his bare hands, never removing his eyes from the victim of that dreadful, crushing warmth.

When the bird spoke, as he knew it would, it was with Reza's voice—a fearsome, exhorting whisper tangled by triumph and yielding.

"Hello? Be warned! You have felt my fire.... You think to come so late and quench it still? You would be the master whose rub will tame this genie? But how could you match a passion so intensified by the yielding of this tiny creature who knew life as we could never know it?... Keep your distance! If you come near me you may die from your neglect of my fire. Hurry!

"Yes? Then, perhaps we both shall die. I of the quenching and you of the fire. Come!

"But I am silly. We both know it. You will win, of course. How could you not? Come. Rage and caress this flesh. Rip and rend it...enter at the tear. My body is not deep enough to bury you....

"Hurry!"

When he reentered the house he could see her in the living room. She had spread a pallet on the rug and was lying naked, motionless, at its center. Her arms were at her sides, her hands tucked beneath her buttocks. As he approached she arched her back and spread her legs until her feet touched the edges of the pallet.

He took a breath, removed his clothes and stooped slowly to his knees. He hovered over Reza like a stark white cloud drifting across the face of the sun.

It was deep into the night before the fire was extinguished and the cloud transformed into vagrant mist. Before sleeping, Michael raised his head from between Reza's legs to look upon the gaping, merciless, unfillable void that lay beyond the sun.

7

We were on the verge of telling about Michael and Reza's first intimacies, of the happiness of those encounters, of the painless passion Michael had enjoyed—the hateful, painless, free-lunch passion that would soon give way (he suspected, he *knew* as much) to the pay-as-you-go emotions of love discredited by neglect. But there are—what shall we say?—constraints being placed upon us. It is clearly Michael's wish that his and Reza's story be told only in the tragicomic mode. Gentle smiles and glances, shuffles, winks and sighs, may be allowed only if they make a point; only if they occasion moral reflection, only if they exact a price.

Reluctantly, we shall yield to these constraints but (*pace* Michael) not immediately. First, we will recount an episode or two of pointless, and (thus) painless enjoyment. For one cannot honor the appropriate strictures of the morality play without some celebration of the noninstrumental nature of love. Otherwise, how are we to recall what it is that has been denied, degraded, and destroyed by those who, as a consequence of this destruction, must suffer that awfullest of literary fates: the doom of having their stories rendered in the tedious idiom of petty moral pageantry?

8

Michael was relaxed, lying on the bathroom floor with his head propped against the bathtub, watching Reza wash her leotards in the sink. This was a morning ritual that each performed for different, opposite, reasons. He very much needed to move off-stage, to escape attention. Reza needed to step onstage, to be adored. Michael said little; he simply watched. Reza would draw a breath and hold it as she reached into the hot sudsy water. She made no effort to note Michael's presence and generally managed, in spite of the intimate space of the bathroom, to ignore him. But she moved (he knew this to be so) differently when he was present. Her stances and postures were almost classic then. She was aware of his presence, aware of being watched. But like all classical theater, this drama would not survive her attending to her audience.

Each morning as he lay, neck wrenched against the cool porcelain tub, looking up at Reza's strong body, he would rehearse the same two thoughts: first he would reflect upon the claim of Dostoevski that if one's existence were reduced to an eternity of life inside a bathroom, still one would cling to life. Yes, Michael would say to himself each time. Of course. A second reflection would always supervene the first: Nicholas of Cusa, a fifteenth-century mathematician and Roman Catholic cardinal, had attempted to characterize the infinity of the world in this manner: The universe is infinite by virtue of having its center everywhere and its circumference nowhere.

He never really examined the connection between these two thoughts. He simply enjoyed their juxtaposition. Reza might have understood these thoughts and the motivation for their ritualistic emergence into Michael's consciousness had he ever mentioned them. He never did.

This dreary, cramped bathroom with bathtub, sink, and single mirror, could serve as Michael's refuge solely because it was rendered infinite by the motion of Reza's body, gliding from center to center, neither reaching nor defining a periphery. Morning after morning, as Michael would stare up at Reza's nude or partially clothed form in a silent, abstract, dispassionate manner, he would be thankful for this shelter. For Michael, this bathroom floor, the ground of this centerless, shapeless infinity, provided his only rest beyond choice, beyond desiring.

9

When Michael thought to place Reza in the realm of public life, when he asked himself what sort of person she was, he would think of her as a poet. Reza was, Michael thought, perhaps the only real poet he had ever known. To him that simply meant that her bare face was her original face before she was born. Michael believed her to be fresh, spontaneous, completely without habits or trite cadences. She was, in spite of the curiously baroque character of her language, immune to clichés. She would often try to speak like the rest of the world, try to use the language in a consensual manner, but it never worked.

Soon after Michael and Reza met she became concerned about the more than twenty years that separated them. "The only reason you want to see me," she once announced to Michael, "is because I'm young and beautiful." Coming from Reza's mouth these so trite words seemed to have been uttered for the first time, their tedious familiarity canceled by the absolute uniqueness of the delivery.

Her love for the language, her almost compulsive need to speak, to make the sounds, was all the greater since, for her, this language was always new. Each sound received individual attention. Names were special. Unreflectively, she knew that names, unlike class terms or universals, point to concrete particulars. A name, properly used, is a no-deposit no-return sign-function, indicating a uniquely insistent particular. Reza would demonstrate her special love for names by making each of their syllables distinct.

Michael and Reza often did their grocery shopping together. Each time they shopped the ritual was the same. On their way to the checkout stand, Reza would pause and say, "I forgot something," or "I almost forgot," or "Oh, yes, one more thing." That was an indication that she wanted something sweet— candy or cookies. She was, though she would vehemently deny any suggestion of the fact, addicted to sweets.

"Ah, look," she had once said, indicating her favorite brand of cookie, "Ap-ple New-tons. These are much, *much* better than Fig New-tons. I give these an A+." It had taken Michael several trips to the cookie shelves for Reza's favorite snack before he realized that Apple Newtons were better than Fig Newtons primarily because "Apple" has two syllables. It was simply a greater joy to say "Ap-ple New-tons."

Many months after Reza's introduction of Apple Newtons to him, not long after he and Reza had ceased their joint shopping ventures and their morning bathroom rendezvous, after he had been denied access to that troubling, uncompleted portrait and Reza's troubled, unfinished spirit was no longer his to share, Michael found himself standing in a supermarket, smiling broadly but without the slightest idea why. Then his eyes gradually focused upon what he must have vaguely noted just before: to his right on the uppermost shelf, among many sorts of cakes and cookies, stacked tightly between the Fig Newtons and the Apple Newtons, there was a new product—"Blueberry Newtons."

Even as he left the store, and for most of the drive home, he listened to Reza's voice as she savored the sounds of "Blue-ber-ry New-tons," and he watched as she reached toward the uppermost shelf, a delightful, eyes-wide smile illumining her face.

10

Reza was a poet, a maker of moments, a shepherdess of those crystalline drops of time, which like the truest of our tears, are quickly borne by desire and fade fast into memory. She understood that it is not the artist's task to set her face against the passage of things, but just the opposite. It is to protect the flow from interruption, to let moments pass as they are meant to pass. To celebrate discontinuance. Such a poet is the true priest and priestess. And from such a poet a poem is Last Rites said over the unrepeatable moment.

11

For weeks after Reza had stopped nursing her daughter, Michael continued to drink her milk. The bond was now irrevocable. She was his lover, his mother, his source. When her milk ran less freely, the flow of blood increased.

They often made love during her period. After, there would be blood on Michael's hands and face, Reza's legs and breasts, in her hair. She would be radiant. "All this blood," she once said. "It's like giving birth. This is how it should always be. Don't you think? We should always make love in the daytime—and in winter. That's when it's best. Don't you think so? And there must be blood."

"I tasted your blood."

Reza reached up and grasped Michael by the shoulders, shaking him to and fro, smiling, laughing, tears glistening. "Yes... *Yes.*" Reza's yes frightened Michael, as much by the immediacy with which it had been uttered as by its intensity. She was saying so much with that simple yes: "Of course you drank my blood," she was saying. "Wasn't it wonderful?," she was saying. Shaking Michael as he sat astride her on the bed, she was saying—her yes was saying, "It was time, was it not? I gave you my milk, now I give you my blood. This is my body... these are the sacraments."

Reza kissed Michael hard, fastening his mouth to hers.

12

Reza couldn't know, so Michael believed, that from the first taste of her milk and now with the infusion of her blood, there could be no thinking of the sacraments. It was her actual, untransubstantiated blood and milk he craved. Michael came to think of himself, sardonically and with but the slightest shadow of whimsy, as a foolish, failed vampire. Reza surely knew the effect she must be having on this sad, impotent vampire. Sucking at Reza's body, Michael would become more and more a victim of his victim's juices. And eventually, at a moment of Reza's choosing (there came to be no doubt in Michael's mind about this), he would enter the Zone of the Undead.

13

When her milk was gone, and when her blood was not flowing, Michael felt empty but empowered. Only then did he grasp the wasted essence of another untimely truth. Passion cannot exist without *passio*, "passiveness." All those promised passion face the same dilemma. Power is passion's opposite. It is a mistake to believe that one can lust after power. The lust for power so-called is the desire to give passion, not to receive it. The powerful are always outside of passion and may only experience it vicariously.

Michael is certainly correct in his analysis of the relations between power and passion. But he should know that none of this is truly relevant. Power games are cliché-ridden spectacles and Reza is unsusceptible to clichés. Reza has no interest in power. Her sole sense of life and of the world about her is focused by a single desire: the desire to enjoy another's enjoyment of her. Not to enjoy her world, not merely to enjoy herself, not just to be enjoyed—but to enjoy herself being enjoyed by another.

More specifically, she desires not merely to hear her words repeated by another, but to listen to those words, the very sounds, their tone and timbre, echoing in an alien (now, no longer alien) voice; not just to feel another's fingers touching her, but to feel herself in those fingers, feel her skin in the surface of that other skin.

Reza could never hesitate to force her lips upon the lips of one whose tongue had just emerged from her most private places, to touch his tongue with her tongue that she could taste, ingest, consume herself from out another's mouth.

Michael can't really be expected to understand this about Reza, for just now he is preoccupied with his own pain. The sad, silly passion which makes him posture so, and about which we shall have a great deal more to say, is quite beside the point. That is because, judged solely in terms of his relation to Reza, Michael is largely beside the point. He is but a means, a medium, a vehicle, permitting Reza to experience herself more fully.

No, it isn't power Reza wants. Were she to consider Michael in the consensual terms of more polite love affairs, she well might. Were she to consider him *at all*, she certainly could. But, in the strictest of senses, there is absolutely nothing personal in Reza's treatment of Michael.

14

It was Voltaire who inspired Michael's plan of escape. With the unsparing logic of an infidel this avatar of the anti-Christ had thought to mock the sacraments: "If in truth," he said, "we do eat the very body and drink the very blood of our Lord Jesus Christ, must it not then also be true that we shit the very body and piss the very blood?"

Bravo, Voltaire.

Michael contrived to fast. Days passed. He fed only on Reza's blood and the remaining drops of milk in her drying beasts. In this way he hoped to insure Reza's passage through him in her purest form.

It was simple. He would ingest Reza, yes, but then he would discharge her, expel her, send her forth forever from his bladder and his bowels.

"This is my body..." she had said.

"I am the Way..." would be his reply.

15

"Ugly...old...man."

When Reza was angry at Michael she taunted him with this litany. Out of some warped sense of deference, Michael would pretend to be hurt. In reality, these words had little effect on him. He had never been vain about his appearance, and age was for him a simple biological given. He felt no special need to share his true vanities and fears with Reza, and he knew she was so little capable of being occupied with another besides herself, that she would never discover them on her own. That presented a very real problem: Reza had no effective means of hurting Michael as long as they were together. But unless he could learn to hate her, he would never be free. He would have to become the aggressor.

Michael was very much aware of Reza's greatest anxiety. She spoke of it often, seeking reassurance from him, which he would gladly provide. She believed that her hair was thinning. It was the only flaw she was willing to confess. Though he believed her fear was groundless, he was most willing, under these special circumstances, to exploit it.

In the midst of one of the routine arguments that now punctuated their days together, Michael thought the time had come. Smiling with unmistakable sarcasm, he reached out and touched Reza's hair, shaking his head in mock sympathy. Reza pushed Michael's arm away and started pummeling him with both fists.

Reaching through her flailing arms (he hadn't planned this), he managed to grab her breasts. "Guess what?" he said. Reza became hysterical. Until that moment she hadn't realized that Michael knew of her second, most painful deformity. Her breasts were of slightly different sizes, one made larger by virtue of a conspiracy between him and her daughter. Michael had never counted these discernibly asymmetrical breasts a defect, having himself been one of their principal architects.

Reza's vanity could not permit such taunting. She had retreated to another room and returned with a heavy glass bud vase containing the two roses—blood red and milk white—

Michael had given her two days before. (It is pointless here to recite the occasion for the gift; indeed, as we have said, we are enjoined not to rehearse the finer moments shared by these two.) Reza swung the vase, flowers still inside, hitting Michael on the elbow. Refusing to grant Reza the gift of his pain, he neither cursed nor cried out.

Reza looked on while Michael went to the refrigerator for ice and methodically wrapped his arm with a kitchen towel. The concern on her face vanished and contempt returned when she saw there was to be no reprisal. Michael left without speaking. The arm, and Reza's spell, were broken.

16

Sadly for Michael, both fractures would mend.

Two months later a healed and weakened lover sought out Reza at her home. Before he could ring the bell, she opened the door. "You can't come in, Mi-chael." Michael moved past Reza into the living room.

"I do not give you permission to be in my house, Mi-chael."

I do not give you permission to have such a warm, soft mouth, Michael thought. Then while simultaneously rehearsing each of the certain agonies she would visit upon him were she to accept, Michael blurted the words he had pledged he would never be so imprudent as to utter: "Marry me."

Reza's face was blank with surprise, then all manner of emotions began registering one at a time, each involuntarily yielding its place to its more intense successor: joy...triumph... vindication...painful sorrow...anger.

Michael hardly saw the blow. It was thrown, fist-doubled, with all the sad, abused, scornful might distilled from months of waiting, expecting, until finally her expectation had faded and her shriveled hope had crawled into a corner of her heart and died.

Michael was stunned as much by his sense of the aptness

of the blow, which landed solidly on his left jaw, as by its considerable force. While recovering his balance, he rehearsed the line of.... (Who was it? He couldn't remember): "The trick of evil is insistence upon birth at the wrong season."

Thankfully, Reza's perfect timing had canceled the effect of Michael's grotesquely unseasonal plea. He didn't want to laugh, but what else could he do? Reza, too, recognizing that there was no real alternative, allowed her tears to give way to a gentle, only slightly sad smile.

Reza was standing quite still, her right hand raised in a pose reminiscent of a Hindu *mudra* for the worship of Shiva. When she finally spoke, her words sounded to Michael like distant, fading echoes. "Mi-chael. It's over, Mi-chael. We both know it."

Reza's next words would be fearfully precise. Standing now in an almost rigid posture, Reza reminded Michael of students in the early grades of grammar school called to the front of the class to recite a poem, or the Pledge of Allegiance. She spoke more loudly than seemed her wish.

"We're through," she said.

After this announcement, Reza moved her head just slightly to one side then turned once more to look directly into Michael's eyes. "Isn't that what they say, Mi-chael—'We're through'?"

Walking out the door, descending the concrete steps, Michael smiled at Reza's deference for his knowledge of how things are said.

17

Broken love affairs have their own mode of continuance, not unlike that of discarded automobiles or refrigerators. Who hasn't considered the possibility that there exists somewhere a kind of infernal junkyard where the ghosts of ill-conceived romances hover and moan? If that is so, then surely the specter of this fractured passion would find its way there to do penance for the insult wrought by these two narcissistic souls upon the spirit of loving.

Michael knew that Reza's life would alter very little. She would find another adorer, one she could more easily control. She would continue to believe that she loved him above all, that she was connected with him in some supernatural way— though her love would now be scented by contempt for his weakness.

He had finally learned that Reza's love for him, as for anyone, was but a mask worn by contempt. His reason for ignoring this insight was, he believed, so reprehensible that he now felt at greater fault than Reza. He had been quite willing to accept the consequences of Reza's selfishness and contempt as long as he was permitted access to her body: to drink from it, to lie atop and move inside it.

Michael's problem now was not with Reza, of course, but with himself. He had betrayed his sense of who he was. He had acted stupidly, cruelly. Such were his memories of passion, however, that even now he could not believe it had been a mistake to yield to Reza's scent and taste, to drink so deeply from the fountain of her body. His passion's penalty was a heavy one: Michael found he could respond to no other odor than that of Reza's skin. The honied froth of her breast milk and her sugary sharp menstrual blood were the only foods he could imagine savoring. Were he obsessed with her eyes or lips or legs he would be healed with the fading of the memory, but it seemed impossible that he should ever forget Reza's odor and the taste of her.

18

"Tantrics have, I now know, a startlingly bad reputation in the West. This can only be explained by the very different attitudes toward the power of sexuality. It was your Heracleitus who said, 'The way up and the way down are the same.' We have a similar view. As I have said many times, we believe that one can only ascend by the same means that has dragged one down. You would perhaps say that this is a convenient rationalization for our sexual alchemy.

"Freud believed, did he not, that the death instinct is the controlling fact of life; that Eros, the drive toward unity and coherence, must ultimately give way to the drive toward dissolution, that sex is a temporary dodge to avoid the ultimacy of decay, and that above all one must struggle against the lure of final dissolution, the comfort of a cosmic afterglow? But Sigmund Freud, the ultimate Romantic, held death, decay, dissolution—the natural consequences of life—to be reprehensible. A bit arrogant, wouldn't you say?

"Our view is quite different: The end of so-called life is so-called death. It is emptiness. The candle is snuffed out. We agree with Freud: Existence involves us in a struggle against dissolution. The only difference is that we do not, as does Freud, endorse the struggle, the struggle that insures that to be is...*to hang on.* Surely, a rather undignified activity.

"You feel that if you don't hang on, existence will be torn from you. That will be that. You will die. Those who still cling to the so very strange Christian view concerning life after death, believe that if you practice your hanging on in a faithful and obedient manner, you will win an afterlife. The belief that one can live forever is a most painful example of *hanging on.*"

Rinpoche waved his arms as if to call a halt to his own speaking. He was silent for some seconds, the first pause of any duration since his remarks had begun. When he finally spoke, his voice was even more deliberate, his words spoken in a different cadence and much more slowly.

"The basic principle is that declared by your Oscar Wilde: The only way to avoid temptation is to yield. For only by satisfying wholly and completely all one's desires may salvation be attained. This must be taken quite literally. The end of our practice—both its goal and its culmination—is the complete satisfaction of desire. For to satisfy—truly to satisfy—a desire is to cancel it. One desires only what one lacks. The fulfillment of all desires is the cancellation of defect and the termination of desiring.

"To be is primarily a function of primitive attachments to the world. These attachments are consequences of the method of Sniff and Grab. It is odor and touch that bind us most firmly to the world. Sexuality is best explained this way. Another body touches our senses; we must, in turn, touch it. Sniff and grab.

"Our most primitive passions are all coordinated with the olfactory centers and the taste buds. In the animal kingdom, to which human beings, before the invention of culture, proudly belonged, a failure of the sense of smell is disastrous, leading one either to miss a chance to escape or, perhaps, to consume the wrong thing. Mischief.

"The sense of smell, and of taste, which is almost wholly dependent upon smell, is the creative mechanism that has raised the human being from out of the evolutionary mire. Before there was anything like a highly complex brain to tell us when to buy and when to sell, there were noses to tell us when to stand our ground and when to flee. Of course, we were hardly human, then. We were frogs and fish.

"This is not a joke. I read in one of your science magazines that the earliest versions of fish noses work almost exactly as do human noses. We humans were literally sniffed into existence by our fish and frog relatives. Your scientists who experiment with frogs—the creature whose olfactory structures we humans inherited most directly—have learned that if a nostril is removed from a frog embryo the frog brain develops with one seriously retarded hemisphere. Human infants born with the condition known as anencephaly—the absence of a brain—are also always missing their noses as well. The conclusion can only be that your Descartes's famous discovery, *Cogito ergo sum*, is a late evolutionary version of the more fundamental, *Odorari ergo sum*.

"Being is grasping. To be is to hang on. We are products—victims—of Sniff and Grab."

19

In the absence of the only desirable tastes and aromas, Michael's world was reduced to a odorless, flavorless mélange of experiences. His fast was now complete.

Out of deference for the forlorn themes of one of his favorite American poets, he called his new regimen the Edna St. Vincent Millay Diet. When friends would compliment him on his increasingly trim frame, he would simply respond that on the Edna St. Vincent Millay Diet he had actually lost 107 pounds in a single day!

Subsequent losses, though not nearly as dramatic, would for some weeks continue to be steady.

20

The phone calls started irregularly at first but soon came once every week, almost always on the same day and at nearly the same time. There would be no response to Michael's "hello," but the line would remain open until he hung up.

When finally Michael had gathered sufficient strength to confront her silence and address Reza by name, she had responded quietly and with equanimity, "It is a small thing, Mi-chael. Don't be upset. I only wanted to hear your voice."

The calls ended. But every week Michael would listen for the phone, suspended between hope and dread. Months passed with no contact between the two.

One day a letter arrived, written in Reza's wispy hand. Michael's eyes moved slowly down the page pausing at each syllable, listening for her voice. In the manner so familiar to him, Reza's words were written increasingly smaller and farther apart from the beginning to the end of the message, like veins running outward from the center of a leaf.

Reza had copied a poem of Yeats, "The Lake Isle of Innisfree," which she knew to be a favorite of Michael's. At the end she had appended these words:

> Innisfree
> is our home.
> Was our home.
> And where shall we go, now?

A painful spasm in Michael's throat imprisoned his defiance. His words, when they finally came, dribbled pathetically from his mouth: "No...*more*..." Then that same spasm, traveling downward from his throat, gripped his legs and moved them stiffly, mechanically toward the door.

21

There was no blood. Nor was it winter. They were to meet on equal terms.

22

Seconds from release, Michael felt her cheek tighten against his face. She was grinning!

"Teach me."

"Jesus, Reza"

"*Teach* me."

It was their game. "Teach me," they called it—*she* called it. She was gently mocking Michael's professorial status. The single rule of the game was that whenever one of them said, "Teach me," the other had to respond with instant wisdom. He had thought some contexts sacred. Apparently, this was not so.

She chuckled. He was shriveling inside her. Sheepishness overtook his frustration and he laughed too. Easing himself out he said, "OK. Ready?"

"Ready."

He allowed his eyes to scan her body. She was perfectly proportioned with long, long legs that wrapped him when they loved.

Michael knows that Reza has no intention of saying good-bye. She has apparently proposed and presumed that by his coming he has consented to a final welcoming, a last, unrenewable hello: a greeting that would cancel both the necessity for any further meeting and (this is her real purpose, of course) all possibility of farewell.

But Michael has another plan.

"How would you like to learn the basic rules of drinking?"

"I would love to learn those rules. How many are there?"

"Two."

"Just two?"

She made room for Michael on her pillow and he laid his head close to hers. She reached under the covers and held his limp flesh in her hand. It was nice being touched while not erect, he thought. Eros and innocence.

She tucked her feet under his legs for warmth. He loved her feet. The rest of her body was dainty, doelike. But she had wonderfully strong peasant feet.

"My father taught me these rules when I was fourteen or fifteen. I've always honored them."

"In the breach."

"Honored, nonetheless. Pay attention: the first rule is Never take a drink when you need one."

"Your father does not appear obsessed by a desire for originality."

"Ah, judge him not until you've heard the second rule."

"Which is?"

"Always drink alone."

Her puzzlement lasted for only a second or two before it was converted to a loud guffaw. As she laughed she squeezed Michael's penis tightly enough to occasion concern. Michael coveted her laugh. It was the sort one hears in a bordello late nights or a truck stop at sunrise. In that laugh was the hint of a coarseness he found irresistibly intriguing. She was most real when she laughed. She laughed from her feet.

"I apologize to your father," she said. "He must be wonderful."

"He is. Now, you have learned the rules of drinking?"

"Indeed."

"You're sure?"

"Oh yes. Thank you. And thanks to your father."

"Questions? Any questions at all?"

"None."

"Then can we fuck?"

"Is that what we were doing? I was certain we were making love."

"Nope. We were fucking."

"Then, by all means."

Suddenly the sea change Michael had experienced so often before. Eyes cast away, then firmly fixing his...bottom lip pouting...furrows and tears.

"Mi-chael. Mi-chael."

When she spoke his name it was all breath and resonance, uttered in the falling cadence of fourth tone Mandarin.

"This is a sin. It is, Mi-chael.... Admit it's a sin or we can't make love."

Michael ignored her and pulled her legs apart.

23

It was the later-to-be-sainted Augustine who, bound to the flesh of his passionate mistress, invented the Ecumenical Prayer—an all-purpose supplication repeated by adherents to every conceivable faith and creed. Augustine had pleaded, "Lord save me...but not yet."

That's as far as Michael would go with Reza. He would confess. But not yet. For the sin he needed to confess was yet to be committed.

Of course, Reza had no knowledge of sin. She could, like all trained Catholics, catalog sins—hers and others—but she had no knowledge of sinning. As capable as she was of violence and anger, of lies and of betrayal, she was without sin. All her actions were instinctive and instincts are, of course, prelapsarian.

Imagine that in the Garden, Eve had brought the fruit to Adam and he alone had partaken. Eve would have remained with the sinner, but outside the sin. Such was Reza's relationship to sin. She knew when there was sin, but lacked the knowledge of good and evil that would permit her to participate in it. Her sinlessness was not manifest in purity or chasteness. It was an atavistic trait. Reza's was a fearful, cold, iron innocence.

The ragged rhythms of their bodies merged subliminally with other, distant, rhythms. They were musical rhythms, vocal rhythms, the sounds of evangelical religion. Gradually, Michael's body took up the meter of the preacher's words, and together they pounded Reza's soul on the anvil of her innocence.

24

From a wooden bench the child looked up to the platform on which stood the latest prophet of the Lord, imported, along with his gigantic canvass tent, to renew the faith of the faithful and to stay the march of lost souls to everlasting damnation. From Reza's bed the man's eyes scanned the rows of repressed mænads with their dresses hiked high, legs slightly separated, fanning thighs heated more by sensual imaginings than by the hot Louisiana evening. The child hadn't noted those exposed thighs nor sensed the furtive passion dispersed by the ladies' fans. The man sensed little else.

Life lies between the immediacy of experience and its recollection, in the space between Eros and the ironic reflection upon one's ever not-quite satisfied existence. Living requires re-membering, placing experiences into new patterns, new associations, new contexts. We are always casting a backward glance. Socrates' only real teacher, the priestess Diotima, told it as bluntly as it can be told: Eros is the stepchild of abundance and need. The fullness of our desire is a consequence of the enormity of our needfulness, the absence of need's object. The older we become, however, the greater is our dependence upon memory. Then desire serves only as an object of remembrance. We remember having desired...or not having desired enough.

It is said that angels have no memory, living as they do in the eternal present. For mortals, resort to memory means that we have lost our grip on the present and are growing old. It is the recognition of the weight of the past. And the desire to return to the past through memory, only to trade in reminiscence for the felt immediacy of the recollected event is surely the best advertisement of the fear of growing old.

Most of us are never permitted to grow old in the truest sense. History and tradition preclude the aging process by rendering us old from the beginning of our public existence. We are given identities shaped by tradition and the great events of our historical past. We are provided public memories that establish well-defined continuities with the past. This is why one could never find a young Jew. Tradition envelopes the Jew at birth. Only those few who are without the communal comforts of tradition and history must directly face the reality of aging and death.

We face two deaths, actually. The point at which desire fades and memory takes command, the still-point between memory and desire, is the *petite mort* that comes before the *grande mort* we call death. But the *petite mort* is more surely death itself. Life fades in the absence of desire. Desire is the motor of life—*is* life.

Memory stores only two items: objects sanctified by desire and the traces, the footprints, of desiring itself. Memory is the echo of desire, so the life dominated by remembering rather than by desiring is the fading echo of life. But if desire is pure and unsullied by memory and the need to re-collect, nothing is ever closed, complete, decided, and the world is new each moment. Without the *petite mort*, without the yielding to memory, nothing would ever die...

25

What had the preacher said? "Unpardonable?" Of course. The man remembered. But it wasn't the memory he sought. "Lest you become as a little child…"

"The sin (the preacher said "see-un") for which there can be no ransom—the sin without pardon, the Devil's guaranteed road to damnation. Your brothers and sisters will want to help you; Jesus ("Jay-ee-zus"—three syllables) will weep tears of pity, and you will cry out 'God, have mercy!; Jesus, have mercy!' But it will avail you naught. For in the very moment you commit that sin you are eternally dead. Brothers… Sisters… Children of the Lord! The love of God is without limit, but forgiveness has a limit. You set that limit. You…and you…and you."

The preacher continued in this fashion for the longest time. The child waited, listening for the name of that unpardonable sin. But the preacher wouldn't say it. He must have said it before, and the child had not been paying attention. What was the sin? Had he committed it?

This was the beginning, the man in Reza's bed now thought: the beginning of the anxiety, and the obsessive concern with understanding. All the bad, and most of the good in his life, the parts he couldn't help as well as the parts he could control, could be traced to that August evening.

Why hadn't the child just asked?

Questions must be timely. Isn't that so? If one asks a question at the wrong time, the answer will surely be a punishment. Had the child asked his question out of season, the answer could only have been that one of the many sins he had committed was this very sin, the unpardonable sin.

26

Do we really wish to answer any of our most fundamental questions? Since one of his early visits to the dentist, Michael had known otherwise. He remembers being confused by the rather severe lecture on the prevention of tooth decay the dentist had dispensed along with the novocain. This man loved his work, Michael could tell. How, then, could he so easily risk losing his profession as he obviously would if his patients heeded his advice?

And if physicist answered the questions of the origin and the structure of the cosmos once and for all? It was clear to Michael that as civilized human beings we are continually in a bind. We claim to be working ourselves out of a job, but that is not at all what we wish.

If one were to ask a professional if he definitely wanted to achieve the ends of his profession, to answer the questions, solve the problems, one would almost always (this was the response Michael had heard) receive answers such as: "Well, unfortunately, not everyone is going to brush and floss after meals and at bedtime, or unfortunately, the universe is a vast complication the laws of which we shall never fully catalogue however much we wish to do so."

But something is wrong with such a response. Our apparent desire to find answers is only apparent. We have to look for answers and solutions, the world is set up that way. But our enjoyment of our missions and professions depends upon our inability to get all or even most of them.

A much more consistent and honest response is that we *want* to be ignorant, we desire to be without answers, and that ignorance is what enables us to seek understanding. An unanswered question is the romance of reason. It is one short step from this quite candid and, so Michael thought, satisfying response to the admission that the greater our ignorance the more intense is the satisfaction we receive in seeking knowledge.

27

As a graduate student, each day while on his way to and from Yale's Sterling Library, Michael passed a relatively small gray windowless building surrounded by a neatly trimmed hedge and a perpetually locked gate. And twice a day for the greater part of those three years, he found himself wondering what this structure could be. There was no sign, no dedicatory cornerstone; nothing to give any evidence of its purpose.

One morning, dignity yielding to curiosity, Michael climbed the fence, stumbled through the hedge and walked purposefully up to the door of this odd edifice, trying to appear as if he might have business inside. The door was locked, of course. Why, Michael belatedly thought to himself, should the door be opened when the gate was locked? His failure to get inside was compounded by embarrassment when he realized that his retreat was not to be nearly as inconspicuous as his assault. What seemed to him to be legions of his fellow students paused long enough to indulge him through the hedge and over the fence.

Partially recovering his dignity, he realized that he was pleased he had not uncovered the mystery. He rather enjoyed not knowing. He was much more concerned with what the building *might* be than with what it was.

Indeed. What *could* it be? Perhaps it was an archive for pornographic diaries of Jonathan Edwards... A tomb where Frank Merriwether and Bart Hodge were encrypted for the everlasting joy of one another.... Where William Buckley knelt to speak with God.

And so it went through many happy days until the moment when, walking with a friend past that mysterious monolith, Michael shared his wonderings only to have his friend, against Michael's most urgent protests, relate the story about the building. Michael had not felt so betrayed since, years before, another so-called friend had distracted him long enough to drop a caterpillar in his ice cream soda.

Blup. Gone. Wasted.

We do not intend to tell the story of the building. Some

of you may visit Yale and be captured by its mystique. Like
any reasonably wise teacher, Michael should not wish to
spread knowledge where ignorance is more productive.

After that disappointing incident at Yale, Michael thought
to choose his friends more carefully. But that proved impossible. For it seems everyone has answers. It is as if they have
failed to know what knowing is about. Nothing ruins a good
question like an answer. You just start wondering good, and
blup somebody shows up with an answer. Victims of information overkill, we now possess thousands, millions, more
answers than questions. This is so because we are now given
answers without their accompanying questions, before we ever
think to ask.

28

But ignorance is not only useful as a lure for increasing understanding or as a method of guarding against the collapse of
one's defenses—ignorance is alluring in itself...

"In the Middle Ages there was a thriving branch of theology called 'agnoiology.' This is the science that treats of the
nature and extent of human ignorance."

Michael felt the groan. He had long since learned to note
the inaudible complaints of his students. This was not the
harmless, indiscriminate groan that came just before entering a
class that one found particularly trying or in response to a particularly heavy reading assignment or before the announcement of an unexpected exam or, for that matter, the general-
ized, archetypal groan resulting from awakening to a beautiful
spring day only to realize that the semester is less than half
over.

This was a discriminate groan, and such only came from
students who had already made some accommodation with the
educational contest. This lament was most often a response to
what could legitimately be considered an unfair demand upon

student attention. It came when there was a general recognition that the professor was about to pound his own drum, blow his own horn, or mercilessly beat once more his favorite long-dead horse.

This was going to be awful, Michael thought: students all at attention, leaning forward slightly, pens at the ready, yawns suppressed. But only because there was no choice, because something was about to be said, something that if missed or misunderstood could threaten the possibility of the "at least a B" everyone expected (but rarely received) from a course in philosophy.

This time the tremor, the rumble, that announced the ubiquitous anticipation of pain was so palpable that Michael considered abandoning the subject. He finally decided to stick with the topic on the unassailable grounds that any treatment of epistemology, philosophy's "dismal science," would be as tedious as any other.

Michael comforted himself as best he could by silently reciting a favorite refrain of one of his colleagues who, nearing retirement, had confided in him: "Sometimes," his friend had said, "teaching is like slowly bleeding to death."

29

Exsanguinating, Michael continued: "For perhaps the first and only time in our tradition there came into being an honest science, one that by turning its back upon clarity and by actively seeking obscurity, had advertised the essential quality of the human attachment to the world of experience. The motto of the agnoiologists was, *Per obscurum ad obscurius*, 'From the obscure to the even more obscure.'"

The students weren't asleep. Quite the contrary, some probably thought they might never sleep again. Boredom can place one in a state beyond sleeping. One must be interested in something in order to go to sleep—interested in the darkness of sleep, or in dreaming. When the last modicum of interest is drained, there is not enough vitality to make the transition from waking to sleeping. Thus, the Zombie.

Michael had witnessed this phenomenon often. And of course, he knew what his students did not—what very few know (hospital orderlies and the guards in death camps, for example, learn this)—namely, that zombies are, of course, extremely susceptible to influence. In one (shabby) sense, therefore, zombies make the best students. In his classes he recognized that the Intellectual Undead, those who passed the hour in the zombielike stupor between waking and sleeping, would be most affected by philosophic ideas. This is certainly no way to train critical minds; there is, however, no better candidate for indoctrination than the zombie.

He persisted: "Buddhism, correctly viewed, is the primary illustration of a religion grounded upon agnoiological principles. For isn't it true that the Buddhist believes that he sees the world by the light of a flickering candle which enlightenment compels him to snuff out. Existence is suffering; freedom from rebirth is the goal. Nirvana, as you may know (eyebrows laboriously raised here and there suggested that few had even heard the word *nirvana* before), means 'a blowing out.' Nirvana is the state, as the Buddha Gotama insisted, wherein 'the candle is snuffed out.' *Per obscurum ad obscurius.*

"If we were to remain true to the tendency to seek obscurity, if we were to carry it to its Buddhist extreme, then we should have to recognize that the search for knowledge is most satisfying when we find ourselves moving away from clarity, away from understanding, away from answers into an increasingly more complex muddle. We do not really wish to move from darkness to light, but from lighter to darker shadows, and ultimately into the darkest of obscurities. An answer is the light at the tip of a questioning candle. The goal of existence is to snuff out that candle. Every candle. *Per obscurum ad obscurius.*

"Yes, Mr. Stackhouse, you have a comment?"

"Does what you're saying, Professor Evers, mean that the people who don't come to college are better off than those that do, or that if they do go to college it's better for them to spend as little time as possible with the books?"

"Nice try, Mr. Stackhouse. There is a Chinese Buddhist *kung-an*—what you know from the Japanese as a *koan*—that might answer your question. A guru is asked by his *chela*, his disciple, 'How, master, do I cultivate true silence?' The master responds, 'A donkey does not achieve silence merely by refusing to bray.' Were you to ask that *guru* how to achieve true ignorance, he would likely respond in a similar manner. It is not as easy as you think to be ignorant. The candles must be lit before they can be snuffed out. And each person must light his own candles."

Class time was up. Michael was preparing to leave when he took one last look at the twenty or so students moving toward the door. No candles were burning; neither did any smolder.

30

The power of the unpardonable sin was, he knew, the obscure power of unconscious determination. In two senses was this so. First, because it was his ignorance that determined the efficacy. He worried, he guessed, he speculated, he wondered. The power of the anxiety produced in the child Michael by his fear of having committed this unknown sin was vast. Soon, however, his ignorance (and its efficacy) was doubled: he forgot his fear and the mysterious sin which occasioned it. He lived his life unmindful that he was still plagued by his ignorance and the anxiety it engendered. All he actually knew was that if he had committed the unpardonable sin, the consequences were irrevocable.

But there are two sorts of irrevocables. One is like having a caterpillar dropped into your soda or being given a secret you wished you never had to learn. Once accomplished, the act and its consequences persist as inevitabilities. The other sort of irrevocable is that which happens only once and then fades: the ephemeral is unrepeatable, unique, irrevocably so.

The child sitting on the hard wooden bench understood the first kind of irrevocability; the man in Reza's bed had come to know the second. And in a few short minutes, as time is measured from Reza's bed, these two irrevocables would merge.

31

Reza's body tightened under him. Michael felt her breath close to his ear. Was she going to demand confession again? No. Her voice was insistent and low, pleading, commanding.

"Mi-chael." Make me preg-nant."

Michael let himself go. At the moment of release his mind was filled with images of Ap-ple New-tons.

32

Plato tells us that all our thoughts are but reveries, dim memories of a realm of forms encountered before our soul's fall into this world of flux and change. We live among things victimized by time and subject to decay. What we love, when we love, cannot be the decaying things of this world of becoming; we love the ideals of which these items are imperfect instances.

According to this vision, the tragedies of the world all result from our mistaking individual instances of ideals for the ideals themselves, so that when the particular is taken from us we believe that we have lost the ideal itself. All we have to do is to recognize that it is the ideal we really love, then we can easily enough find another convenient window through which to view it.

Further, we are given to believe that we can free ourselves from the power of idealized individuals by seeing them actualized, temporalized, subjected to passage and decay. For example, we can be free of our unrequited love if we picture the lady picking her nose, or sitting on the potty. For those who have accepted Plato's vision of things, this almost never fails.

Unfortunately, Michael has long since ceased to believe in Plato's Hoax. The notion of an ideal world beyond this world, eternally protected from corruption and decay is nothing more than a comforting rationalization for those who can't look directly into the face of things. There are, in fact, no ideals, no untainted possibilities. There is only this and this and this...

Most of us are too conscious and too fearful of our decay ever to learn this lesson. We will continue to interrupt experience, to put the brakes on as it were: to say to the moment, "Hold thou art so fair," even were we to realize that our soul will be required of us. We will conspire with desperate, decaying moments and the beings that inhabit them—to idealize, to offer life after death. We will presume to love and by that love immortalize, as we falsely believe we have been immortalized by our desire.

Michael knows the truth. And so he realizes that Reza's power over him is wholly temporal. To turn away from the processive, event-ridden, occasional flux of their lives together would be to surrender Reza to timelessness. She would become the Eternal Feminine: the only woman Michael could never love.

This was his choice. He would idealize her. And be free of her. Michael knows who Reza is and exactly what insures her uniqueness. He will take that from her. It is to be his sin.

His unpardonable sin.

33

The phonograph was on top of the second bookshelf. Reza had to stand on a chair to operate the machine. When he came up behind her she was intent upon cleaning a record with a paper towel. He put his face next to her bottom. He could smell the two of them mingled in her. He reached between her legs and put his fingers inside her, raising his hand but arresting its movement just before it reached his mouth.

"Teach me."

He could feel her body smile. She turned round on the chair. He put his tongue in her belly button. She shivered.

"Ah. The teacher would be taught?"

"It is so. If you have wisdom to spare."

"More than enough. And certainly you are in need." Reza closed her eyes for a moment, reflecting. Then, her arms rising slowly over her head, she whispered, "Today's lesson... The lesson for today is..."

She is much better at this game than I, Michael thought.

Stepping regally from the chair, she said, "Well, now. Since we seem to be on the subject of rules today, how would you like to learn the first principle of ballet?"

"The first principle of ballet?"

"The very first principle, yes."

"Teach me."

Reza bowed deeply and began a pirouette. "Attend to me, my rapidly aging friend."

To Michael her voice sounded vacant and flat, as if she were reading another actor's line from off a cue card.

"The first rule of ballet is... 'Ow do you say eet in eengleesh.... The very first rule is..."

IT'S NOT HOW HIGH YOU JUMP BUT HOW LONG YOU STAY IN THE AIR.

No more vindicating irony than this: that Reza's final words before her apotheosis, the last words she would utter on this planet, should be unoriginal, borrowed from some high-culture comic. George Bernard Shaw, perhaps.

As Reza spoke she leapt from the floor. Michael watched her breasts press downward, then rise, lifting her toward the ceiling. Every muscle taut, her eyes gently fixed on a point in space light-years distant, she reached the highest point of her arc...and paused.

34

Reza would no longer be a poet, no longer a maker of moments. Michael would no longer inherit from her, absorb her. He had stolen her ephemerality and had rendered her eternal. Reza could never again play about his consciousness like Avogadro's number or the fine structure constant (the thought of Karla—of Adrienne, really—still caused him wrenching pain). She was no longer an endlessly open, increasingly precise, but never, never exact process of approximation, no longer a river on its maiden voyage to the sea. She was now fixed, permanent, finished, complete. Unreal.

A closed issue. From among the infinite series of droplets of becoming Michael had selected a single one and immortalized it. From the stringless string of pearls strung out through time, he had chosen a single pearl, consigning it to the Repository of Eternal Ideals—Hell Itself.

The idealized memory, of course, would not completely vanish, but all the better. The memory of a denatured Reza, drained of her milk and blood and left suspended at the apex of her arc, motionless and imperiously beautiful, soon would have the same scentless, tasteless, effete status in Michael's consciousness as that of the Eternal Feminine whose frigid, pale form he had first encountered in *Faust*, Part II.

Michael knew that the unpardonable sin is the cancellation of immediacy, its apotheosis, its idealization. It is the feeding of Fat Dharma, the Carrion God. Plato's Hoax persuades us that ideals are superior to the flux of circumstance. Fat Dharma is the benefactor of this lie. Our ideals are excuses for us, but they are food for Him. All of our experiences are thus aborted, stillborn, rendered innocuous and repetitive.

Michael knew his sin to be unpardonable. And since the essence of all sinning is to stay the flow of reality, to render permanent what is meant to be ephemeral, every sin is unpardonable. Fat Dharma forgives no one.

But few of us are ever free to sin. For it is no easier to sin than it is to be ignorant, or to attain true silence. Most sin is original, in the sense that almost all of it came in the beginning. Sinning is so difficult because the world contains so little uniqueness and immediacy, so few insistently particular beings against which one might offend. Thus, it is understandable that, though Michael did not welcome the sin, he could not but feel privileged that he had been afforded the opportunity to commit it.

35

At last Michael understands the dynamics of sin. The locus of the event that taught him was the triangular space defined by the evangelist's tent, the desk at which (simultaneously reading Aristotle and the *Lotus Sutra*) he had first encountered Fat Dharma, and the now exhausted fountain of Reza's body.

IV

The Rhetoric of Rainbows

1

1. All meaningful events are either accidents or coincidences.

   1.1 A coincidence is the intersection of two or more accidents.

2

Michael awoke in unusually high spirits. Reza had been out of his life for some time and, except for an occasion on which a colleague had mentioned the character of Faust while discussing the myth of Prometheus, which had made Michael think of Goethe's silly doctrine of the Eternal Feminine, which in turn had led him to entertain the ever-fixed, everlastingly pale image of Reza suspended in her flight (the image causing Michael to laugh out loud and his colleague to ask what was so funny), he had not given her a single thought.

The reason for Michael's mood on this particular morning, however, has less to do with his having conquered the memory of Reza and more to do with last night's dream which was vividly imprinted upon his consciousness.

Unlike many others who dreamed often, Michael was seldom disturbed by his dreams. He often wondered why his dreams were so discursive, so rational, why they all had pleasant endings. He would have enjoyed, now and again, a dream less logical than his were wont to be, without the all too obvious moral, with a slightly fuzzier climax. In his waking life he was always teaching or preaching to others; in sleep, denied an audience, he would exhort himself. One can hardly awake truly rested after a night filled with exhortiums.

He considered the possibility that he never slept in the truest sense and that his dreams were little more than reveries. For we all believe with Heracleitus that, "Awake, men live in a common world; asleep, each turns aside into a world of his own." Michael, however, occupied the same world both asleep and awake.

Plato, elaborating Heracleitus's insight, had said, "A tyrant behaves as a person behaves in his dreams." It would be an innocuous tyrant, indeed, who took Michael's dream-behaviors for a model. As an adolescent, he had wondered if he were the only one who had no private world to turn to, who was always in the common world, always aware of himself and those around him.

The problem, of course, was not in Michael. The insights

of Heracleitus and Plato are simply dated. There was a much greater spontaneity in dreams in the early days of our civilization when the emergence of self-consciousness from out of the chaos of dreams and imaginings was a relatively recent event. But lately, Freud, Jung, et al. have invaded our dream-worlds with their catalogues and sample cases. Now even our most bizarre dreams are unlikely to have as much as a tincture of originality.

Dreams are now surface phenomena. Once the meanings of dream-symbols and archetypes have been given a common interpretation, dreams can no longer be symbolic. Drained of their mystery and evocative power, symbols function as dead metaphors that have passed into the realm of the literal. Such is the consequence of our bloated consciousness.

In his most recent dream, Michael had found himself at a masquerade party. He was embarrassed because he was wearing no mask. His embarrassment turned to panic when the host announced that the evening's entertainment was to be a guessing game—the individual whose identity was discovered by the largest number of partiers was to be put to death. The person who identified the most guests would be his executioner.

Each of the participants was asked to write his guesses on a piece of paper which was then placed in a cigar box. (Michael thought that when he recounted this dream he would have to substitute something like an antique portmanteau for the cigar box.) Michael could do nothing but await the inevitable which, he soon realized, would never come. His was the only identity never once discovered. Everyone assumed that the guests at a masquerade party would all wear masks. The person wearing a Michael mask certainly could not be Michael.

As irony would dictate, the fellow who made the most correct guesses also was most often identified. His was a forced suicide. Michael reflected: In life, of course...

3

So begins this morning's oneirocritical exercise. Before brushing his teeth, before his first taste of coffee, even before getting up to pee—or in the act of peeing—Michael *will* examine his dreams...

In life, of course, the timid avoid the risk of suicide by refusing to guess identities at all. Murder is not so easily prevented. Socrates had a most accurate sense of who was behind the masks he encountered on Athenian streets. He, however, wore the mask of irony as if it were no mask at all. He was completely visible. Thus, the hemlock.

Appearance is a mask of reality. Order is the mask of Chaos. In the beginning...there were no masks. The Buddhist *chela* is asked, "What was your original face before you were born?" It was a maskless face.

Our myths are the masks of our common world. The masks we share. We must presume that a mask hides rather than reveals. Yet we believe this cannot be so in the case of our myths since myths purport to tell us what lies behind the mask. The dark, formless void lies behind the cosmic mask of created order. Or does it?

Myths reveal reality by masking it. Is the myth advertising a reality so similar to the mask as to be indiscernible from it? What if order and harmony were there all along? What if each being could encounter a primordial harmony suited to its original face? Then the myths of creation advertise nothing more than *an order not mine*. Behind the mask is one's original face. Distinct. Insistently different. But ordered nonetheless.

Michael remembered visiting an exhibit of Iroquois face masks at the Whitney Museum of Modern Art. These were masks carved from living trees and then ritually fed until used in religious ceremonies. What made them seem so real? Wasn't it their very seeming? The chasm separating seeming and being was no longer present. There is no chasm, really. The chasm itself is only a seeming. Masks are the only reality. Why should there be something behind them? The mask is alive and will continue to be so as long as it is fed. The Iroquois show forth another reality by donning the mask. They become the effigy. Perhaps, then, masks are not meant to hide but to *present*.

We have little choice but to feed masks, our own and those of others. Only through this conspiracy can we defend against infinity. The demands of the infinite, the obligations of the absolute, are resisted even more than the unknown. The courageous few who recognize infinity shining through the masks do not seem to realize that infinity itself is a mask.

Thankfully, there is another way to unmask the world. If not a better way, then a richer, intenser, more complex way. It is Iris's way. The way of the rainbow.

4

Her name was Iris, but almost from the beginning, when they first made love, when he first touched her skin and felt (as much as saw) her Mexican colors, Michael called her "Arquita."

Iris's skin was all shades of cinnamon: darker in the arms and shoulders and knees, lighter neck and thighs. She was a rainbow of cinnamon, a spectrum of moist, round colors. She even smelled of cinnamon. Michael's face moving down her body from her hair to the arches of her feet drifted through fields of scents shading discreetly, but with distinctive boundaries, one into another.

In Spanish "rainbow" is *arco iris.* So Michael named her Arca—Arquita. Iris's third-generation Spanish was obviously no better than Michael's; he had to discover his mistake for himself. By feminizing *arco,* "arch," he had rendered "ark" instead. And through this blending of romantic intent and grammatical indiscretion, he discovered her real name.

A rainbow announced the end of the forty days' rain. And an ark protected Noah's cargo. Arquita was a securing vessel come to celebrate the end of a storm. In the beginning Michael gave no thought to the most profound sense of Arquita's name. She was indeed an ark—an untouchable holy of holies.

Is there a word for the feeling one gets when trapped by the power of another whose ability to give pleasure and pain is exactly equal, whose disruptive and securing powers are of exactly the same strength?

Michael was led to think of the fourteenth-century medieval philosopher, John Buridan, who attempted to illustrate the dilemmas associated with moral decisions through the use of a famous analogy subsequently known as "Buridan's Ass." (In fact, the animal discussed at some length by Buridan in his commentary on Aristotle's *De Cœlo* was a dog, and a number of other elements of the traditional account differ significantly from Buridan's actual tale, but here as in so many other instances in history, the embellished account is far superior to the original. Since we know this, Michael "knows" it, as well. But he has long ago forgotten this fact and remains content with the emended version.)

Buridan's ass stood exactly halfway between two equally desirable bales of hay. It stood until, weakened by hunger, it could no longer stand. There was no reason for it to choose one bale over the other, and so the will was paralyzed. Michael, a far greater ass, had placed himself at the exact center of an equilateral triangle whose vertices were formed by an untouchable ark, an insubstantial rainbow whose source he could vainly pursue for the rest of his life and a vessel that could receive him only under the Rule of Noah: Yes, another pair of nostrils sucked at Arquita's skin.

But we shall not...there will be no need to recount any intimacies other than those Michael and Iris shared.

5

He came home after six weeks absence and found her sitting in that loose-fitting frock with gigantic sleeves that put her on display every time she raised an arm or bent forward to speak. She wanted him to ache. He obliged, though he couldn't be sure the ache would be soothed. She often refused to be touched. And some parts of her were always off-limits.

"Michael. *Michael!*"

"What?"

"Your hand. It's on my knee."

"Yes."

"Would you *move* it?"

"Of course." Michael was puzzled.

"I never let anyone touch my knees. I sort of trust you so you can touch my ankles. But when you start getting too close to my knees, you'll know it."

"What is it with your knees?"

"What do you think? Your kneecaps could be just ripped off in a second. Then where would you be? Most people think that the eyes are the most important things. Not me. It's my legs. Without eyes you can still listen and find out what's coming.... Sometimes it's better not to see what's coming. You don't have to see in order to run. But what if you had your eyes but no legs? Then you would see, but you couldn't run."

"That's the problem, then: to see but to be unable to run?"

"If I lost my legs, I wouldn't want my eyes anymore."

"There must be something perverse in me after all, Arquita. All I can think about now is being the one to touch your knees."

"I know. That's why I don't tell many people. As I say I sort of trust you."

"Your knees are safe with me, Arca."

"I don't want to talk about it."

6

Long before he had been caught trespassing upon Arquita's knees, Michael had occasion to learn of the territoriality of promiscuous women. Such women, otherwise disposed to offer their bodies to whomever, whenever—and often—invariably have distinctive body parts they consider precious and unassailable.

These sacred areas never have any direct connection with the primary genitalia. On the contrary, the erogenous areas of promiscuous women are, by definition, free-fire zones, offering no constraints upon hostile armies; they are all welcoming resorts for recreation and relaxation.

Even with such women, however, there must be limits.

The untouchable areas could be toes, wrists, temples—any local surface or feature. These arbitrarily selected areas are always invested with a virginal aura. They are the place of purity's last stand. As long as these are not touched, kissed, caressed, or fondled, the women can believe that they have not yielded everything and that they are not (whatever the appearances) persons of easy virtue.

The promiscuous must maintain control, and so must at least partially numb their genitals. But all that libidinal energy has to go somewhere. The trick is to invest it in a place that may be protected from erotic engagement. Arquita's refusal to let her knees be touched was a defense against the collapse into an erotic ecstasy that would have signaled her loss of control.

The most promiscuous woman Michael had ever known, the only woman who was completely possessed by her need to have men, maintained control in just this manner. By her own defiant admission, almost any man at almost any time on almost any pretense could get this woman into a bed or the backseat of a car, or onto a desktop or floor, or into a linen closet (or against the wall in a dark corner of Central Supply at Spirit Valley Community Hospital, where Michael had met her). While in any of these places anyone could do anything they wished with or to her, constrained only by the limits of imagination, physical dexterity, and locale...and oddly, by the inviolability of her ears. Julie would not allow her ears to be touched. Any attempt to caress or nibble at them would certainly have led to a cry of rape.

Michael and Julie would meet once or twice a week at her apartment. At first he found her attractive, but he soon realized that their intimacies could not continue. For immediately after they would begin lovemaking, Julie would press her hands over her ears and hold them tightly in place until the end of the enterprise. Michael couldn't help thinking how much she looked like the hear-no-evil member of a trio of monkey figurines he had been given as a child.

His affair with Julie ended when Michael involuntarily laughed at exactly the wrong time and then proceeded to compound his sin by confessing the reason why.

7

"Most days are Tuesdays. Even if they start out as a Sunday or a Friday, they mostly turn into Tuesday real fast."

Michael wasn't in the mood for this desperate whimsy. He wondered distractedly if Tuesdays and kneecaps had anything in common. But he didn't care. He tried to ignore her.

"Today is Tuesday." (It *was* Tuesday.) "But not for the reason you think."

"Oh?"

"Calendar Tuesdays are weird. They only pretend to be Tuesday. But they usually *are* Tuesday, anyway."

"Ah, reality masked by a mask of the same countenance."

"What?"

"Tuesday wears a Tuesday mask."

"Sort of, I guess. But the Tuesday mask is special."

There was no getting out of this. Michael yielded to what promised to be one of those mind-bending exercises in self-referenced free-association Iris was so often compelled to perform. "What are the qualities of Tuesday? What is 'Tuesdayness,' Arquita?"

"Tuesdays are letdown, leftover days. They're empty days and empty days are dangerous. You know, if you leave any empty spaces bad things will come and fill them. That's why I always make sure my closets are full. If your closets and cabinets are full nothing can get in and hide. Tuesdays are hard to fill, so things can get in and hurt you. I'm afraid of Tuesdays."

"And you say most days are Tuesdays?"

"Yeah, for me. Most days usually get around to being Tuesday—Satansday." Iris paused, leaned forward, as if straining to hear, or perhaps to see, something afar off. Almost immediately she again sat stiffly straight in her chair as she added, "Maybe that's sacrilegious. I'll take it back. I just think that Tuesday was the day God chose to create empty spaces."

8

Iris closed her eyes, breathing deeply. When she took deep breaths she seemed to let only half the air out again. Deep inhale, shallow exhale. "You want a blow-job?" Her eyes were still closed.

Michael was by now accustomed to this sort of timing. For Arquita, sex was a gift. It secured her relationships and cost her nothing, since it meant so little to her. Oral sex was best since it took less time. And it was least threatening, since she was in control.

Tuesdays are for blow-jobs, Michael thought.

She was deservedly proud of her oral talent. Michael had often attempted to influence her to use the term, "oral sex." "That sounds disgusting," she would say. "I give blow-jobs."

She had been a bit more discreet in the beginning. The evening of their first encounter she had said, "Shall I put my head in your lap?" At first Michael hadn't known what she meant, she had asked so sweetly. Then, he thought he should mention the antagonism between zippers and male genitalia, but soon realized that she had mastered every nuance of her art.

After Iris's initial performance, Michael could only sit or lie or stand or kneel in a kind of benumbed awe which ever so gradually became mixed with a sense of disaffection, an alienation first from that engorged muscle—no longer Michael's but hers: it moved or failed to move more at her bidding than his; whatever pleasure she derived came from it, not from him. She loved it, not him. Michael grew jealous of it (a primal instance of "penis envy"). Finally, as the distance between himself and that part of him increased, both Michael and that part of him were alienated from Arquita.

9

Often, after one of her incredible oral displays, Iris would simply turn over and go to sleep, leaving Michael spent but wide awake. She had obliged him by feigning the intensest of emotions, the most provocative gyrations and postures, pornophonic sounds, both articulate and merely guttural. Still, there had been little real sensuality in her performance. He would wonder what she had gotten in return.

Michael finally realized that the economy of sex was a most straightforward and simple issue for his Arquita: She would do him a favor (blow-job); in return he owed her something (security). For her part, she didn't have to worry about Michael for awhile. She had stolen his power and short-circuited any aggression that could possibly spill over in her direction. She was relaxed and could sleep because she could now "sort of" trust him.

Sex, for her, wasn't sensual at all. It was an act of self-defense aimed at maintaining her autonomy. It was as if she had sought to prevent rape by offering to fellate her attacker. It wouldn't be sex, and it wouldn't be offensive, if the attacker submitted to the blow-job.

Didn't she understand what she was doing to him? Didn't she know that all he wanted was to be the one to touch her knees and, beyond that, to have something other than make-believe sex with her—to fuck her out of her pretense, to the point of at least one involuntary twitch or grimace, one uncontrived sigh? Of course, she understood. But Michael knew that were he to seek control she would simply leave him. Iris counted on his knowing that.

So Arquita's wonderful body, that untouchable ark, protected now by sleep and by Michael's reluctant gratitude, belonged only to her.

10

We think that love and sex surely ought have something to do with one another. Of course, the Greeks knew this was not so. In the dialogue called *The Symposium*, Plato has Aristophanes tell the wonderful tale of the round beings, each of whom owned two distinct sexual identities paired in three ways—male-male, male-female, female-female. Jealous of their strength and aggressiveness, Zeus divided them into two parts in order both to limit their power and to double the number of sacrifices the gods would receive. The desire that urged these severed beings to seek reunion Aristophanes called eros.

The problem was, of course, that when they did reunite, these sundered creatures would refuse to let go. No longer anatomically able to fit into a single harmonious sphere, they were forced to wrap themselves desperately around one another, clinging tightly, fearful of separation. They began to smother one another or to starve themselves to death. Zeus had to intervene once more. He invented the orgasm as an automatic mechanism of release. They had rewon their autonomy through sexual climax. Between the periods of orgasmic union, they could go about the business of the day.

According to this account, orgasmic sexuality is an afterthought. Love is for union. Sex is to gain release. They are opposites. Contradictories. One is an expedient to cure the problem raised by the other.

This is, of course, not to say that we should decry sex without love. It is sex without passion that does most harm— more harm than even that wrought by love without joy. Passionless sex is an empty gust at best.

11

It was inevitable that Michael start to resent Iris and the power he had yielded to her in return for one-sided pleasure. He began the fight to regain control of his private parts, but the struggle only led to a most ludicrous détente. Neither his nor any longer hers, Michael's organ lay suspended in whatever space houses objects admixed of flesh and fantasy. Each of them now came to it for their separate aims—pleasure for him and power for her. But it no longer gratified either of them. It gave power to no one and pleasure only to itself. Michael and Iris were unwilling voyeurs.

Locked outside her body and kept in ignorance of her substance, Michael was forced to fall in love with her style. And though his feelings were no longer sexual, it was nonetheless passion that he felt. Passion is, in fact, little more than an intense appreciation of style. The less substantial the motivating object, the more intense passion must be. That is the power of fantasy.

A rainbow is insubstantial. It is all style and no substance. For all that, rainbows are precious and real. Arquita was real.

12

Michael had fallen in love with Iris in absentia. Driving through St. Louis on his way to Chicago to visit the seminary from which he had graduated, he decided to see the famous arch. As he approached one of the anchors of this awesome parabola he recalled his part in the construction of another remarkable edifice, erected in the central quadrangle of the University of Chicago. About four in the morning, at the end of a heavy snowfall, eight or ten of the seminary students, standing on the roofs of two strategically positioned vans, completed a nine-foot-high penis, sans prepuce, and endowed by its creators with dramatically dimensioned snow balls.

Michael had not been able at the time to account for the feeling of *mysterium tremendum* that had overwhelmed him when, standing with his colleagues in a circle at the base of this gigantic snow phallus, gross product of their collective desublimation, they had recited a hastily revised Lord's Prayer which began "Our Penis, Which reaches to Heaven..." and which had then continued to decline both in literary and theological merit from that low point.

That Michael should entertain this memory while approaching the St. Louis Arch was probably due to his having read an article in which a female critic, dismissing the obvious allusion to "vaginal symbol," had likened the arch to a "a limp phallus, a permanently flaccid penis, announcing the declining potency of all sky-piercing structures which have long since exhausted the thematic variations on the Tower of Babel."

At the time he thought the essay clever. Now, overcome by the magnificence of the arch, he was retroactively offended. Here was no mindless celebration of sexual accouterments. This straining, bending metallic bow offered a far more primordial message. This was a monochrome rainbow.

Freud's perverse genius transformed eros into the motivation for reaching outward and upward, for erecting spires and towers to touch, to penetrate, to violate the sky. But in Hesiod's *Theogony*, we find the original sense of eros. In that myth, Chaos comes into being with the separation of the earth and the sky. Chaos is separation and *eros* draws earth and sky together, overcoming the yawning gap, the gaping void of Chaos. And in that myth Iris ("rainbow") is a messenger between gods and human beings, between heaven and earth. Because the rainbow touches both earth and sky, it unites the two. A rainbow is the shadow and reflection of love.

Of course, Michael knows a rainbow doesn't last, isn't real. It is only an illusion that appears rarely and fades rapidly. But, at least it is an illusion we all can share. That makes it more than real enough. And even if the messenger is illusory, the message doesn't have to be. A rainbow (so Michael, standing before the St. Louis Arch suddenly had realized) is the sign, the consequence, and the reward of love.

13

Iris had a fascination for television that Michael had never encountered even among children. She would watch for hours, sitting only inches from the TV, twisting her body in her chair, making both of her hands into fists, holding them tightly together before her mouth in agitated anticipation of the next twist in the plot.

Iris loved to *be* asleep. She thought herself safe while asleep. She hated *to go* to sleep. The transition from sleeping to waking was too threatening. She needed noise. Noise served as a kind of guarantee that her world was not vanishing as she fell asleep. Only if somehow assured that it would be there when she returned, could she rest.

She would never fall asleep without the television on. One of her worst fears was to wake up to an "empty" TV—all snow and sounding of static. For then the Arimaspian eye would have turned around to make of her the only reality.

Television was more than a kind of comforting reassurance that the outside continued after sleep. Iris didn't distinguish it from the rest of the world. It was as real as was anything else. Even *more* real by virtue of its richer content—fantasies and anomalies, places and people encountered nowhere else. Cartoon characters.

And demons.

Michael and Iris had rented a movie. It was a horror film. Iris loved horror movies. But she would only watch films she had seen before or that had been screened in advance by Michael or a friend. She had to be certain that everything would come out all right. In this particular film, familar from several viewings, Iris was faced with one of the minions of Satan advancing upon his unsuspecting victim. Iris's face mirrored the horrified countenance of the virginal prey as she raised her fist toward the screen and said, "OK, buster, if you come after me I'll say one 'Hail Mary,' an 'Our Father,' and a 'Glory Be' and you'll be dust!"

"And you expect the demon to snarl and drool in place while you go through all that?"

"Don't make fun."

Michael ignored her plea. "Iris, do you actually believe that your religion can protect you from the dark, empty forces that surround us all, that even now...?"

"Hush! Of course I do. I always say a novena to St. Jude when I'm in trouble."

"Isn't Jude the patron saint of lost causes?"

"Yes."

Iris looked at Michael, waiting for him to speak. He didn't need to. He realized that, in the beginning, before the intervention of the saintly mediators, Iris thought all her causes hopeless.

14

Friedrich Schleiermacher, a nineteenth-century theologian, had thought the feeling of absolute dependence to be the wellspring of religious sentiment. Iris's sense of dependence, though limited, was nonetheless powerful. So she had the power to create God. And to destroy Him. Forget the Our Fathers and the Glory Be's—one Hail Mary could turn God to dust. Of course, Roman Catholics may already have long ago accomplished that.

Iris didn't feel the need for God. For all practical purposes, He was suitably, fashionably dead. The saints were quite another matter. Faith in a saint requires something less than absolute dependence. Saints are for people who can't trust in cosmic proportions. Each of the saints has his or her specialty. One doesn't tax a saint outside the area of his expertise.

So the best Michael could be was a saint: one of the saintly band, earthly and spiritual, that ministered to Arquita's needs. And as saints are but the masks of God—who Himself does not exist except as the terminus a quo of the masking activity—Michael was made into a mask.

Of course, no one who really knows Michael would believe he has any reason to complain. He has, after all, spent the better part of his adult life preparing for just such treatment...

15

Those training for the solitary life of the scholar have little use for social skills. Typically, social events among intellectuals in training are mildly desperate affairs at which everyone starts off determined not to talk shop only to discover that no one really cares about anything else.

At one such joyless event during his graduate student days, the following game was included among several feeble efforts to avoid early capitulation to intellectual showmanship: Each person was given a pen and paper and asked to write ten terms that were *not* descriptive of his or her personality. The lists were then distributed among the guests who were supposed to guess the identity of the person from the list of irrelevant characteristics.

Here is Michael's list:

1. deliberate
2. meticulous
3. painstaking
4. particular
5. fastidious
6. conscientious
7. scrupulous
8. exacting
9. punctilious
10. advertent

He was picked out rather easily both because of general awareness of his impatience with detail and, more significantly, because he was thought to be most likely to come up with ten synonymous terms off the top of his head.

Michael was usually quicker, more sensitive and more knowledgeable than his intimates, particularly the women who sought him out. To compensate, he was continually pulling his punches, feigning ignorance, enthusiasm, or surprise. His friends, especially females, invested altogether too much in his opinions and judgments. If he did not actively avoid candor, he could easily offend those close to him.

Whatever charm he possessed was born of high intellectual seriousness—the sort of appeal that wears off rather rapidly.
And once he had handicapped himself sufficiently to insure
reasonable harmony in his relationships, the women who had
been attracted to him because he was sensitive and intelligent
were certain to lose interest. He in turn would feel disdain for
his lovers when they did not become fully actualized under his
nurturing presence.

16

The abused cliché, "Those who can, do, those who can't, teach," contains some skewed wisdom. The truth has nothing whatsoever to do with questions of talent or ability; it is, rather, altogether a question of commitment.

Michael's choice of teaching as a profession dated from a moment in early adolescence when his father had said, with a humorous intent Michael had missed because immediately so engaged by the wisdom of the statement, "Listen, son, you've got two choices in this life: You can either keep changing your jokes or your friends." Michael had realized then that he was too lazy continually to learn new jokes. Teaching would suit him well. He would be guaranteed a regularly changing inventory of "friends."

The teacher depends upon transitory commitments. Short-term impressions. Student populations change every semester. Who couldn't sustain a relationship for that length of time? The *guru* releases his *chela*, the professor bids farewell to his students—then each moves on to impress new minds with the same old jokes.

Michael was a teacher. Not only in the classroom, but outside of it as well. He could redirect people's lives, alter their values, solidify their relationships with other people, renew their marriages, and give them reasons for believing themselves to be worthwhile. What he could not do, would not do, was to commit to any relationship long enough to be changed himself. He was the teacher, the guide. Often, when he raised to consciousness this sad fact about himself, he wondered how his friends could stand him. Then he realized that, of course, his friends were teachers too.

Those not scornful of teachers are envious of them. And rightfully so. After all, six or nine hours of class a week, plus an occasional committee meeting, a month off for Christmas vacation, three months free in the summer—such an undemanding schedule leaves one with lots of free time for reading and reflecting and, most importantly, for writing those books which are the sole sources of the scholar's vague fame.

17

"Well, I feel that Socrates..."

"*Mr.* Evers..." Everyone knew what was coming. Students sat frozen in their various postures, fixing their eyes on the ceiling, desk, or floor while their colleague received the Message: "In this class you are not asked to feel, but to *think*. And when you *do* think you are asked to think about the text. Your heart-felt opinions, however inspiring you may believe them to be, are of no interest to us here. Now, again..."

Michael's years as a seminarian at the University of Chicago were filled with encounters of just this kind. He studied philosophical theology, which meant that he read the works of the great philosophers and theologians. These texts had meanings which, upon excruciatingly precise analysis, could be exposed. His professors were not interested in comments about the texts or their historical background. It was the text, and only the text, which was to be understood.

And always the great, *primary* text—whenever possible in the original language. No secondary sources, no surveys or commentaries were allowed. In the words of one of Michael's seminary professors, a distinguished New Testament scholar visiting from Tübigen: "Vell, gentlemen, *gut*. At Zhicago, I understant zat you schtick to zeh texts."

After three years of "schtickink to zeh texts," Michael completed his seminary degree and went off to Yale to work toward his Ph.D. The severe contrast between the two schools set the tenor of Michael's later philosophical career.

18

The scene again is a seminar room, this time in New Haven. The professor is somewhat younger, Michael slightly older.

"Yes, of course, Mr. Evers. But I should like to learn your *opinion* of that argument. How would you *e-val-u-ate* it? Do you, Mr. Evers, find it *per-sua-sive?*"

Michael innocently reiterated the Message: "I do my best to analyze textual meanings; I want to avoid as much as possible introducing my own opinions."

The professor seemed unimpressed. "And where did you come by such a methodology, Mr. Evers?"

"At Chicago."

"Of course." The professor rolled his eyes and wrinkled his nose just enough to make it clear how scornful he was of such an approach to philosophical education.

"Very well, Mr. Evers." The professor said this with an almost world-weary condescension that suggested he had given this lecture before. "We now know what *has been* expected of you. May I inform you what *should have been and indeed will be* expected? At Yale, Mr. Evers..." The professor straightened in his chair, apparently uplifted by the mere thought of glorious Mother Yale. "we are not required to hide ourselves in the interstices of the text. You see, at Yale, Mr. Evers, we are expected to have..." The professor's upper teeth lightly touched his bottom lip. His chin raised slightly, then lowered, then raised again—higher this time—as he concluded his sentence, "*views.*" The word was sounded quite slowly, with two syllables, taking perhaps three or four seconds to pronounce. It sounded like, "*v-yooze.*" "At Yale, Mr Evers, we are expected to have *v-yooze.*"

The word wasn't actually spoken, it was thrust from the professor's mouth in the manner of a plush red carpet rolled forward to receive a guest who, though at present most undeserving, would nevertheless attain royal status once he had set foot upon it.

Perhaps that metaphor is too grand. To be more consonant with Michael's ambivalent feelings, one might rather say that the professor's pronouncement ("At Yale, Mr Evers, we are expected to have *v-yooze.*") reminded Michael of a frog's slow-motion demonstration of the correct manner of catching a fly.

19

Michael's education at two great universities had taught him three fundamental truths:

THE FIRST TRUTH: By 323 B.C.E. (This was the year of Aristotle's exile from Athens. He died a year later.), the definitive concepts, principles, and values had already been developed. Thereafter, thought had taken on the character of variations played upon a small finite number of principal themes. As a Chicago graduate, Michael was dutifully persuaded of this fact.

THE SECOND TRUTH: If one is to be responsible as a scholar and a teacher, one cannot simply mimic the great voices of the past. One must have (there is no choice)—*v-yooze*. As a Yale Ph.D., Michael, reluctantly at first, but then most readily, yielded himself up to this credo.

These apparently contradictory pedagogical advices led Michael to

THE THIRD TRUTH: All the important *v-yooze* having already been taken, there being nothing new under the sun, one's only choice is to chart galaxies whose worlds are warmed by other stars.

Michael's attempt to weld these three truths into a viable means of preserving both of his deeply felt loyalties at least partially accounts for the borderline, even bizarre, character of many of his *v-yooze*.

20

Soon after acquiring these three pedagogical truths, Michael realized that, both in order to develop his own *v-yooze* and to assure himself of their originality, it would be necessary to read as much as possible. He resolved the "so many books, so little time" dilemma by taking a speed-reading course. Increasing his reading rate by a factor of more than ten in just a few weeks, he set out to read ten times the complement of books that otherwise would have been possible.

He studied closely the writings of the philosophers and theologians—Plato, Aristotle, Augustine, Aquinas, Calvin, Descartes, Leibniz, Spinoza, Kant, Hegel, Kierkegaard, Wittgenstein, Heidegger, Tillich, and so forth. With respect to collateral fields such as science, history, and literature, however, he had to move more rapidly. He sped-read the entire *Principia* and *Opticks* of Newton but concentrated only on the discussions of absolute space and time in the former and certain of the anomalies related to Newton's theory of vision in the latter. He read all of Poincaré's *Science and Hypothesis,* considering only the discussions of non-Euclidean geometries in any detail. That way, he knew he would never seem altogether superficial if the occasion arose for him to discourse upon "Newton and the Rise of Modern Science," or "Poincaré's Contribution to Relativity Theory."

He read all of Herodotus and Thucydides, Gibbon's *The History of the Decline and Fall of the Roman Empire,* Spengler's *Decline of the West,* and (in spite of Sumervell's splendid abridgements) seven of the ten volumes of Toynbee's *A Study of History.* After skim-scanning these works (at least glancing at every page), Michael collated passages from them which treated of the importance of great personalities. Thereafter, if engaged in a conversation with, say, a colleague in the history department, he would attempt to turn the discussion in the direction of heroic interpretations of history.

He would march through (at his new streamlined pace) the entirety of the *Inferno, Purgatorio,* and *Paradiso,* slowing down only long enough to memorize a few, randomly selected passages from each. Milton's *Paradise Lost* would be swallowed whole, and in record time; only the most dramatic of the Satan passages would be digested. Then, if ever the occasion arose, he could offer the few lines he had memorized, hoping to leave the impression that, had he wished, he could have quoted these poets at far greater length.

There are difficulties with this method of preparing to don the mask of the Genuinely Well-Educated, some of which, even now, Michael fails to appreciate. For example, such an approach to learning gives one a "meroscopic" intellectual outlook. If he were candid, most of Michael's judgments concerning this or that area of his knowledge should begin: "Judging the whole from one of its parts..." That is to say: It is invariably the case that most of what Michael has skimmed, scanned, browsed, surveyed, perused, and glanced at has been forgotten. Thus, while he may claim to have read enormous amounts of material, he is usually forced to assess the meaning of that material—a scientific theory, the vision of a playwright or poet—from but a single chapter, a few lines of dialogue, or in the extremest of cases, a single poem.

To cite a rather embarrassing instance: Michael counts William Blake among his favorite poets. But he does so on the basis of one, brief poem—in fact, on but the first two lines of that poem. He has read other of Blake's poetry, but remembers with precision only this single poem. The lines Michael remembers as quintessential Blake are:

Never seek to tell thy love.
Love that never told can be.

Michael interprets these lines, rightly enough, as a prophetic challenge to Elizabeth Barrett Browning's offer to list the ways of love.

Now, one doesn't have to be a Blake scholar to see how badly Michael has misconstrued that poet's intent. Indeed, Michael himself has read (scanned) more than enough by and about Blake to realize his error. But he fails, for instance, to recall that the lines he believes so well characterize the sense of love he shares with Blake are from an early draft of a poem intended for *Songs of Experience,* which was later inked through and discarded. Further, he has forgotten that all of the poems

concerning the theme of secret love included in that work—
poems which he once rapidly skimmed through but as quickly
dropped from his memory's store—were written from the opposite point of view. Consider "The Sick Rose," for example:

> O rose thou art sick!
> The invisible worm
> That flies in the night,
> In the howling storm,
>
> Has found out thy bed
> Of crimson joy,
> And his dark secret love
> Does thy life destroy.

Indeed, the very first poem in *Songs of Experience* (after
the "Introduction," that is)—its title is "Earth's Answer"—contains these lines:

> Does spring hide its joy
> When buds and blossoms grow?
> Does the sower
> Sow by night?
> Or the plowman in darkness plow?
>
> Break this heavy chain
> That does freeze my bones around.
> Selfish! vain!
> Eternal bane!
> That free Love with bondage bound.

In these poems which, in order to protect his (mis)under-
standing of "the central focus of Blake's poetry," he has conveniently forgotten, one finds the same cloying bombast that
Michael so abhors in Goethe's *Faust*. Clearly, then, Michael
totally fails to understand Blake, and so should not go about
quoting him as if he could count upon his authority.

More significantly, he should not attempt to act on the
basis of his insights into the nature of love (which is precisely
what he is currently planning to do) comforted by the illusion
that he is bolstered by the authority of the Blakean vision.

21

Michael knew well that Iris counted the ways of love, including among her reasons for loving him several that suggested virtues he didn't begin to possess. He found this fact most disconcerting, for though he is clearly disposed to inflate his intellectual attainments, it is simply not in Michael's nature to exaggerate his moral worth.

Once, when Iris was telling him of his kindness and sensitivity (more, he suspected, to reinforce than to celebrate these qualities), he decided it was time to correct the record.

"Let me tell you a story, Arca."

"How does it end?"

"Iris, dammit. Just listen."

Michael reached over and lowered the volume on the television. Iris wrinkled her forehead and thrust her head back, sighing. This was going to be tougher than he had thought.

"While doing alternative service as a conscientious objector in the early stages of the Viet Nam war, I worked as an orderly on a terminal cancer ward."

"You told me that."

"*Listen.* I found dying acceptable. It was the rotting that was so hard to take. The smells were unendurable. And it wasn't just because of the odor...." Michael attempted to recapture that odor, struggling unsuccessfully against the strains of the "A Minor" flooding his mind.

"You know, when you smell something, little particles of what you smell get in your nose and go down your throat. A sniff is the same as a bite. When you smell a rotting man you are actually eating his flesh. Not much. But enough to make you a cannibal, or worse—a ghoul. Anyway, the stench is not just stench. Its rotten food."

"That's gross and you're sick. I'm going to sleep."

"Then by all means allow me to talk in your sleep. There was this one fellow who had cancer of the larynx. I would have to clean his tracheostomy tube with pipe cleaners to keep the breathing apparatus clear."

"I don't want to hear this." She was about to get out of bed. Michael grabbed her.

"Listen to me. This is very important."

"I want to go to sleep." Michael ignored her.

"Once when I was doing this fellow's trach tube, he started coughing, and the whole metal disk came out along with phlegm and bloody tissue. Some of his flesh stuck to my shirt. The fear in his eyes stopped me from turning away. I didn't feel nauseated but I wanted to throw up. I *wanted* to. I wanted to hug him and throw up on him. To make him feel better. He was choking. Something—the collapsed larynx, I guess—was preventing him from breathing. I put my finger inside his throat to clear a path for him to breathe. I screamed for help. He was holding my hand with both his hands, using my finger as a Roto-rooter. I...we were digging flesh from his neck and the hole got bigger. Then...I...put *two* fingers in his neck...we...I.... Have you ever used a Ouija board?"

No answer. "When you and your partner both have your hands on the wooden disk it moves first to this letter then another, spelling out words. You know that you aren't moving the disk—and your partner swears that he isn't. It was...like that. I think it *was*. It couldn't have been me. I don't think it was him. The ouija spirit came and held our hands still— mine...and his grasping mine. It held our hands still. I tried to vomit. Nothing came. My mouth was dry—I couldn't even spit on him. He seemed so alone.

"He died...so fast. Someone finally came. I guess I was lucky. It was Dr. Ermias. I told you about him—my chess partner. He looked at the mess I...we...the ouija spirit had made. My hand—the one the spirit had held—was covered with bloody tissue and what looked like pus. The man...I didn't tell you his name—it was Mr. Grodjah...was doubled over with his head sort of jammed between the bedside stand and the bed. I looked at Ermias. His forehead had deep lines which got deeper, then vanished as he fixed me with a familiar gaze—the look he always managed when, about to checkmate me, he would take pity and move another piece. There were to be no attempts at resuscitation. Mr. Grodjah was allowed to experience his first moments of death undisturbed.

"There is something I can't explain. Whenever I think of that man I remember...the picture comes into my head...there I am calling him filthy names and throwing up all over him while he is dying. I know it didn't happen that way, but that's how I remember it. Isn't that strange? Before he dies he smiles at me and winks. Then it's over. I *remember* it that way. Even though that part didn't happen. The other funny thing is that, until recently, I had forgotten all about the ouija spirit. How could I have forgotten that?"

Michael turned to Iris. She was asleep. Or pretended to be. He touched her arm. She rolled over on her side, away from him. He didn't feel as well as he thought that he might.

22

Jorge Luis Borges said, "Life is anachronistic...(and, therefore) all men are born at the wrong time." Odd then, that, though we do everything we can to delay it, to throw it off schedule, death is always timely.

Cicero, reflecting upon the career of Socrates, had claimed that philosophy is nothing more than learning how to die. That is, the philosopher is one who learns to accept the timeliness of death. Philosophical discipline stands somewhere between the stoic or pitiful desperation of unbelief and the plasticine comforts of religion. Montaigne wrote a wonderful essay on this very theme.

When Hamlet, certainly one of the least attractive characters in literature, soliloquized to the effect that life is to be preferred to death because we cannot be sure that dreams in the afterlife will be less horrible than the pains of living, he merely parodied Socrates' last public address:

> Wherefore, O judges, be of good cheer about death, and know of a certainty, that no evil can happen to a good man in life or after death....

> The hour of departure has arrived, and we go our ways—I to die and you to live. Which is better God only knows.

Fear of evil dreams results from a bad conscience which is usually a consequence of not thinking things through. Socrates could leave questions open because he was a thinker, and for a thinker there can be no evil except the refusal to think. A world open to investigation is harmonious and ordered sufficiently to serve as a subject of inquiry. Whether death is a dark emptiness or a continuation of a journey, it is a good—just as are productive conversations and dreamless sleep deemed goods. The thoughtless person expects evil, because he lives the confusion he believes the world to constitute. Still, one may admire the agnostic with all his clinging to life more than those who too easily yield to spiritual comfort. At least the consequences of unbelief are often the struggle to maintain life whereas religion makes it all too attractive to give up the struggle in return for promised peace.

Fear and aggression keep people alive. Religious belief often urges a letting go of life. Still, those who struggle without the comforts of religious belief or the always unearned gifts of grace or miraculous intervention, usually become terrified and mean toward the end. They cling to life until one wants to say, "Don't you think you've had enough? Haven't you sufficiently embarrassed the medical profession, ridden your family with guilt, made enough of your friends question their spiritual sentiments? Won't you please just turn over and die?"

If the comforts of institutional religion allow one to yield oneself up unafraid, and if the lack of those comforts thrusts one into the undignified struggle to survive, then religion, powerless over death, merely offers an etiquette of dying. Thanks to religion, we do not as often have to hear fingernails scratching at the inner edges of the sill that separates death and life— the spheres of absolute and relative indifference.

23

Michael turned off the television, removed his trousers and shorts and got into bed wearing only his T-shirt. Iris was sleeping, naked, on her side. Michael touched her back with his fingers and moved close enough to smell her cinnamon skin. He straightened the sheet and blanket, making sure her shoulders were covered, then fell asleep with an arm around her, his hand lightly touching one of her breasts.

He wanted to dream. The thought of suffering the darkness of sleep on this particular evening undisturbed by internal images of sight and sound frightened him. Arquita needed the television as a proof that the waking world remained intact while she slept; Michael needed some reason to believe that there was something besides the public realm, a world rich enough to afford him privacy, a world where solitude did not require escape.

He didn't dream. But even though he did not in any strict sense *have* a dream, he manifested all the preconditions of dreaming. He experienced everything but the images and the associated subjective forms of feeling. His eyes moved at frequent, erratic intervals. There were alterations in temperature, pulse, and blood pressure. Slight changes in the respiratory rate could have been noticed. Brain wave monitoring would have shown distinctive patternings. There were transient muscle twitches and, now and again, what might have been sighs—once there was a loud snorting delivered (if it is correct to attribute something like intention to the unconscious Michael) in the manner of a scornful rebuke.

But there was no dream. The physical correlates we associate with dreams do not themselves constitute dreaming. They can exist, as was the case for Michael on this dreamless evening, without recollectable images. The sleeping Michael was not host to any images or to any focused emotions at any time during the night. He will not recall having dreamt, nor is there any reason to believe that hypnosis could make him recall having dreamt. He will, in fact, recall *not having dreamt*. And, because he had hoped to dream, had actually anticipated dreaming, he would be disappointed.

Some events *almost* take place, but never quite realize consummation. These truncated events are more than simply causes without effects, or uncaused effects. They possess a very real, though untapped, significance *as events* in spite of the absence of any efficacy.

Michael's "dream" was such a truncated event. But how can we be certain that Michael did not dream simply because he lacked the images? Perhaps the effects upon the body were the same as would have been so if the images had been present. But that can't be so. The specific effects of dreaming upon the body require the mediation of images; the body requires meaning as much as does the mind, if physical balance and harmony is to be realized. In simple perceptions there may be redness and roundness, but the associated image of a ball, sustained by its attendant concept, is required if the perception is to have any efficacy. There were no images. Michael, we must realize, *did not* dream.

The dream that never manifested itself, that never will be a factor in Michael's conscious or unconscious mind, the dream whose uncoordinated fragments will have only scattered and transitory effects upon his circulatory, respiratory, and nervous systems, is a truncated dream. It may be spoken of as a dream only in the sense that it may be constructed from its inefficacious, inconsequential conditions (this we shall immediately proceed to do) and may thereby serve to tell us something that Michael could never directly learn about himself—or rather, the self he would have been had he dreamt this dream. Thus, what the dream will tell us can only in the loosest sense be said to be "true" of Michael.

We seem to be left with a question: If Michael manifested only the potential for this dream, if it was but an unrealized capacity that he possessed on this almost dream-filled dreamless night, and if, finally, we are justified in calling this a dream only after proceeding through an act of construction, then who shall we say owns this dream?

24

Teeth. Grim, jaundiced, liver-yellow teeth...not simply stained. Stains are superficial; this yellow was pervasive. It touched every cell of every tooth from crown to root: the enamel, the dentine, the pulp—all yellow. But these were, in spite of their grotesqueness, *clean* teeth—immaculate, polished yellow teeth without chips or cavities (at least none visible). It was for this reason that their yellowness was so disturbing; it was for this reason that one dreaded the sardonic, lips-retracted, seconds-long smile of Dr. Ermias.

One could have reconstructed Ermias's face, his body, his very posture from those teeth—after, of course, having sketched the teeth themselves from their yellow hue. Incisors sharper than usual, the whole set of teeth longer and narrower than should have been so. As was true of Ermias himself: long, thin, slightly bent frame, convex, powdery textured face, like the yolk of a boiled egg but with lancet features that cut small openings in the air as he moved his head this way and that, long thin hands with fingers that punctured the spaces around him as he spoke in that acrid, acid-lemon voice. Parchment-old...ancient...ageless...timeless Ermias.

Thirty-four.

Dr. Ermias smiled often, always with that suggestion of defiance that accompanies proud deformities. To become friends with Ermias, it was essential that one accept his teeth and his defiant smile, to become, if not respectful, at least indifferent in the face of those teeth, and above all not to enter one's own teeth into competition with his. The trick, Michael had found, was always to smile second. To be the first to smile could be interpreted as a challenge to Ermias: "Hey, Doc, let's see those weird teeth," or it could mean: "Fortunately, I have clean, *white* teeth, so I can smile whenever I wish. Do *you*, however, dare to smile and expose those monstrous, mutant teeth of yours?"

And the Queen's Pawn. Chess was the only bond between them. Michael was not experienced but he had the sort of tactical mind that could often choose the better of a series of possible moves. His one-move-at-a-time manner of playing was thoughtful enough, and unorthodox enough, to provide some small challenge to Ermias's classical style of play. After some months of playing Ermias (never once beating him), Michael's game had improved sufficiently so that he could defeat any of his other friends. Neither Ermias nor

Michael could find a better opponent, so they spent their slack hours sitting at a table in the hospital corridor facing one another across a chess board.

The corridor became progressively dimmer as here and there lights in the patients' rooms were extinguished in preparation for sleep.

The chess pieces seemed strange. They were the usual size and in the familiar Staunton style, but they looked and, so Michael noted as he was setting his pieces on the board, *felt* strange. They were too shiny, too smooth. As he reached for the White Queen's Pawn to make his opening move (Ermias always let him begin), his attention was drawn to Ermias's pieces, and he understood. They were not black, but yellow—jaundiced, egg-yolk, parchment yellow.

25

Michael's hand had been poised for several seconds directly over his Queen's Pawn.

"Do you think, Michael, that taking your time at the very beginning will save you? No. It's what you do *after* the first move that gets you into trouble. But at least it appears you are beginning to doubt the value of your usual resort to the Lady's Pawn."

"One minute." Michael felt uncomfortable. Hadn't Ermias *noticed* yet? "Look, I always play white, why don't we change for once. It might even make for a more interesting game. I'm always forced into defense anyway."

"Next game, Michael. This one is already underway."

Michael's hand began its final descent toward the Queen's Pawn but it stopped less than an inch from the piece then made an unintended veer to his left, grasped the Queen's Knight and deposited it onto Queen's Bishop Three. He recovered from his own confusion almost immediately when he noted Ermias's puzzled expression. Michael leaned back in his chair and stretched before asking through an exaggerated yawn, "Surprised?"

Ermias gave Michael an indulgent nod, then muttered, "From an intelligent boy, stupidity is always a surprise."

Steinmetz, one of the other night-shift orderlies, had been standing nearby reading a large, rather old looking book. At this moment he rushed over to Ermias, shuffling from side to side, and handed him a folded piece of paper he had been using as a book mark. Steinmetz whispered in Ermias's ear as Ermias read the message, all the while Ermias's head nodding in assent. He waited for Steinmetz to leave before he spoke.

"Your question, Michael, is this: "What is the worst act of which a human being is capable?""

Michael was silent. He wasn't sure whether he should respond. He did not know it was a dream. (Indeed, he could not know it since, as we have said, this is not *Michael's* dream.)

Ermias's features softened, his voice became as gentle as was possible for him. "You must tell me, Michael. What is the greatest fault?"

Michael was becoming anxious. They often talked as they played, but there was something altogether too formal about the beginning of this conversation. "Well.... I'd say that it isn't murder or rape or incest. Maybe, lying. *Lying.* I think lying is the worst human act."

"You will tell me why this is so?"

Michael was warming to his inquisition. "Because a lie is the offer of a false foundation for someone to build upon. If appearances don't match what is real, then we build on sand. And a lie continues to be a part of our foundation. Then when we run into a crisis or problem, we respond using that defective ground as the basis of our judgments. We are off by an inch at the bow but by many feet at the target, as the Zen archer has it."

Michael was impressed by his sudden wisdom. He hadn't the slightest idea where the allusion to Zen archery had come from.

"Lying, is it? Ermias turned his head in the direction of Steinmetz, standing only a few yards away. Ermias's nod sent

Steinmetz scurrying away. "But, come now. The liar lies for control, for power. Surely, that's so. And usually this is done for survival, not for domination. The purist who claims that lying is truly evil wants the same thing, does he not—power and control over his own existence? It is naive to expect the weak to tell the truth?"

"Naive perhaps, but what is the alternative? Should we indulge weakness?"

"Surely, the alternative is to choose intimacy with persons of strength. If one is the victim of lies, isn't it his own fault? Most of us relate to the weak so we may be in control. Then we complain when we are betrayed..."

"More often the weak choose the strong."

"The same thing. One waits to be chosen so that he will not have the responsibility of commitment."

"Yes, but the weak are so much more interesting than the powerful, the aggressive, the competitive. The unalienated can afford to tell the truth because the truths they have to tell would never shock anyone, would never challenge anyone. Who could ever care for their truth?"

Ermias turned his head to one side, addressing the lamp that served to illumine the chessboard in the now darkened corridor. "Quite a Romantic, this boy. He longs for the harshness of truth...its *bite*. He thinks we are without comforting truths, I suppose."

"Truth itself is always a comfort. The content of a truth is quite irrelevant. Truthfulness is the point. It is the offer of reality, of what is real."

"Do you suppose we could tell the truth even if we wished to? Look at the difficulties. First, we more often than not haven't the slightest idea why we do what we do. So the only things we can be truthful about are the events themselves—not their meanings. And certainly the motives that occasion them are far beyond our grasp. Second, merely *saying* the truth is not enough, we have to *tell* it. We have to be believed. It is likely the case that we as often disbelieve the truthful as doubt the liar."

"If that's so its only because we have been made doubters by becoming too familiar with lies. Politicians and generals are liars by definition. They can only tell the truth if it serves their interests. And that is not telling the truth, only *saying* it."

"How do you suppose we got to this sad point, my boy?"

"There must have been an Original Lie."

"At last, a worthy idea. He can't play chess, this boy, but he can produce philosophic reflections. Michael: I would think that you are quite correct. There must, indeed, have been an Original Lie. Furthermore, it must have come before the Original Sin. Wouldn't you agree?"

"The first lie *was* the Original Sin!"

"No, No. Quite impossible. To sin one must have a choice. There is no escape from lying. No, the initial lie wasn't whispered by the serpent in the garden. It was sung by the earliest poets, those protophilosophic spirits who emerged from the silent womb that sent forth speech. The first sentence uttered by the first reasoning creature was a lie. It was this lie that made necessary the metaphors of the Garden and of the wilderness of the exiled couple. Before there could be sin, there had to be this lie."

"You know the lie?"

"I do."

"You will tell me?"

"No patience. No sense of the artfully constructed account. No..."

"The first lie. The Original Lie..."

"Be quiet, Michael. It will be said. I cannot believe, as apparently you still do, that intriguing questions have equally intriguing answers. Being well over thirty, I know that all questions worth asking have no answers; they must, therefore, be their own reward. The question you have asked, however, definitely has an answer. So much the worse for the question."

Michael started to reply but was distracted by the sound of humming drifting down from somewhere just above him. It was Steinmetz, floating like a rumpled white balloon, his head occasionally bumping silently against the ceiling. He was humming what Michael reckoned was a theme from Mahler. Probably the *First Symphony*, he thought.

26

"Questions with answers are less valuable than questions without answers?"

"Of course."

"Then, if a question is left unanswered, even if it has an answer, does that make it more valuable?"

"Clever, Michael. But, no. I think not. It is, however, sadly true that we are sometimes reduced to hiding from answers just to keep our interest alive. But that is, I'm afraid, cheating." (Michael could certainly benefit from this lesson were he privy to the counsels of this undreamed dream.)

"OK. Then I will allow you to tell me about the Original Lie."

"Thank you. I will be brief. The Original Lie was expressed in the very first utterance. Language used to *refer* to a world of arbitrarily existing experiences and objects presupposes the Lie. Names are lies. And it is with naming that all of our problems began. The belief that truth and falsity may be distinguished is a consequence of the act of naming.

"Adam was set lose in the Garden with the power to give names. But God already had sinned. It is He who had called the pair by the names Eve and Adam. Mimicking our first ancestors, we carve out the world into this and that set of objects and events by the expedient of naming. We love to give names. Names are the lies we most like to tell.

"The perniciousness of naming became apparent only with the birth of the philosophic spirit. Philosophers began to develop theories about the relationship between appearance and reality. The question was asked, 'How do we come to know?.' The science of epistemology was born from our failure to understand that the basis of all presumedly certain knowledge is the arbitrary act of assigning names and then treating the names as if they have some necessary relationship to the world.

"Friedrich Nietzsche embodied a final exasperation with the philosophic enterprise. He simply drew the conclusion required by the chaotic relativism of the philosophic tradition. The truth concerning a thing, said Nietzsche, would be realized once every creature had asked the question, 'What is that?' and had received an answer. Once one added all the answers, that thing would be defined. This or that answer is not true, cannot be true. The truth of a thing is the gathering of all responses with respect to it. No particular perspective can give us truth. *Everything*, in the sense of the sum of all perspectives, is true."

"If everything is true, then nothing is false."

"Listen to what I have said, Michael. 'Everything,' as a sum of all perspectives, is true. *Each* thing, in the sense of each particular perspective conceived singly, is false."

"But that can't be so. If truth is the sum total of perspectives on a given object, then truth would involve contradiction, since we certainly may make contradictory claims about any given object."

"You seem to be grasping the very center of our dilemma. The perniciousness of the Original Lie is to be found in the fact that "truth," characterized by consistency, by noncontradiction, is an anthropomorphic invention. What is thought to be true about the world is that which helps human beings accommodate themselves best to their planetary environs. Of course, the desire to survive is a perfectly acceptable motivation for any given action. But it is perhaps somewhat ignoble to glorify this by allying such a desire with the dispassionate search for objective truth in the manner that the philosophers and poets have done.

"The only truth worth celebrating is that masked by the Original Lie. Such truth is nameless...can never receive a name. What could we call it, then, but Chaos?"

27

"It seems the poets might be excused from your critique. They do not seek truth in names. They are the creators of metaphor and imagery."

"So the poets would have us believe. Unfortunately, poets have been seduced by the same lie as the philosophers. They believe metaphors to be but masks of the literal—a pleasant coating on the pill of so-called objective truth."

Steinmetz had floated down and was hovering only a few inches above Ermias and Michael. It *is* the *First Symphony*, Michael thought.

"Poets, no less than philosophers, are ideologues. Both reinforce belief in the literal, the referential."

"But you seem to be acting on behalf of the philosopher in your attempt to uncover the Original Lie? Couldn't a poet attempt the same exposé?"

"Well said, Michael. Quite true. The exposure of the Original Lie would be both the last philosophical act and the final poetic expression. After, there would be no need for either poetry or philosophy."

"We would be reduced to silence, I suppose. Since the use of language involves us in lying."

"Language is not the problem in itself. It is our misunderstanding of its function that betrays us. Lao-tzu's book, the *Tao Te Ching*, tells us, 'The way that can be spoken of is not the true Way.' A Confucian critic is said to have chided his Taoist colleague with the query, 'If it is true that the way that can be spoken of is not the true Way, how is it that Master Lao wrote five thousand characters concerning the Way?' To which the Taoist replied, 'I make for you a beautiful embroidery of drakes and pass it along to you for your admiration. I cannot, however, show you the golden needle by which it was made.' We may certainly employ language—as long as we recognize that it's source is not to be identified."

"Don't we attempt to refer to the source of language when we seek truth?"

"No, No. If we look for the golden needle, we will always be both inspired and frustrated. Looking for the source of language is like traveling down a road toward your own hometown—you are returning after many years. You come round a curve in the road and encounter a huge sign that announces that your town is only 33 miles away. Ah, but there is a problem! The sign blocks the road and it is impossible to go around it. Language is at one and the same time a signpost and a barrier.

"Language is mostly sound; sound is mostly breath. Breath sounds are vibrations, periodicities, cycles of energy that extend outward, in principle without limit. Songs and chants are true language. Real communication involves establishing resonances. God said, 'Let it be.' That command breathed life into the Void. It established the resonances that language is meant to serve."

"That makes sense. In intimate language the quality of the sound and the subjective feelings evoked by the sounds are most important. 'I love you' is the greatest of clichés, yet these can be the nicest words to hear."

"'I love you' is hardly a cliché. It is, rather, what the Hindus and Buddhists would call a *mantra*. It is a chant used for purposes of invocation and union—that is, for the purposes of calling forth love and establishing resonances with one's lover."

"As long as I am singing or chanting, then I'm OK? But the moment I start talking about this or that, I involve myself in lying. Is that what I am to believe?"

"Between intimates lying is difficult. Between friends and lovers, speaking is always an act of celebration in which the topic of the conversation is secondary to the formless ecstasy of participation."

28

It was the buzzer for Room 412—Mr. Grodjah. Steinmetz was nowhere to be seen. Glancing at the board as he rose, Michael noted that his Queen's Knight was the only piece that had been moved. "I'll be right back," he said.

As soon as he entered the room, he saw the blank space on the wall over Mr. Grodjah's bed. The crucifix had been taken down. Next he saw Steinmetz shriveling in the corner nearest the foot of the bed. He was luminescent pale, face and arms. Drool had soaked his shirt and was still flowing from the sides of his open mouth. Michael noted with a detached curiosity that Steinmetz seemed not to have a single tooth in his head!

Michael turned toward the figure of Mr. Grodjah who was holding the crucifix in his left hand, his arm extended in the direction of Steinmetz. He thought Grodjah looked more like a reclining conquistador claiming territory in the New World in the name of the Holy Roman Church and on behalf of Ferdinand and Isabella than a cancerous, old, dying man defending himself against the assault of a toothless vampire.

Mr. Grodjah raised his right forefinger to his mouth, urging Michael to be silent, then beckoned him with the crucifix. Michael approached without the least anxiety. Steinmetz's face contorted and he uttered a rather listless snarl. Michael could not suppress a contemptuous scoff. He had never thought of Steinmetz as anything but a harmless middle-aged vagrant, and though it would never have occurred to him that he was a vampire, the discovery certainly hadn't shocked him. Besides, Michael thought, what harm could a defanged vampire do?

As Michael approached, Mr. Grodjah pulled the sheet down to the middle of his chest, exposing a gaping, putrescent hole in his neck. Michael couldn't tell whether the wound was due simply to the work of the cancer or if Steinmetz had been gumming at it. Grodjah pointed to his neck. Michael saw something white—a tightly rolled piece of paper—protruding from one edge of the hole.

A sad, angry moan, occasionally modulating into a kind of chant, was coming from Steinmetz, though his lips did not move. As Michael reached for the paper the chant became louder, culminating in a shriek just as Michael removed it from the rotting crater in Grodja's neck. Michael had finally begun to be affected by this scene. He had suddenly remembered (realized?) that vampires weren't real and that this should not be happening.

Steinmetz smiled as he walked toward the bed. His color had returned (but not his teeth). He took the crucifix from Mr. Grodjah, climbed up on the bed and hung it in its place. Then he reached under the sheets and gently removed the bedpan on which Grodjah had been reclining, covered it with a towel and walked out the door. As Michael was leaving the room, he glanced back. Mr. Grodjah's finger was again touching his lips.

29

Michael was reluctant to unroll the paper. It was, he was thinking as he returned to the table at which Ermias was sitting, simply not the appropriate time...

As a matter of fact, the message was never read. Michael's *in potentia* dream ends here. This creates an interesting problem. We are describing the construction of dream images from inefficacious, and inconsequential, physical correlates. But there are no correlates permitting the construction of Michael's act of reading the message. In what sense may it be said that the message existed?

In the waking world, our consensual world, a tightly rolled piece of paper tucked in one's shirt pocket would either contain or not contain a message. But in a dream it is not clear in what sense a message could be said to exist except in and through the act of reading.

A dream is once removed from reality. A truncated dream is twice removed since, apart from the sort of construction in which we are presently engaged, no dream could be said to exist. The precise nature of the message on that unexamined piece of paper in Michael's truncated dream is three times removed—if, indeed, it could be said to have any relationship to reality at all.

30

The rules of dreaming seem to be quite different than the rules of waking life. Were one to say, "I saw the President of the United States eating a hamburger at McDonald's yesterday," one might reply, "You probably were mistaken," or at the very least, "Are you quite certain it was the President?" But if one said, "I dreamed I saw the President of the United States eating a hamburger at McDonald's," no one would object. Dreams are self-validating.

One could, for example, dream that Cleopatra was hiding in one's closet—without the slightest evidence of there being anyone at all in the closet, much less Cleopatra. Dream-claims do not require evidence.

"I dreamed of Cleopatra."

"How do you know it was Cleopatra?"

"In the dream I just knew!"

"Was it really Cleopatra?"

"Don't be silly, it was a dream. But *in the dream* it *was* Cleopatra."

"What did she look like?"

"I never saw her, she was hiding in my closet."

"You never saw her? Did she speak? Did she announce herself as Cleopatra?"

"She didn't speak. She didn't make a sound. All I remember is that I was sitting in my bedroom and Cleopatra was in my closet, hiding."

The proof that Cleopatra is hiding in one's closet is simply that this is what the dream *was*: a Cleopatra-hiding-in-my-closet dream.

31

Now to return to our dilemma. Michael's dream manqué contained the belief that he had received a message from Mr. Grodjah. So, he did in fact (in dream-fact) receive a message. But it was unread. Have we any means of finding out what the message said?

Yes, with a high degree of probability. Having complete access to Michael's every psychic, every neural nuance, it is a small matter for us to deduce the contents of a message Michael would have dreamed had he, under these specific conditions, truly dreamed. It is our judgment that the unread message in Michael's undreamed dream must have contained these words:

OM AH HUM

Actually, these are not words at all. They are "syllables" (*bija*, in Sanskrit). We would call these morphemes or quasi-morphemes. Michael (not the dream-Michael, the sleeping Michael) is equipped by his eleven-week retreat into Buddhist meditation to recognize the message as the *mulamantra* ("root-mantra") of the Tantric Buddhists. This mantra is associated with the mysteries of body, speech, and mind (*om, ah, hum*) and correlated with the "power centers" of the brain, throat, and heart, respectively.

OM AH HUM is a mantra of identification that unifies the aspirant with the essential vibratory character of physical bodies, oral expression, and thinking itself. The root-mantra is used as an invocation when the name of a buddha or *prajña* (the female aspect of the buddha principle, a *dakini*) is substituted for AH.

We do apologize for this somewhat involuted excursus, but the importance of this dream manqué, including the unread message, will become clear not many pages from these. We can say only this much now: it is of great significance for Michael (and equally so for us) that the message, the *mulamantra*, dwelt (and dwells) in a realm of existence as far removed as is conceivable from the realm he is accustomed to consider reality.

32

Michael awoke from his dreamless sleep surprised to find that Iris was already out of bed. The bathroom door was closed. He rapped on it and said, "Good morning, Lady Rainbow."

Iris was silent for some seconds before she spoke. "Go away, Michael. You gave me bad dreams."

"I'm sorry, Arca. Open up."

"Too late for 'sorries,' Michael. I'm mad."

"What say we establish a temporary truce—just long enough for me to pee?"

"You'll have to find another place to pee, you bastard. This is my bathroom and I just may never come out."

Listening to her muffled words through the door, tears came to his eyes. How he loved her loneliness!

"Come on, Arquita, the bathroom is no place to hide. No one can hide in a bathroom. Listen..." Iris turned the water on to drown out Michael's voice, which didn't help his struggle for continence.

He raised his voice to as loud a volume as he dared. "You can't hide in your bathroom because, in the first place, it has no windows. Without windows it is impossible to hide. Hiding requires that one be able to peek out, to watch for intruders. Don't you think? You don't even have a keyhole. So, give it up!"

Iris started humming. She was, indeed (as she had so often insisted), tone deaf.

"Listen to me, Arca." Michael was shouting now. "You are forgetting one of the fundamental truths concerning human beings: We are what we eat. The corollary, of course, is that we *were* what we excrete. The very bathroom you are currently occupying opens out to an underworld sea of communal refuse. We are continually sending ourselves forth into that sea. So, you must realize that a bathroom is the least private place of all. It is, you see, a communications center."

Michael began his peroration. "We humans are always in process. Being is the memory of becoming, its detritus. Being, Arquita dearest, is shit. And you now seek private sanctuary in the Temple of Being, the tabernacle of our common humanity?

A futile gesture. Nevertheless, I shall respect your wish."

He put on his pants and prepared to go in search of the nearest place to pee. As he silently closed Iris's front door, he thought he could recognize the melody of "The Eyes of Texas" announcing itself from amid the atonal chaos of Arquita's humming. Michael smiled. He wished he could stay and listen.

33

Only minutes after returning to his apartment, Michael received a phone call from his sister. Their father had died. He left immediately for his father's home. From there he traveled to Gransfield, Louisiana, for the burial. He tried several times to call Iris, but there was never an answer. He tried to call her from Louisiana—without success. She finally contacted him on the day of his return...

But that part of the story need not, cannot, be told...

V

Consuming the Past

1

Descending the steps from the plane, Michael breathed in the muggy summer air and watched heat waves rising from the airport apron. As he stood looking for directions to the lounge entrance, he could sense the heat coming up through the bottoms of his shoes. The paranoic tremor he had immediately dismissed as excessive was instantly transformed into a panicky acquiescence. It would be futile to run back inside the plane—his past had already invaded his lungs and entered the bloodstream, was even now coursing toward his brain; it had seeped through the soles of his feet and was rapidly numbing the leg muscles. As he walked toward the airport lounge he could not help wondering if a truly discerning eye might detect in his gait the staggered rhythms of a zombie.

2

Michael rented a car and proceeded directly to the funeral home. His father's body had arrived that morning. As he drove through the middle of the town he was surprised to note that the buildings he had assumed must surely have been razed, or collapsed of their own accord, were still intact, listing in the same manner as when he had seen them last, in the same need of paint and plaster and tile. One might look in vain for a poorer town, one with more shacks and shanties, less white trash, fewer idle blacks.

He was vaguely irritated when he realized how easily he could recall the way to Wiley's Funeral Parlour. When he discovered that his struggle against remembrance was to be futile, his irritation grew, though it was somewhat mollified by the seductive innocence that attaches to all but the most painful reminiscences of childhood.

Michael cannot explain his abhorrence of his childhood environs, nor his reluctance, even under these special circumstances, to return. He has simply come to accept these as givens. And there will be very little in what happens in the next few hours that could serve as an adequate explanation. All he knows at this point is that, had he a choice, he would not have made this trip.

There had been no choice. On the evening of the day Michael had received his Bachelor of Divinity degree, his father read aloud the words *summa cum laude* on his diploma and announced, "I've decided to let you preach my funeral." At that time, Michael thought to himself that Congregationalist ministers were expected to *conduct* funeral services, not to *preach* them, but that he would be willing to make an exception in his father's case.

"That's a promise, old man." Michael had said it casually, with no insight into just how difficult that promise would be to keep. Nothing more was ever said. But nearly twenty-five years later when, at the age of eighty-nine years, seven months and a day, his father died, that promise was still firmly in effect.

He conducted the service (he had actually "preached" a little), in the Texas city where his father had lived his last twenty years, then proceeded to Gransfield, Louisiana, his father's first home, to see the body safely in the ground. His sister had been forced to stay behind because of the illness of one of her children.

His first visit to Louisiana in over twenty years will be brief. His return flight departs in less than nine hours. He already knows that this will be too much time. It had been silly of him to believe that he could be protected from the contaminating effects of involuntary memories.

3

The car moved past the ravine that cut through the southeast corner of the city limits. As a child, while visiting relatives in this small town forty miles from his home, Michael and his cousins had often spent much of the day at the bottom of the ravine building hideouts and swinging from the vines that cluttered the denser parts of the empty river bed.

4

Barely out of his car he saw a large dark suit moving toward him with a gracefulness that belied the formless hunk of ruddy flesh stuffed inside it. "Mr. Evers?"

"Yes."

One huge hand reached forward to grasp Michael's, the other rested on his shoulder. "Our sympathies, Mr. Evers. Why don't you come on in and talk with Brother Shakian. He's supposed to help with the service, I understand. He tells me he remembers your daddy."

Shakian? Michael immediately recognized that name. Assyrian. A Baptist preacher. An unlikely person to have been accepted into the tight white circle of Gransfield, Louisiana. But he had been. He became the preacher of the First Baptist Church perhaps fifty or sixty years ago. His role as moral measure of the community had included one rather novel dimension: He had served more than once as the excuse for the white citizens of Gransfield to exercise a decency that common custom and tradition would otherwise have prevented.

For example, if a Mexican visited Gransfield (as once happened while Michael was in town), he could be accepted because he was simply thought to be Assyrian, "a relative of Brother Shakian, maybe." If a *hiyellah*, on her way to visit family in Atlanta, stopped for a meal, she could be served with a minimum of consternation since "she sorta looks Syrian, don't ya think?"

Civil Rights had likely changed all that—at least on the surface (where it counts). Michael wondered if Brother Shakian had suffered any loss of prestige since the townsfolk no longer had any need to rationalize supererogatory virtue.

Shakian looked eighty-five, at least. He was shiny bald, his loosened tie curving out from his vest, gold chain, with a Masonic pin attached, dangling between his left vest pocket and the pocket of his trousers. He and Michael talked for a while about the division of labor at the graveside. The committal service would be brief. Michael would read from the Scriptures, Brother Shakian would offer a prayer. The casket would be lowered.

"Goin' t' be quite a reunion today, Brother Evers. The blessed part of a funeral is that it brings families together."

Michael smiled and got up to leave. He was thinking how happy he would be if he could simply avoid his relatives altogether. They were farmers and preachers, and their wives and offspring. He wouldn't be responsible for the twenty and under, of course. And it would, on the whole, be flattering to those who had reached maturity in his absence were he to fail (as he surely would) to recognize them. It was the remainder that concerned him: those he could be expected to know. He wasn't eager to spend the afternoon trying to attach the correct names to faces reddened, puffed, and wrinkled by twenty plus tractor-sitting, gospel-waving, butter-churning years.

5

After the first mile and a half, the cemetery road was unpaved. Michael was driving slowly and the red dust of the road enveloped his car, finding its way inside in spite of the tightly closed windows. He ran his tongue along his teeth to rid his mouth of grit. The taste was a familiar one. Everything was too familiar.

The cemetery was small by contemporary standards. Members of the Evers family had been buried there for the past hundred years and more, so there would be many more dead than living at today's service. The large monument just inside the entrance of the grounds was that of Gadsdon Evers, a casualty of World War I. The remainder of the Evers's graves, and those of the other inhabitants as well, were considerably more modest.

This cemetery was far less gaudy than those serving the wealthy urban dead, which so often have the appearance of uncoordinated floral gardens choked by marble weeds.

Every time he entered a cemetery, he felt himself a part of a conspiracy against the helpless dead. It was not the cemeteries themselves that offended him as much as the trite character of the feelings they evoked in him. This is but to say that Michael saw what any clear-sighted person visiting a cemetery must: shiny stone and comforting rhetoric on the outside, rotting flesh and crumbling bones within. And what could be more clichéd than this vision?

The living contrive to hide from their own fears by perpetrating the grossest of insults upon the dead, knowing all the while that—soon or late—they too must suffer those same insults. And to complain about this is to yield oneself up to an overdrawn rhetoric no more deserving of attention than that of the burial artists themselves.

Death need be no great problem, of course. We might believe, with Socrates, that "no evil can befall a good man, either in this life or in the next." But of course, lesser instincts, subject as they are to much greater refinement, teach us that some evil is essential if we are to live at all well.

Our accounts of the glorious afterlife benefit those who don't find it necessary to go too far down the wrong path. Hell is for those who overdo the evil we all must serve if we are to be candidates for the only immortality that really counts: that which remembrance guarantees.

Were it not for the desire for fame, which Milton (himself a chronic sufferer) called "the last infirmity of noble mind," our funerals might be more honest. But since the hapless, defunct body is a monument to its deeds, we can't very well let it decay before it is safely hid beneath a less corrigible stimulus for celebration and remembrance. Embalming fluids, lacquer, wax and cotton wadding, cosmetic skills, all serve to keep the original monument intact until it can be hidden and its replacement installed.

All this is embarrassing for the members of that measureless fellowship who have no share in fame. Religion answers the problem as best it can by arguing for a Democracy of the Dead. But no one really believes in such equity.

The ideal funeral would consist in the burial of the unembalmed, cosmetically untreated, nude corpse in a shallow grave. His or her name could be scratched with a stick in the soil on top of the grave. The first rain that fell, the first strong wind that blew, would take the name away. The name should decay before the flesh that served as its terminus. Any memories that persisted would then be freed from the artificial stimulation of sites and monuments.

The Democracy of the Dead.

6

Michael had once thought cremation an answer to the tawdry resonances of funereal rites. But cremation represents only a slightly more fastidious attempt to avoid inevitable insult.

Traditionalists delude themselves into believing that the embalming process, and a hermetically sealed casket, will defend them against maggots and microbes. Others wish to escape both the injury of the scavengers and the insult of the embalmer's hand by being transformed to ashes. There is actually no difference between the two. Each attempts to win what is oxymoronically called "a dignified death." For if there is any quality or virtue that could be singled out as altogether inappropriate for human beings, particularly the defunct, it is dignity.

The permanent denial of dignity in life makes any idea of dignity in death absurdly anticlimactic. Moreover, though death is doubtless our greatest fear, it is hardly the severest threat to our dignity. That honor is, of course, reserved for shit.

> No wonder I have lost my wits:
> Celia, Celia.... Oh, Celia Shits.

Jonathan Swift's epitaph for dignity.

Crouched on a pot, straining to extrude chunky turds of body-processed viands—vichyssoise or a light quiche, no doubt—Celia strains as well to maintain her poise, her grace, hoping to lose none of her innocent allure. Could she but prove Swift's desperation false and inspire recantation:

> My wits have now flown back to me
> For Celia shits...
> With dignity

Not likely. No one shits with dignity. Our only choices are:

1. Ignore our need to shit.
2. Celebrate that defect in some scatological manner.
3. Despair.

Michael recalled those infamous letters of James Joyce containing encomiums to the "brown spot" on Nora's panties. Imagine (we don't have to imagine, we can read the letters if we wish) the thrill that Nora felt when she learned that not only was her sweetheart aware that she shat, but that he actually admired the plainest evidences of it. By sad contrast, the unfortunate Celia had no choice but to keep up the pretense— to hope, intensely and in vain, that her secret (the only secret lovers hesitate to share) would remain undiscovered.

Oh, Celia...

7

The intellectual world is becoming more and more conscious of the subject of shit. One can hardly read a contemporary novel of ideas (that is, of course, the genre represented by this work) which does not treat the subject exhaustively. One should not, therefore, judge Michael harshly for the indelicate theme of this metaphysical aside.

Michael would stipulate the obvious fact that we try to hide from shit in much the same manner as we hide from death. And he would doubtless accede to the further, truly ironic conclusion that it is easier to mask death than to mask shit. Shit, after all, is an unmixed evil and there are no grand myths to teach us otherwise. Death, so we are grandly told, is not necessarily evil. And though we can hide the *fact* of shit better than the fact of death, it is altogether different with respect to the *consequences* of each.

The correlation of shitting and dying is more fundamental than we might wish to believe. Death is the end result of Nature's digestive processes. Dead things are turds, extruded by the natural world. "All flesh is grass…"

Dead flesh is shit.

A cemetery is a field of toilets tunneling toward repositories of Nature's Own Shit. We waste all that granite and marble. Gravestones ought be made of porcelain.

> No wonder we all lose our wits:
> Nature, Nature…

It is really not so very difficult to appreciate Michael's motives for having begun to think of shit in a cemetery. And it is certainly worth noting that the same rationale lies behind the thoughts of shit that assail many unfortunates upon entering a library.

8

Michael is standing next to the grave of an older sister: Dorothy Kay Evers, "Born December 16, 1931, Died December 27, 1931." "Eleven days," he said aloud. "My older sister died at the age of eleven days." He is still thinking about the Metaphysics of Shit (a topic now sardonically, but respectfully, capitalized in his mind).

He had once read an interesting anthropological work attempting to provide a comprehensive definition of the concept of "culture." Any fool—foolish anthropologists excepted—should know enough to approach this subject with the same caution we would expect an extraterrestrial to employ if attempting a characterization of human nature by researching the Yellow Pages of a telephone book. Too many cultures, too many variables. No constants.

Well, almost none. Shit is certainly a candidate. Not the natural phenomenon, of course. That is a given and of no consequence. It is the *meaning*, the *function*, of shit that is surprisingly uniform from one culture to another. In particular, there is some evidence that excretory functions are raised to the level of collective consciousness in times of cultural decadence. For example (and this is directly from that distinguished anthropological work), the discovery of the value of urine in tanning and in the tempering of metals was made, on at least two separate occasions, by societies near the end of their civilized tenure.

No wonder that James Joyce, one of the narrators of the decline of the West, was fascinated with Nora's brown-stained panties. No wonder old men become obsessed with their bowels, begin to retain their urine, suffer constipation. They are at the end of their tenure on this planet. They no longer need to excrete. They are themselves being excreted. For this were we born, and for this came we into the world...

9

Michael heard car doors closing and looked toward the sound. "Here we go, Dorothy Kay. How about we just trade places for a little while?"

He walked toward his father's gravesite. He had not noticed the arrival of the casket, positioned now next to the canopied open grave. At first he didn't recognize anyone, then he saw a woman of about eighty walking between two much younger men, each holding one arm to steady her. The men turned out to be his distant cousins. They were dizygotic twins with almost no discernible resemblance one to the other. The woman was the family favorite, Aunt (Michael's aunt) Hettie Mae.

There was nothing to be done. He had to speak to her, give her a big hug, tell her how well she looked, kiss her at least twice, ask after her children, and then stand humiliated while she told the Story—every detail of which Michael could (though he never would) recite from painful memory.

We trust none of you is pathologically curious because we intend to draw the curtains while Michael is suffering his ritual encounter with Aunt Hettie Mae. The event is, we assure you, trivial enough. And its omission can save Michael from fortuitous, public humiliation.

"...and later that afternoon I caught Mikey trying to bury his Easter suit in the backyard."

Hettie Mae was the only one who laughed. Though much too loud for a cemetery, her laughter was far from sadistic. She probably didn't know how much suffering the Story caused.

Michael knew why the strange relatives standing by her side hadn't enjoyed the Story. They feared Hettie Mae's telling of it might indicate affection for one, a potential rival, who had invaded their territory from out of what should have been the settled past.

Hettie Mae was one short step away from poverty, so it was not from pecuniary ambitions that these relatives vied with one another. The fawning behavior of these relative-strangers had little to do with desire for a place in the will.

They merely wanted to be favorites of the favorite. These relative-suitors didn't realize that Michael was more than willing to yield any claim he might have upon the favor of Hettie Mae.

10

We have already noted the connection in Michael's experience between embarrassment and reflection. Thus, even before his aunt had finished the Story, Michael was well into a defensive reverie: He was reflecting upon the linguistic accident that led to the confusion between the Latin *obsequiœ* and *exsequiœ*. The first carries the meaning, "submission," the second, "funeral rite."

The word *obsequies,* not (as should have been the case) "exsequies," has come to mean "funeral rites." This odd fact is solely due to the sloppiness of some Latin lexicographer. Of course (now simple pedantry ceases and speculation begins), accidents of the language often are most fortunate. The pun tells us a great deal. What, after all, is more obsequious than an obsequy? What better example of submission than death? What better evidence of death than absolute obsequiousness?

"You sit next to your Aunt Hettie Mae, hon, and you can tell me how pretty I look in my new dress. Let's hope your daddy likes it, too. It took me all yesterday afternoon to find something to wear. Your daddy always was a lot of trouble."

11

Aunt Hettie Mae tugged lightly on his coat as Michael rose from his chair. He turned and bent down to receive what he knew would be last minute instructions. "You stand up straight, hon. And don't mumble. Me and your daddy will be listening."

He stepped to the front of the canopy and looked at the farmers and preachers assembled there. He was surprised by the tender, grateful feeling that arose in him. That feeling was born of the realization that the entire contents of his father's memory were deposited in the minds of those seated before him. As he opened his Bible, he felt a twinge of remorse for having selected this particular reading:

I have seen everything that is done under the sun; and behold, all is vanity and a striving after wind.

God has made everything beautiful in its time; also he has put eternity in man's mind, yet so that he cannot tell what God has done from the beginning to the end.

The fate of the sons of men and the fate of beasts are the same; as one dies so does the other. They all have the same breath, and man has no advantage over the beasts; for all is vanity. All go to one place. All are from the dust, and all return to dust again.

In the morning sow your seed and at evening withhold not your hand; for you do not know which will prosper, this or that, or whether both alike will be good.

For if a man lives many years, let him rejoice in them all; but let him remember that the days of darkness will be many. All that comes is vanity.

Michael closed the book and turned his back upon the celebrants, carefully avoiding their faces.

12

As he took his seat, Hettie Mae leaned toward Michael and whispered her judgment (whether based principally on form or content he didn't know): "About a B minus, hon."

Brother Shakian had been standing just behind Michael. He now stepped to the front, raised his right hand forward and above his head, and closed his eyes. Michael noticed that his eyes were so tightly shut that his face was distorted, his lips stretched around his teeth in what at any other time would have been seen as a broad grin.

> We have come, Oh Lord, to bury our departed brother.

> Father, when a man of almost ninety dies a peaceful death in the bosom of his family, we don't have to ask about the meaning of that death. Instead we ask, and it is right that we do, about the meaning of his life. Yes, of life itself.

> When the preacher called Ecclesiastes told about the meaning of life, he said, "Vanity of vanities, all is vanity and a striving after wind."

> It didn't seem to him like the righteous were making any headway against the unrighteous.

> It didn't seem to him that the godly were any better off than the ungodly.

> It didn't seem to him, Father, like You treated Your children any different than You treated the animals.

> All the preacher saw was that in the end death caught up with every living thing.

> We look out at the work of Your hands and we see, with the preacher, that everything is beautiful in its time. But then we forget and want it always to be *our* time. We remember how when Brother Job, like the preacher, complained about all his sufferings, You spoke to him from out of the whirlwind, Lord, and said: "Job, where were you when I laid the foundations of the universe?"

Michael couldn't help smiling at Brother Shakian's rebuttal. Good for him! Let the old guy defend the faith.

Against the darkness, the stillness, the emptiness, of the world before creation, this single life whose end we celebrate today stands forth as a miracle.

And all of us would give thanks to You for this one life, lived almost to ninety years, even if it was the only life there ever was or ever would be.

But the gift of life is ours as well, Father. The life of the flesh, of these bodies.... Miracle added to miracle.

And You have promised eternal life to the faithful—everlasting beatitude purchased for us by the blood of our Savior, Jesus Christ.

Ah, blood at last! But almost in passing. Michael had been waiting for the bloody parts. All Baptists loved to talk about blood—and to sing about it.

As a child-Baptist Michael's favorite hymn had begun:

There is a fountain filled with blood
drawn from Emmanuel's veins
And sinners plunged beneath that flood
lose all their guilty stains.

The image these lines had conjured in him as a child returned now in all its crudely quaint detail. Michael had to tighten his jaw to keep from laughing out loud. He tried to empty his mind; instead, he was assaulted by another hymn:

Are you washed in the blood, in the soul-cleansing blood of the lamb?
Are your garments spotless, are they white as snow?
Are you washed in the blood of the lamb?

But Shakian would not satisfy Michael's lust for blood. There would be no fountains full, hardly enough to wash a single garment. The prayer was winding down. Brother Shakian had shifted into the unmistakable cadence of an evangelical preacher. That he could accomplish this shift and still manage, unlike the majority of downhome preachers, to keep all the syllables in his words was an impressive accomplishment.

> Grateful for the promise of eternal life—yes, we are that, Lord. But we have a duty to give thanks for life itself—life that comes with no promises.

> Heavenly Father, we weren't around when You laid the foundations of the universe, so You couldn't ask our advice.

> If You want to take our lives away, or let us suffer all manner of pain, we won't be spoiled children and complain.

> For we have witnessed a miracle.... Miracle added to miracle.

> Heaven is a gift, Father. We know that. Salvation is by Your grace and by our faith in Your son, Jesus. Yes, Lord! We know.

> We have no claim on paradise, Father. We are not Your only creations. Gransfield is not the earth, the stars, the sea...

Michael wondered if Shakian was stanching the flow of blood to impress the returning liberal fallen-away theologian. And he wondered if this prayer was an exercise in apologetics, a demonstration that an Assyrian Southern Baptist with a degree from an obscure Bible college could be as articulate as anyone. Mostly, Michael wondered how Shakian was able to pray and grin at the same time.

Shortly, all wondering ceased. Michael's shoes had begun to pinch him. And he began to feel the heat from the grass burning the bottoms of his feet...

13

...feel the scalding tar on his bare feet.

It was the first day of "seasoning." No one wore shoes in the summer, so feet had to be prepared for the blistering streets and sidewalks. This was accomplished by walking on the hot oil and dirt roads, hopping to the grassy edge when the pain was too much to stand. Two or three days of this and the skin was thickened, the tarry dirt was ground into your feet. You were ready for summer.

Walking to Creech's Grocery Store to trade in pop bottles so he could make the picture show, he was rehearsing the lineaments of the new economic situation: Fares at the movie house had increased from nine cents to fourteen cents. Refunds were two cents a bottle. Twenty-four cents, or two cartons of bottles, had been enough for a ticket, popcorn, and a cold drink. Now he needed twenty-nine cents, which required fifteen bottles. Too many bottles to carry comfortably (it was almost exactly a mile to the store)—and that penny left over, which would be useless to any but gumball enthusiasts, which he definitely was not.

Michael was not questioning the justice of the fare increase, nor would he have thought to complain about the increased inconvenience of the transaction that was meant to insure his seeing the next-to-the-last episode of *Sheena—Queen of the Jungle*, neither was he practicing stoic resignation. Resignation was a feeling he could not have understood.

A soft-drink carton in each hand, one extra bottle stuffed in each carton, and the fifteenth bottle pressed uncomfortably under his left armpit, Michael was experiencing vaguely, almost inchoately, a belief he would later thematize in more than one of his books, a conviction that had its origins precisely here on this hot dirt road and at this very moment.

The as yet unformed doctrine born in him as he calculated the latest threat to his standard of living would eventually find expression in this manner: The world in which we find ourselves is a blind play of natural forces over which we neither have nor need to have control. The motivating force of life is neither reason nor love nor any of the rationales invented to camouflage our dread. The motor of life, and of all existing things, is the blind compulsion of brute circumstance. And the pain and mystery of life, at least human life (though Michael the elder would think this applied to all things, human and nonhuman, with or without souls, with or without the "gift" of life), proceed from the fact that, having realized the truth of the matter (the truth that at the heart of things lies a contradiction), we are constitutionally unable to accept it since we can never truly know absurdity. For, to believe that life is absurd is to have a coherent hypothesis concerning its meaning. What would it be to experience that presumed absurdity immediately and directly?

According to some (Aristotle probably said it first), the mind takes the form of that which it knows. What would it be like to take the form of absurdity, to know from the inside the blind compulsion of brute circumstance? It would be to know the original Chaos, prior to the imposition of order. It makes sense to Michael, the philosopher, to say that the object of knowledge is primordial Chaos. Chaos, of course, is strictly unknowable. And yet, the knowable universe that forms, we believe, some reasonably coherent whole is but one of a billion billion possible orders that could be construed. Eros, what Plato thought of as the desire for completeness of understanding, must ultimately lead us to break out of this single-ordered world and to come to know the myriad and shifting orders each on its own terms, each with respect to its own laws and rhythms.

The Chinese sage, Chuang-tzu, famous for his butterfly dream, told a story which had captivated Michael from his first encounter with the tale. The story concerns the Southern Ruler and the Northern Ruler and their host, Lord *Hun-tun* (Lord "Chaos"). The two rulers, it is said, had many interesting discussions while visiting the Kingdom of Lord *Hun-tun*. At the close of their conversations they counseled together as to how they might repay the kindness of their host. "See here," said the Northern ruler, "Lord *Hun-tun* has no orifices. Let us dig him some." The Southern ruler thought that a fine idea, and so every day for seven days they dug a hole in Chaos. And at the end of seven days, Lord Chaos lay dead.

The seven holes in our heads determine the order of the world and at the same time destroy its spontaneity. Without the comforting filters of the senses, of knowledge, of reasons and reasonings, the world would be an unorganized hotch-potch: quite friendly, of course, hospitable, a very good host. We are, however, inconsiderate guests who in our haste to offer appropriate thanks bring to an end the fruitful chaos of existing things and provide in its stead: the World.

The Cosmos. The Greek word *kosmeo* is a verb that in Ancient Greek meant "to set in order, to arrange, to adorn." The word "cosmetic" derives from the same source as "cosmos"—a fact more interesting than it first appears. Faces unabetted by the powders and paints of the cosmetician, possessed only of those unsightly holes, are already victims of cosmetologists who wish to mask the presumed imperfections of Chaos. What actually lies behind that mask is the true face of things, the innocent face of unadorned reality.

Neither Michael the philosopher nor the pop-bottle entrepreneur would ever simply resign himself to the facticity of things. Resignation is a response to an alien order—an order not mine. It is stoic, submissive, and not a little sad. Both Michaels accepted (the elder, as I have said, had written books celebrating this acceptance) the sum of all orders, the Blessed Multifariousness. Neither would wish to see orifices distorting the face of Lord *Hun-tun.*

Accepting the Blessed Multifariousness requires tolerance of the intensities, complexities, and outright contradictions of experience. The world, the single-ordered one, born of the seven orifices is altogether too knowable. Ignorance is harder to come by than we realize. We are surfeited with, inundated by, knowledge. Truth be told: We know too much, and that too well.

About the World, the Cosmos, the Mask.

Concerning that which lies behind the mask, however, we know nothing. The real friends of Lord Chaos understand that curiosity drives one to look beyond the comforts of cosmological order. Knowledge is not born from the orifices; it is only occasioned by them. The desire to know is principally a *desire,* and it is quite independent of the holes in our heads. Desire, mercifully blind compulsion, is our original face lying beneath all of the masks—both those we hide behind and those behind which we refuse to look.

Such are the thoughts born here with this young disciple of the Blessed Multifariousness, hopping from road to grass and back again, balancing three-more-than-usual pop bottles, anticipating that whatever changes were to come between now and next Saturday (the day of Sheena's final episode), he will either meet the challenge or he won't and that both eventualities have an equal claim upon the hospitality of (though he has yet to meet him personally) the gracious Lord *Hun-tun*.

14

Brother Shakian was completing his (almost bloodless) prayer. Michael, his eyes still closed, smiled to himself and silently echoed the preacher's "Amen."

15

The reception was held at the home of yet another unknown relative. Michael couldn't believe he was becoming accustomed to this, but something surely had happened. He had increased his level of charm to a point approaching scintillation. He teased and hugged and cajoled and traded stories, some of which, against his finer instincts, he exaggerated without conscience or simply made up.

All the while Michael was holding forth, Aunt Hettie Mae was sitting in a large leather chair with a matching ottoman which served as a temporary perch for those who, as was expected of them, paid her court. He had sensed from the beginning that she was waiting for him to seek an audience. Out of some unaccountable feeling of perverseness, however, he refused to do so. The more charming Michael became, the more racket came from the chair and ottoman. He was deeply engaged in the combat before he fully realized what was at issue.

Michael's earliest memory of his aunt was of her frequent, usually successful, attempts to shave a second or two off her record time for playing Chopin's "Minute Waltz." Michael recalled standing beside her piano with his sister and cousins, joining in the congratulations and applause, never fully appreciating (nor could he upon reflection even now appreciate) his aunt's achievement.

Hettie Mae had been quite beautiful and as a young woman had been the toast, and the talk, of Gransfield. Of all the stories that had circulated among the family, Michael's favorite was the one about Hettie Mae and Brother Colson. He had once won a $50.00 prize in high school for a short essay recounting that incident. He had already moved to Texas by then, almost a thousand miles away, so his telling of the tale did no harm to Hettie Mae.

16

Michael could only recall the gist of the story, of course. But, since we have the minutest access to all of the experiences embedded in his brain—including those he himself could never reach—we will provide the polished, final draft verbatim.

DEDICATION SUNDAY

On June 13, 1926, the newly built sanctuary of the Gransfield Baptist Church was dedicated. The minister, Brother Colson, had come only eleven months before. In that time he had managed two very impressive accomplishments: the funding drive that led to the completion of a brand new sanctuary, and making the eighteen-year-old Hettie Mae Evers the new church secretary. For some, the latter was the more impressive achievement since it involved the not inconsiderable task of persuading Mable Whitenby, the church secretary for over nineteen years, that "the Lord is truly grateful for your long years of service, but now He wants you to rest from your labors for awhile."

For most of the eleven months after the preacher came (right up until the scandalous Dedication Sunday) Brother Colson and Hettie Mae were seen regularly together, driving around town on "church business," usually (but not always) in the subdued, sometimes sullen, company of Brother Colson's wife. A member of the congregation had once encountered Hettie Mae and the preacher sitting together in a cafe in Big Willow. "Sister Colson's goin' t' meet us in jest a few minutes," the preacher had said.

Now, Brother Colson was a very popular preacher and in the beginning most of the members of the congregation were willing to give him (and Hettie Mae) the benefit of the doubt. But even the most loyal supporters of Brother Colson received a shock when on Sunday, June 13, immediately after finishing the dedicatory prayer and cutting the ribbon in front of the entrance to the newly completed sanctuary, the preacher turned around, walked passed Sister Colson, who had already begun to move in his direction, right over to where Hettie Mae was standing, wrapped in perfect knowledge of what was about to transpire. The preacher took Hettie Mae by the arm and escorted her into the sanctuary. The congregation followed, Sister Colson entering last.

It was less than two months later when Brother Colson announced that the Lord had called him out of the ministry and into insurance. "Just another way to serve as God's helping hand," he had said. He and Sister Colson moved to Bogalusa in south Louisiana, a town that bordered on "Catholic country" and which was about as far from Gransfield as a Baptist might safely go and still stay in the state.

As for Hettie Mae, when the new preacher came (it was Brother Shakian just out of Bible College), she had happily agreed to yield her post to Mable Whitenby who, having rested more than long enough from her labors, thank you very much, was most eager to take up the Lord's work once again.

Just over a year later, some two weeks before she was scheduled to marry the man who eventually became my uncle, Hettie Mae had rescandalized Gransfield by running away with an encyclopedia salesman (or did he sell band instruments?). They married and lived in Houston for about four months. Then Hettie Mae divorced her salesman and returned to my uncle. Everyone knew she had rejected Houston, not the salesman, and returned to Gransfield, not to my uncle.

Aunt Hettie Mae and Uncle Shelby were married in the main sanctuary of the Gransfield Baptist Church almost exactly two years after its dedication. The date was June 17, 1928.

It was a Sunday.

It is testimony to Hettie Mae's undilutable charisma that not only was there standing room only in the sanctuary but the well-wishers pretended to wonder how in the world Hettie Mae *ever* persuaded Brother Shakian to break long and powerful tradition and perform her wedding service on the Lord's Day.

Michael had long believed that it was Hettie Mae's return to Gransfield after having decided against a more sophisticated manner of living that lay at the basis of the tension between him and his aunt. Though hardly urbane, he was, nonetheless, the one relative who had clearly rejected his Baptist homeland with no thought of a backward glance. If Hettie Mae were forced to concede value to the world beyond Gransfield, a world she had herself given up, it would at least be necessary that this world in turn, in the person of one of its dedicated converts, agree to pay homage to the Belle of Gransfield. Otherwise, leaving Houston, and the salesman, could not be justified.

17

After little more than an hour, Michael began saying his good-byes. On no account would he allow himself to miss his plane. When he approached the throne at last (as he knew he must) to bid Hettie Mae farewell, he could tell that she was more than a little offended that he had not attempted to spend time with her. He offered his hand, which she promptly grasped, pulling him down on the ottoman.

"Buddy died of cancer." Buddy was her son, a man in his mid-fifties, still known to his mother, and to the world, as Buddy. His only slightly younger brother was called Donny.

"I know."

"He died real fast. But he suffered so much."

"Yeah."

"When you get old you begin to think that all the pain in the world is right there in your joints. But then one of your babies dies.... Your daddy didn't suffer, did he?"

"No ma'am."

"I saw your books. You gonna be famous?"

"Certainly not rich."

"The Evers family don't know how to make money, hon. Of course, we never seemed to know much about being famous either."

Preachers and farmers, Michael thought.

"What are you writing now, Michael?"

"I'm working on a couple of things."

"Well, if you run out of people to dedicate your books to, you keep me in mind. You can just say, 'To my favorite aunt, who let me wear my Easter suit to the rodeo.'"

Michael winced. "I'll certainly consider that." He tried to be light. His hand was still in Hettie Mae's. He looked at her sparkling sad face and wondered if she had ever read Byron's *Don Juan* and, if so, had she paused at the line

> And if I laugh at any mortal thing,
> 'tis that I may not weep.

18

On the way to the airport, Michael loosened his tie and was relieved to discover that the constriction in his throat was eased. He had feared it would be permanent. As he became more relaxed he thought to himself that the trip had gone about as well as it could have. He had, he believed, kept contaminating influences to a minimum.

19

Michael may not have been quite as successful as he thought, however, for now that the traditional twelve-month mourning period has come to an end and the stone is set on his father's grave, and it is his duty to visit the site a second time, he finds himself eager to return.

This time he plans to drive, taking the southern route through Cajun country. He had lived for a year in southern Louisiana when he was twelve and wants to revisit the bayous and wander the Creole roads.

Louisiana is actually *two* states. In the south, it is Cajun, Creole, and Roman Catholic. In the north, mainstream Southern culture reigns—Protestant to the core. When he makes his way northward, where the South begins, he intends to take some time to reminisce. He thinks he might even visit the graffitied walls of his grammar school and see if a few of the stains and etchings for which he could claim responsibility are still to be found. And he certainly intends to reacquaint himself with the cuisine. (The rule of Southern, as opposed to Cajun, cooking is simple: You pour gravy on top of anything that pork fat isn't *in*.)

All in all this journey should not be like a year ago.

It should be different.

20

This is to be a working trip, as well. Three months ago Michael received an invitation to deliver the Pherendon Lectures in London. He plans to use this trip to reflect upon the topics of his lectures.

The Pherendon Trust, a foundation dedicated to "the sharing of artistic, philosophic, literary, and historical enterprises between Great Britain and the United States of America," sponsors an annual lecture series given alternately by an American in London and a Britain in New York. The lectures, usually four, are then enlarged and published in book form under the auspices of the foundation.

Michael knows very little about the trust other than that its founder, Lord Cecil Pherendon, had been an engineer, a communications technician who had made his fortune by investing capital initially acquired from working in the American television industry. It was, however, Alfred Pherendon who had persuaded his father to set up the trust and it was he, while still a student at Cambridge, who had developed most of the ideas for cultural interchange that formed the bulk of the Pherendon Trust activities.

Michael is somewhat puzzled by his appointment as Pherendon lecturer. Though he has given invited lectures at a number of universities across the country, he knows he has nothing like the sort of reputation that would have led to such an invitation.

21

He has no intention of visiting any large city, so when he approaches a sign telling him that New Orleans is thirty-five miles east, he turns north. Traveling the small country roads is relaxing. On occasion, but not nearly as frequently as when he had lived in this area as a young boy, he has seen someone navigating a long narrow pirogue into the swamp.

22

The small cafe was sitting back from the road, its rear portion jutted several feet out over the swamp, supported by large wooden piles. The cafe itself was almost hidden by very tall, very old cypress trees. The trees in turn were nearly invisible beneath the moss they so graciously hosted.

As he approached the entrance, Michael noticed a small wad of cotton dangling by a string from the top wooden frame of the screen door. He smiled as he recalled the rationale behind the contrivance: Flies were supposed to mistake the cotton fiber for a spider's web and stay clear of the door. As a child he had thought this theory both silly and unsound. Now, however, seeing no flies in the immediate vicinity of the door, he found himself almost willing to believe in this miracle of Southern technology.

23

Before he even noted her presence in the cafe, she was seated at his table reaching for his iced tea. He had been distracted by an oddly pungent odor streaming from what the menu had, with excessive confidence he now thought, designated chicken fried steak. The woman took a sip of his tea then said, "Good for you. I always smell things myself. And not only food neither. Everthin'. I trust my nose a lot more than I trust my eyes and ears. Smell is the only one of the senses that won't let you down. If it smells like shit, you can be sure it's shit. And if it smells like perfume...well, then, it's perfumed shit."

There is a kind of charm—this woman had it—that is both instantaneous and irrevocable in its effect. Two equally powerful feelings announced themselves to Michael. They didn't struggle for dominance as respectable contradictories well ought to do. Rather, each settled separately into his mind, paid passing homage to the other and waited for subsequent events to vindicate its, or its alternative's, claim upon his psyche. These feelings could be described in poetic form, of course, but the most accurate expression of them would have to be something like, "Go for it!" and "Run while you can!" respectively.

Michael tried to look at her, but she was holding his ice tea glass in front of her face. "Should I ask your name or would you rather skip that part?"

"Don't you want to know my sign first? Aint that the way it goes nowadays."

"That's been out for a while."

"Yeah? What's in now?"

"People like to trade medical histories right away, before things get too serious."

"Beg your pardon?"

Michael wasn't quite prepared for such naïveté. "Look, why don't we try the straightforward approach. I'm Michael Evers."

Silence.

"OK. Should I call you ma'am?"

"I don't think you could learn to say ma'am right."

"Just you hold on, ma'am." Michael did his best to resurrect his accent. "I was born in this state."

She didn't seem much impressed. "A Loo-ziana boy. Don't look like it. And it sure sounds like it didn't take. Maybe I just better take me a whiff." She leaned across the table. Her face was inches away from Michael's She wasn't smiling. Neither was he any longer.

As she moved closer, Michael watched from what seemed an infinite distance as her body made that irresistable movement he knew so well. It was an almost imperceptible posturing, something like a bow, a folding inward. She was leaning toward the immediate future, submitting to it in all its anticipated detail, yielding herself up to what surely must come to pass.

She put her nose close to Michael's cheek and sniffed at him, as one dog smells another. Then she moved her head back and looked directly into his face. He waited for her to speak. The silence would have finally become embarrassing for him were he not suddenly assaulted by another, intenser concern: He couldn't move! He took a deep breath and closed his eyes. When he tried to open them his lids held fast...

24

He was in a room with a large window covered by translucent curtains and a canvass window shade with a small embroidered pullstring. The shade was three-quarters down and the window had been raised even with the bottom of the shade. There was just enough breeze to move the curtains. The bed had fresh linen with that smokey scorched smell that comes from boiling the laundry water over a pine and hickory fire. Michael immediately recognized the room. It had been his as a child.

She was lying on the bed, head half-raised by two very large pillows resting against the cast-metal headboard. Her hands were clasped behind Michael's neck. He looked down at

her breasts (freckled, as he knew they had to be). They were
squeezed together by the pressure of her arms. As he watched
a moist glaze began to form on her upper chest and neck.
Reluctantly, as if doubtful that he could survive his first complete vision of her, Michael looked at her face. She was smiling:
a glorious smile, punctuated by the lingering surprise at being
entered by another...

His eyes opened. He was still paralyzed. She had moved
her chair around the table a bit and had reached for Michael's
arm. Holding his wrist between her thumb and forefinger, she
began to rap his hand against the surface of the table. She
seemed moved now as much by Michael's desire as by her own.
What was he feeling, then? Was it her, or her feeling of him?

Her smile slowly yielded to another, equally primordial
expression. Her bottom lip quivered, then tightened. The sigh
came from somewhere beyond her body and passed through
both of them, like an ocean's first wave at the moment of its
creation.

How long until she spoke? Softly, so softly. "Whatever..."
He could hardly hear her. He leaned forward. She raised her
voice. She was smiling. "Whatever I smell...Michael...it sure
aint shit!"

Beneath his laughter and behind her smiling eyes, a feeling arose, intense and pervasive, a feeling that canceled from
this moment on the boundaries permitting the fiction that here
were two separate beings.

25

"You want to call me Genie?"

"If that's your name."

"That's it. Except you spell it with a *G*. Everbody gets it wrong."

"*G-e...?*"

"*n-i-e.* Genie."

Why not?, he thought. *Why not?*

26

"There must be something you need. A toothbrush?"

"I'll use yours." The idea of sharing a toothbrush with her thrilled him even more than the thought of lying beside her.

"You're ready to travel, then?"

"I'm ready to travel."

They were silent as they drove through Evangeline country. It was night and the moon, though only three-quarters full, was extremely bright. As he surveyed the streamers of moss cascading from the cypress trees bordering the two-lane highway, he recalled the line his tenth-grade teacher had used to illustrate metaphor: "The road was a ribbon of moonlight." Yes, he thought, the road *is* a ribbon of moonlight, and the sky ribbons of moon-soaked moss...and my life frayed and tangled ribbons of memory and desire.

"Won't you tell me something about yourself?"

Genie had been staring straight ahead. She turned almost imperceptively to the side, away from Michael, and said, "Sometimes, I'm easy."

"But I bet you get considerably more difficult as time passes."

"I can see we've been together too long. You're about to get to know me." She turned on the radio and began to punch the buttons in sequence. She had already looked through the cassettes Michael had brought with him—mostly chamber music. "Tell me when you hear somethin' you like."

"Anything with Hank Williams lyrics will do fine."

"You still tryin' to impress me, Loo-ziana boy? I guess you're a fan of the Long family, too."

Genie finally settled for the syncopated rhythms of a Cajun fiddle and harmonica.

27

"Are you getting sleepy, Genie?"

"You're the one that's been drivin' all day. It's time you got some rest. But you better stop at the next place you see. Not a whole lot of motels out here in the swamp."

It was three-quarters of an hour before they came upon the Palomino Court. Genie pointed it out. "What about the 'Palomino'?" She accented the second syllable.

Michael smiled. The motel looked very old and in need of paint.

"Say yes, Michael." She was like a child, now—eager and demanding. What magic did she see in this place?

He wouldn't disappoint her. "Yes, the Palomino." He followed Genie's pronunciation.

The room wasn't bad at all. Once inside they discovered a sliding door opening to a large courtyard with heavy wrought-iron benches. In the center of the courtyard stood a small bower, or "summer house." An odd structure, it reminded Michael of a pagoda, but not, he realized, because of any real architectural similarities. Eight thin columns formed the frame of the shelter. Extending above the edge of the roof, these columns supported what looked like small turrets. The frame of the pagoda, almost completely covered with some kind of large-leafed ivy, had been lined with lights of various colors, but the lights shone so dimly, and so many of them were hidden by the ivy, that the effect was somber and eerie.

The metal rod that formed the center support inside the summer house extended up through the roof, making a point about six feet above the center of the building. A small blue light dangled unsymmetrically from the top of the rod. Only while entering with Genie to take a seat on one of the painted iron benches did Michael realize that, out of ignorance or perversity, or from an extremely risky aesthetic sense, the central support of this quaint curiosity was serving as a lightening rod.

The moon was at its zenith, not visible from inside their shelter. Michael felt more comfortable with the moon out of sight. He thought Genie did, too. They held hands. It was the first time they had touched since she had so firmly held his wrist in the cafe.

Michael wondered how the motel had gotten its name. Mercifully, there were no equestrian motifs to be seen. The word *palomino,* he remembered, originally derived from the Latin *palumbes* and the Spanish *paloma,* meaning "dove." He decided that would be the meaning of the name. He and Genie would spend this evening at "The Court of the Dove."

When they finally went back to their room, Genie undressed silently and got into bed. Michael followed her, hoping that she was not one who fell immediately to sleep. She was. Several minutes later, as Michael too was on the very edge of sleep, he remembered that they had failed to brush their teeth.

Tomorrow, he thought. First thing.

28

Michael was up early. He decided to work a bit on his lectures. He hadn't brought any books with him, only a typed précis and assorted handwritten notes scrawled on sheets of unlined paper of various sizes. He is currently sketching a brief description of his lectures to send to the Pherendon Trust lectures committee.

THE DIACHRONOUS WEB
A Prehistory of Postmodernity

LECTURE I: STRANDS OF MODERNITY

Principal meanings of modernity: 1) Rational interpretations—Descartes- Kant- Hegel axis, 2) volitional analyses of the sort Max Weber and modern existentialism provide, 3) aesthetic construals—Stendhal, Baudelaire, et al., and 4) economic interpretations—Hume, Adam Smith—counterdiscourse of Karl Marx.

LECTURE II: A TANGLED WEB

Strands not only incommensurable in theory—their instantiations entail serious practical conflicts—theoretical sophistication and "hyper self-consciousness" of modern intellectual confronts him with demand to give consensual interpretation of mod. social, polit., and cult. institutions whose continued legitimacy depends on realization of consensus.

LECTURE III: UNTANGLING THE WEB

One man's crisis, another's long awaited revolution— Efforts to reconstruct the dirempted value spheres and regain cult. consensus are countered by a second movement (flying the paisley colors of postmodernism) which finds in the condition of psychic fragmentation a new aesthetic pluralism. Some think postmod. promises renewed cult. creativity—others label it tasteless and frenetic attempt to make a virtue of necessity by claiming, "Any (and every) thing goes."

LECTURE IV: POSTMODERN ANTICIPATIONS

Postmod. sensibility promotes pluralism, which celebrates tensions and contradictions among opposing visions— social and cult. artifacts are "texts" with multiple codings with no privileged meaning—all important concepts are clusters, webs, constellations, collages, with no univocal meaning or single-valued significance—intellectual world is segmented, fragmented, and plural—in no real sense a "world" at all—only deferred perspectives, receding in all directions, always ever-not-quite realizable—posturings and positionings in which all coherence is gone—each of us a hydra-headed narcissus...

Michael reached for his pen. As much as he liked the image, that "hydra-headed narcissus" had to go.

29

In spite of the dry philosophical prose Michael most often produces, writing is for him essentially a spontaneous, unconscious enterprise. He hasn't the slightest idea where his best ideas come from. Some weeks ago, when he sat down to formulate the outline of his lectures, he found himself writing "Diachronous Web" at the top of a blank sheet of paper. Since that time he has been engaged in discovering what that title might mean.

Many disillusioned intellectuals (of which Michael is surely one) do in fact consider contemporary culture to be a complex of values and interests each of which defines its own historic route of meaning and interpretation. Few poets, novelists, and philosophers any longer offer a ladder of knowledge which may be used to arrive at significant values and understandings. Our contemporary world is decidedly horizontal; each of us treads the surface of a web with divers threads, leading us in multiple directions. We confront an inexhaustible network of strands, with a center and crossover paths, with causes and conditions, with anchorings and functionings—each individually knowable, yet incomprehensible in its entirety.

To say this is to say that our human ambiance does not add up to *a* world, but *many* worlds, each defined by its own separate strand of significance, each a temporal route moving along its own distinctive path, each requiring a different story be told.

To adapt to such an ambiance one must, indeed, become (pace Michael) a "hydra-headed narcissus."

Michael is quite content with his title and doubtless will benefit from its promising fecundity. Perhaps it is just as well, then, that he has forgotten how the image of a web came to be so firmly embedded in his consciousness.

30

Hiking alone in the mountains of northern New Mexico, the legs of his denims wet and heavy from almost an hour's trek through the dew-soaked grass, he was forced to stop abruptly to avoid running face first into a spider's web. The silk strands of the huge web stretched several feet across the trail from one small tree to another. The morning sun shining through the drops of moisture coating its delicate filaments sent beads of light flashing outward from the center of the web.

The web was empty but for a small, grayish white pouch of silk through which Michael, on close inspection, could discern the lustrous black fragments of a spider's carcass mingled with a glut of eggs. He winced at the image of the ugly rite this carnage advertised...

The male is strumming the strands of the web at one of its anchoring points. His serenade enthralls the uninnocent mother to be.... Now he follows the silken path to the very center of the web to be joined there with his dozing consort.... A pulsing, drying spasm...half the feat accomplished, its sequel on the way.... Too weak to flee, the male anticipates the portentous stirring of his cannibal bride as soon, with a ravenous solicitude, she will wake to her wedding feast....

31

He sat on a metal chair outside the room so he could see Genie through the partially opened curtains. An unconscious conspiracy between the two of them had led to the covers being pushed, symmetrically, to the foot of the bed. Genie was lying on her back, wearing only the bottoms of her underwear.

She was thin and Michael could see the lines of her pelvic bones through her panties. She must be in her early thirties, he thought, but her freckles made her look much younger. Her left hand grasped her thick brown hair slightly above the nape of her neck. Her right hand was tucked between her legs, fingers just inside the crotch of her pants. A wisp of brown pubic hair curled up from between her thumb and forefinger. Michael stared for some moments at that vague, helical lock. His hand, too, now rested between his legs, its furtive rhythm intensifying his gaze.

32

"Remember: Each of the forms we find in our textbook—curves, planes, and solids—is to be found first in Nature." Miss McCrory said that fervently and with tedious frequency throughout both semesters of geometry. Michael knew better. Natural lines are always somewhat crooked; circles and spheres turn out to be ellipses and ellipsoids—irregular ones at that. Nature is definitely the wrong place to look for geometrical perfection. Nature has no true geometry, at least not in Miss McCrory's sense. What then of this natural helix born between those freckled thighs?

He called up the image of his geometry text and rapidly turned its pages:

> *Helix*: the curve formed by a straight line drawn on a plane when that plane is wrapped around a cylindrical surface of any kind.

He rehearsed the formula:

$$x = a \sin\Theta, \, y = a \cos\Theta, \, z = b\Theta.$$

Is nature that which strains to realize perfect form, as Aristotle believed, or does it serve as the imperfect model of the true supranatural forms, as his teacher Plato taught? That pubescent helix mocked both thinkers. Whatever mystery life holds has little to do with the mathematically perfect forms, with universals, classes of things, or with the general principles employed to bring order from the chaos of particulars. All form-dependent thought (and what could thinking be without forms, without concepts?) is a series of impertinent asides.

But this is real: a degenerate helix, existing finally through anticipations of its smell and feel and flavor, and not by virtue of the spiraling symmetry it so badly approximates.

33

Michael worked for about two hours. It was now past seven-thirty. When Genie awoke he caught her attention through the glass patio door and waved hello. A few minutes later he went inside and telephoned for something to eat.

Breakfast was a glorious parody of Southern cooking—which is but to say that it was absolutely authentic: eggs fried in sausage grease (accompanied, of course, by the greasy sausage), steamy hot-buttered grits, biscuits and gravy, fresh whole milk, and chicory coffee. Even the toast was made Southern style: three or four small pats of butter had been placed on the bread which was then broiled in an oven. The jam was made from muscadines—tart berries, like small plums, that grow on vines in the moist areas of the Louisiana forests and swamps.

Michael knew well enough that he should despise the thought of consuming such unwholesome food. And he did. He could not, however, bring himself to despise his memories of having eaten it so many times in the past.

In his defense, Michael reasoned as follows: this model breakfast could only exist for him by virtue of the memories he owned. This eggs-grits-sausage-gravy-biscuits-jelly-coffee-milk mélange was simply a collection of childhood memories. Thus, reconciled to the reality of the situation, he could relish his meal. He wasn't, he now knew, eating the food.

He was consuming his recollections of it.

34

After breakfast Michael went out to his car for his camera and spent quite some time attempting to persuade Genie to let him take her picture. She wouldn't relent.

"OK, Genie. Then let's sit for a little while in the summer house."

"Michael, no. Here." She gestured toward a nearby tree. "Let's sit under this tree. This could be anywheres."

"What have you got against our summer house?"

"Nothin,' Michael. Really. It's only that as long as I'm just *any* place, I'm safe."

What she was really afraid of, Michael thought, was being *some* place, then having to leave.

35

Michael turned on the television to see if he could get a weather forecast (clouds were forming in the north). He found a news program originating from Alexandria, the largest city in the vicinity. It was a live remote broadcast. A heavy-set man in work clothes, sleeves rolled high up on his burly arms, was being interviewed by a reporter in front of a large burning church. The man was introduced as "Brother Samson," the head minister of the ill-fated Methodist Church.

Brother Samson listened with agitated impatience to the reporter's question concerning the possible causes of the fire and when she had finished he firmly wrested the microphone from the woman's hands and, very nearly shouting, said, "The Devil made himself a big mistake this time!" Then, turning directly toward the camera, he continued, his voice lower now, almost level: "You listen to me, Satan. You really made a mistake: We've got plenty of insurance, and we're going to build up the temple of the Lord *bigger* than it was." The microphone was in the preacher's left hand, and he was shaking his fist at the Devil who, he doubtless assumed, was out there watching to see how much havoc he had finally wrought.

Home at last, thought Michael, remembering how when he was a very small child he had sat with his mother in a Baptist Church in Shreveport, Louisiana, and had watched the preacher, Brother Buchannan (Brother Buck), shake *his* fist at the Devil. Michael recalled how he applauded loudly and shouted, "Ray!" His mother had been amused, making a slight pretense of displeasure only when the more staid among the most righteous (a not insignificant number at any Baptist gathering) began to stare indignantly. Meanwhile, Brother Buck, to his eternal glory (so Michael hoped), looked down from the pulpit and said, "If I could get that kind of support from my deacons, this church would *fly*!" The reporter had regained her microphone and was addressing the camera (could she see Satan out there, too?); Brother Samson was standing fierce-eyed in the background. Michael reached up to turn the television off, pausing long enough to clap his hands.

"Ready, Miss Genie?"

Genie's voice came from behind the bathroom door. "Yeah. Anythin' about the weather?"

"Afraid not. But there is some good news: Satan's on the run."

36

Just after noon Michael and Genie came upon a sign that indicated that Kinny Lake Circle Drive was to the right.

"A drive around the lake, my lady?"

"Thank you, Michael." Genie touched his arm. He was continually surprised at Genie's instincts. He hadn't the slightest interest in traveling around Kinny Lake but had made the offer on the off-chance that Genie might. Genie immediately sensed his indifference and accepted his offer with a grateful acknowledgment of what she took to be his consideration. Now they were circling the lake, Genie thrilled with the scenery, Michael happy with her pleasure and with the manner in which she had credited him as its source.

He didn't even ask if she wanted to look inside the Antique and Curio Store. He drove the car to the side of the shop. As he was getting out he noticed Genie's face. Her eyes widened, then squinted, then widened again, as she scrutinized the shop and its environs. He could see that she was extremely excited; nonetheless, she waited for him to open her car door. It was as if she were registering every second of this event, recording it, creating a memory she would later rehearse in the minutest detail. Michael found himself falling into the rhythms of her movements and observations. He slowed his pace and articulated every posture and motion as finely as he could. They were together now in a solitary drop of time, inside which there could be no before or after. This event was to be both composed and performed in a timeless present.

The shelves and cupboards within contained a motley collection of bottles, vases, lamps, photo albums, jewelry, china, statuary, books, and magazines. Genie wandered here and there, looking at every item. Michael carefully examined the objects that appealed to him, asking for Genie's evaluations. Michael noticed that Genie would take the objects from his hands but would not herself pick them from the shelves.

When Michael entered, the owner greeted him in the friendliest of manners then returned to his chair. Michael was glad that they would be left free to browse. The owner was quite old and had the air of one unconcerned about profits on the grounds that he was well past the age when they could bring him any real pleasure. Once, however, noticing Michael's interest in an art deco lamp, he announced from across the room, "Them's real rare. Harder to find than a gold nigger." Michael looked at Genie for corroboration of his interest. But Genie was concentrating her attention on a small, gold fili-greed wine glass. She had stared at it for a minute or two and then, as Michael somehow knew she would, she picked it from the shelf. Holding the glass in both hands, she slowly turned it round and round.

"Look, Michael." Genie held the glass high in her left hand, slightly above her head. Michael moved toward her, but didn't try to take the glass from her.

"It's beautiful, Genie." Michael knew instantly, even before the lines appeared on Genie's face, that he had said something stupid.

"Not beautiful, Michael, *old*."

37

Every time Genie spoke, Michael felt that both his insight into her nature and the complexity of that nature increased enormously. Looking at her now, with the small glass in her hand, he understood so much that he had only vaguely sensed before. Genie's fascination with the antique glass had nothing to do with its shape, its decoration, its function. She coveted the object simply because it had persisted. It had survived its past.

Genie seemed incapable of owning a past. Not that she was without memories. On the contrary, she must, Michael thought, have the richest collection of memories. But memory alone cannot guarantee persistence. There must be continuity. The irony is that the surest way to avoid continuities is to collect a disparate array of memories.

Now Michael understood why he had loved her from the beginning. Fearing the continuities of the past, Genie had realized by default the manner of living that Michael would have sacrificed all his learning and accomplishments to achieve. Fear of betrayal, of abandonment, of having and losing, had made Genie a vagrant. Yet she could enjoy vicariously the persistence guaranteed to others because that is what she would wish for herself if the world, her world, could be differently conceived, differently constituted.

Michael longed for that which Genie would love to escape. He loved what Genie was, but not what she wanted. He was trapped by persistences and continuities. He had survived his past, but wished to be free of it. Genie could not risk maintaining a past. She lived from moment to moment, here and there.

When he finally spoke to Genie, his voice was distant and abstract, though not without tenderness. "The glass is my present to you, Miss Genie."

"Oh, no, Michael. I can't own it."

Of course not, Michael thought to himself, surprised by the bitterness he felt and unsure at which of them it was directed. Of course not, you could break it.

38

"Never been this far north before."

"What are you saying?"

"Aint been much above Baton Rouge."

"Genie. Surely you've traveled out of state."

"No sir. Aint been to London, England, neither. But you been all over."

Michael knew that her mention of London had not been by chance. "Why did you say London, Genie?"

I read the stuff in your little bag. You're goin' to London, England, to give some speeches. And there's other stuff about China and Japan, and I don't know where all else."

"You went through my things?"

"Sure I did. I get up a lot at night. Last night I got up and took your bag into the bathroom and tried to find out about you."

Michael wasn't at all disturbed by Genie's rummaging through his things. He was rather charmed by it—as he knew he would be charmed by anything she said or did.

"You could have asked me about myself. What would you like to know?"

"Sometimes people lie, Michael. Things never do. I need to find out what I have to without askin'."

"Well, sometimes *I* have to ask."

"You aint afraid you'll get lied to? A guy that trusts his nose like you do can't trust people all that much."

"Oh, I'm lied to all the time. And I never like it. In fact, I hate it worse than anything I know. But I think people ought to have a chance to tell their own stories. When you find some-one who isn't afraid to tell the truth you've got yourself a prize. Besides, I think I trust most people. I trust *you*."

"C'mon, teacher. You goin' to bribe me to tell the truth? People say, 'I trust you' to make you feel bad if you lie."

Michael silently conceded that Genie was right. And he knew that she would never tell him the truth about anything important no matter what bribes he offered. If he demanded the truth, she would simply swear that she was telling it. She would then continue to lie to him, and her biggest lie would be that she had now, thanks to his insistence, learned to tell the truth. Best not to offer the bribe.

"It's a beautiful madstone. I hope you don't mind if I wear it."

"What?" Michael glanced at Genie. She was tying Rinpoche's gift around her neck. "Genie?" Michael slowed the car and parked on the side of the highway.

"You don't mind, do you?"

Michael *did* mind. At least he did at first. But when he saw Genie's expression and the way she held the stone figure up to her face, he conceded. "What did you call it?"

"It's a madstone, Michael. What do *you* call it?"

"Madstone?"

"Yeah. We got all sorts of 'em where I'm from. They're mostly for protectin' you from a hex. Is that what this one's for?"

"It was a gift. It's religious...." Michael realized he couldn't explain, so he let it go at that. He wanted to change the subject. "Genie, you haven't even asked me where we're going."

"I don't care where we're headed, Loo-ziana boy—long's I can get off when I want to."

"Sorry, Genie, I forgot. You're not interested in *some* place—just *any* place. But do me a favor, OK? Don't get off too soon."

"Who knows? I might just go all the way to London, England, Michael."

39

The rain they had been expecting all morning was starting now. The smell of the wet pavement drifted through the air-conditioning vents. Michael was thinking of a line from Cervantes's *Don Quixote*: "The road is better than the inn." True enough. But not for Genie, he thought. She is certainly no traveler. She wasn't interested even in being *on the way* to some destination. She was a wanderer. Oceans, deserts—the swamplands where he had found her—were all places for wandering. No roads there. You can't wander on a highway. Even a well-worn path in the forest is too confining. Oceans and deserts and swamps defy any attempts to explore them, to chart them, to tame them. They were Genie's territory...they were just *any* place.

Genie's eyes were closed, her head bowed low on her chest. Before falling asleep she had reached her left hand over and grabbed the hair on the back of Michael's head, in much the same way that she had held so tightly to her own, a few hours before, at the Court of the Dove.

40

It was all different this time—the town, the cemetery road. He wasn't so much a foreigner. Traveling with Genie helped. He had been talking to her about his childhood in Louisiana, about his family. She was getting to know him (if she was listening, if she was believing what he said), not as he had become, but as he was when he lived here. He did have a Louisiana identity, forged from Louisiana memories. And it wasn't completely abhorrent to him after all.

"Michael, I don't see why you want to see your daddy's grave at night. What if the graveyard's closed?"

"Are you afraid to go into a graveyard at night?" Michael was gently mocking her use of the somewhat spooky-sounding *graveyard*.

"No sir. When I was little our church had a ce-me-ter-y." Genie gave equal stress to each syllable.

Michael remembered that in the South cemeteries are not nearly so separated from the communities of the living. When as a child he had lived in the southern part of the state, there had been a cemetery only a few hundred yards away from his house.

"I bet you're not one to cry at funerals, Genie."

"Yes I am, except I never cried after the first time 'cause it was too selfish. You're 'spose to be cryin' for the dead person, but I was cryin' for me. It wasn't that I wanted to be dead. It's just that things were settled...decided...for dead people. Funerals always reminded me that things weren't decided yet for me."

Before Michael could reply (he wasn't sure he wanted to), they arrived at the cemetery. A chain was stretched across the entrance to protect the sanctity of the grounds from overheated adolescents in search of a place to park. They stopped the car just outside and stepped easily over the chain, Genie's hand in Michael's.

"Show me your daddy, Michael."

Michael took Genie by the arm and they found his father's grave marker. Genie watched in silence while he traced the carved letters with his forefinger. L-e-m-u-e-l. He smiled, remembering that in the family Bible, the traditional authority for things such as this, his father's name was simply Lem. They hadn't checked his birth certificate, but likely it was Lem there as well.

Michael hated to admit to himself that he had always been a little ashamed of having a father with such an unsophisticated name as Lem. He was suddenly touched by a feeling of remorse at having failed to insist that *L-e-m* be carved on the gravestone. He smiled ruefully when he thought how many more serious lapses of filiality he might have chosen to regret. Then, as suddenly as it had appeared, Michael's remorse vanished, replaced by a feeling of peevish ecstasy. He set about to make things right.

The soil just at the base of the head stone was moist. He dug with his fingers, scooping up a handful of familiar red Louisiana clay. His hands remembered making bears and elephants and ash trays with clay just like this—some forty miles, and nearly forty years away. He worked quickly and after several minutes had neatly filled the *u-e-l* on the marker. He stood up and scrutinized his work by the moon's quiet light. Then he whispered, "Goodbye, old man," adding in his mind, as if he hadn't yet earned the right to say it aloud, Lem.

41

"You said your big sister was buried here. Show me her grave, Michael." Genie's voice was insistent.

"She is buried...over here, I think." Michael wasn't sure he could find the grave at night. He remembered it was toward the front of the cemetery. As they approached the vicinity of the entrance, Michael stooped to read the name on the headstone in front of him. Genie wandered through the next row of markers. "Dorothy Kay would be about seven years older than I had she lived. You know, there is some kind of mystery about the circumstances of her death. I was told that she died in the hospital from injuries suffered during delivery. But neither of my parents was ever willing to talk much about her. I always thought...Ah, here it is."

Michael looked up at Genie. She was standing perfectly still, almost at attention. She seemed transfixed by the sight of Dorothy Kay's grave. As he stood and started to speak, Genie reached out and took hold of his arm. Her eyes remained focused on the grave marker as she raised Michael's soiled right hand to her face and slowly rubbed the nearly dry clay onto both of her cheeks.

A beginning. But of what? Michael knew only part of what was to come. Naked warm skin and friction's numbing fire—these he knew. The desolating agony of remaining always outside. Best let it end here, he thought. He wouldn't say yes to it.

He couldn't refuse.

Genie took Michael's hand once more and thrust it into her mouth, moistening the remaining bits of clay with her tongue, rubbing the clay onto her teeth with her fingers. When she was done, Michael somehow grasped what he was to do. Scrupulously, he began licking the clay from her face, examining her cheeks by the moon's intensifying light, making certain that he had removed every bit of it.

Michael reached around Genie's neck and pulled her face toward his. He was shocked by the roughness of his movements. A noise was coming from her throat, a low throbbing whine that Michael felt as much as heard. He held his open mouth tightly over hers, sealing her lips while they exchanged the muddy liquids.

Dizzy, on the very edge of understanding, Michael found himself pleading with his sister's grave and ghost, begging the moon for the dark comfort of ignorance. No matter that Genie's arms were now at her side, Michael knew that the sound coming from deep within her would not let him go.

Genie stepped backward, pulling Michael with her. Then she slowly began to kneel on the ground. He placed both hands on Genie's head and turned her face upward. Moving her head to and fro, he watched the moon's reflection play upon the surface of the crystalline darkness her eyes had become. The sound grew louder and Michael felt his body begin to shake. Again surprised by the violence of his action, he ground Genie's face into his crotch, thrusting her head back and forth as he felt himself swell. She gnawed at him through his open trousers; then her teeth touched his stiffened flesh.

Michael was thrown backward on the grass, Genie spread on top of him. She gouged him into her then sat up straight, her arms thrust back in the manner of a diver about to enter a pool. Michael's hands were shoved up under the waist of her dress and he tugged at her breasts. Her nipples were moist, wet, running. He wanted it to be blood. He was tearing at her clothes, at her flesh. Beyond this grinding, gouging, pounding rapture, Michael wished that nothing would remain.

The whining in Genie's throat was abruptly stilled. Michael slowly looked up into the twin faces—Genie's and that of the moon shining beyond her. Huge veins began to pulse through the moon's horrible, dark face. Or was it Genie's face? A mouth opened. The moon's mouth? Then he inhaled the corpse-breath and understood for one brief, fearsome instant what beginning this was. Mercifully, the knowledge sank beneath his consciousness just before stealing his sanity.

That sound again. The air no longer fetid. The end of the beginning. Genie's head jerked back then forward on her chest, then back once more. Michael felt himself flooded with a scalding hot torrent that washed over and mingled with the countercurrent he had sent to meet it.

42

The moon was approaching its zenith. They had begun to walk, Genie's arm around Michael's waist.

"Genie's not your real name."

"Nope. I gave it to myself. But I expect not for the reason you think."

"Well, let me see. I know quite a bit about genies. Maybe I can figure it out."

"Maybe."

"Genies are mischievous spirits. They come out of Islamic theology."

"A-rabs, right?"

"Uh...Yes." According to these people God created two sorts of beings—human beings and genies. It's closer to *jinni*, but that's not important. The genies were made two thousand years before Adam. Unlike Adam who was made from the earth, these spirits were born of fire. They had the ability to change shapes, to appear in human form or to become any sort of animal they wished. They stayed hidden in rocks and trees or hovered about in the air. They could be good or evil, as they chose. But since they were invisible most of the time, they could easily be offended by some unaware human who might violate their territory or unknowingly take something the genies considered to be theirs. Much of their time was spent getting even.

"Well, so far none of this seems to apply to you. You're not a vengeful person, are you? Let's see, what else do I know about genies? Genies were certainly not all bad. They often served as a means of creative inspiration. Of course, even that had its dark side. Mohammed, for example, was worried for a while that the messages he thought were divine and which became the basis of the Koran—the Muslim bible—came from genies. The author of a false theology? No, that can't be you."

Michael paused to see if Genie was still listening. "Most people, of course, know about genies from the *Arabian Nights* where they are depicted as victims of Solomon's power. He was able to seal them inside jars and toss them into the ocean. Occasionally, a jar was washed ashore or fished up from the bottom of the sea by some sailor or fisherman. Then a genie might win its freedom in return for a little wish fulfillment.

"You know, we never read about all the genies that stayed trapped inside their jars. It seems to me that some of them must have gotten used to their confinement, as long-term prisoners sometimes do, and would have refused to leave even if someone sought to liberate them. Ah, but in your case..."

Michael was startled by a sound coming from behind a nearby grave marker. His scalp tightened, the hair at the nape of his neck was raised. Instinctively, he reached for Genie.

She was gone.

Michael was too confused, too distracted, to notice the small, gray-white rabbit skittering through the bars of the low iron fence that separated the far edge of the moonlit cemetery from the darkening woodland beyond.

VI

Speculum Dementiæ

1

He doesn't remember running, but he ran as fast as the darkness would allow, back to his car. At the entrance, abating his terror, he paused to gaze for several seconds in the direction of his father's grave. He would not remain long enough to recover any composure. He raced the engine as he backed away from the cemetery. The sound of the tires spinning on the rocky, hard clay surface made him realize that he had to control himself. He fixed his eyes on the center of the road and drove at a steady rate of speed. If he screamed, as he thought he might, he was promising himself that it would be a controlled, deliberate scream.

It wasn't Genie's disappearance that was causing Michael's terror. He hadn't yet begun to absorb that event. His panic had a more immediate cause. *It* was hanging there, around his neck. He inhaled the odor of the leather strands, felt the knot just below his hairline, the cold dull pressure against his chest. Unmistakable.

The madstone.

He didn't have the courage to reach up and grasp it, to test his certain feeling by running his fingers over the surface of the stone, reading the convoluted markings he knew from the embedded memories of a thousand fondlings. He wasn't going to touch it. He had never worn it, never would have thought to wear it.

Only two possibilities: magic or insanity. He made the reasonable choice. Until this moment Michael had never once feared the loss of his mental stability. He had often enough experienced exaggerated anxieties over the possibility of the loss or diminution of his mental powers—his memory, his creative insights, his talent for seeing connections and ramifications—but he had never believed it likely that he could lose *control*. Psychosis was simply *out of the question*.

Now, he knew differently. Nevertheless, beneath his unyielding terror and the almost certain insight that he had lost his mind, there was a sense of relief. His thinking mechanisms seemed intact. His brain was sorting, analyzing, remembering, abstracting, generalizing, holding up a vast number of possibilities; he was considering (and, thereby, canceling) the innumerable causes (emotional, psychosocial, biochemical) for his newly won insanity. He might be raving, but *by Jesus*, he was raving brilliantly!

Michael smiled lopsidedly, stretching his lips tightly over his teeth. He giggled for several seconds, tentatively at first, then with greater conviction. It was a rehearsal. He was curious to see how madness would suit him. Not bad...*not bad*.

There were no psychotics in his family. Of course, his adopted family—philosophers and their ilk—owned more than their share of crazies. It was not by nature, then, but through professional experience that he had been raised to this bad eminence.

2

Of all the impaired philosophers Michael could recall, two stood out above all others: Friedrich Nietzsche, of course, was everybody's favorite ranter. The second, less known perhaps, was John Ruskin.

Everyone knows about Nietzsche, the presumed victim of tertiary syphilis, whose final collapse in 1889 was signaled by his rushing tearfully into the street to embrace a horse being beaten by its owner. Michael had always doubted the charge of syphilitic dementia. He believed it far more likely that Nietzsche, goaded perhaps by the offending organisms, had simply *thought* himself into insanity.

There are firm principles meant to ground and secure one's thinking. For most it is a religious or political faith, or the simple inertia of customary belief. But even philosophers, those charged with the unusually bold attempt to think beyond the confines of common sense and received opinion, must have their securing foundations.

A is *A*. For sure. That's the Principle of Identity. Comforting, isn't it? Then, of course there is the Principle of Sufficient Reason, a most popular crutch among scientists and lay people as well. (This one says that whatever happens comes equipped with an explanation, if we are but clever enough to find it.) These principles are invariably capitalized, in the hope that no one will question their authority.

Nietzsche had not been intimidated by capital letters. He thought himself beyond the comforts of First Principles, beyond the myths of Order and Rationality, beyond the Laws of Nature and, indeed, of Nature itself as a single ordered world. He chose to think himself into the Chaos of sensibility prior to sense, into the realm of the Vast Indifference, the Blessed Multifariousness, which is the primordial condition, the state of things prior to our insistent ordering of them from the human perspective.

Nietzsche had the eye of an artist—a true artist, not the timid, programmatic pretender-poets who are so overburdened by the exhausting reservoir of styles and techniques from out of the too honored past that they cannot help but *know* before they see, and so cannot see.

Much of the pain of living can be avoided if we know what we shall see, or not see, before we have occasion to look. Closets are scary to children because they don't yet know what couldn't reasonably be hiding there. The greatest threat to the artist is that the desire to see will be destroyed by the gift of antecedent knowledge. On the other hand, if one wishes to see, to truly see, the risks are great indeed. Nietzsche's insanity was the consequence of his decision to look at things unprotected by advance knowledge of what he would see.

3

An adventitious spirochete invited Nietzsche into the abyss. John Ruskin was beset by an even more invasive presence: a woman, a child actually, whose name, appropriately enough, was La Touche. Rose La Touche, thirty years younger than Ruskin, a strange exotic child, was as effective as the organism (that for history and the public world) poses as Nietzsche's assassin.

Rose was never Ruskin's wife. Moreover, his wife of some five or six years, Euphemia Gray, was never his wife in the truest sense either. That marriage was finally annulled. According to Effie Gray, on their wedding night Ruskin had fainted at the sight of her pubis, accoutered in a manner such as no one tutored by Italian marbles could ever have expected. There was to be no consummation.

Rose died insane in 1875 at the age of twenty-seven, eleven years after she had refused the proposal of marriage Ruskin had tendered six years before, two years after they met. That is to say, the woman Ruskin first loved was eight years old.

In 1878 Ruskin experienced his first wave of sympathetic insanity that continued episodically for the next ten years, until his final relapse in 1889, this time resonating not only with the ghost of Rose La Touche, but with Nietzsche's flagrant spirit across the channel.

In his last years Ruskin was known to have incessantly repeated two words while walking up and down the stairs. In rhythmic sequence, as his foot touched each succesive step, he would utter, "Black, White...Black, White...Black, White." His loving eyes had looked too intently upon the world. He sought rest among the shadows.

The Chinese philosopher Wang Yang-ming said that "to see is to love already." Yes, Ruskin had loved all and seen all, as had his German cousin, until burned out by the light, his world collapsed into chiaroscuro.

Who can say that Ruskin's world was really lost to him? In the simple contrast of light and dark, all things are found.

The indefinite variety of colors and shapes all hide in the shadows. Ruskin still had the world with him, reduced to its essentials. Like a seed from which all complexity could blossom.

Michael knew too well that he possessed neither the courageous eye of Nietzsche nor Ruskin's stoical eye. The truth, of course (and in his present state truths seem to float like crystalline clouds before his eyes), was that he didn't deserve insanity. If he were losing his mind, it was for the wrong reason. His vision was not pure.... He hadn't seen...

Perhaps he wasn't insane. It could be magic...

Yes, magic. If...

4

There is, of course, a third possibility, Michael. But we shall not force you to entertain it.

5

He had begun to feel cold. He reached to turn off the air conditioner and settled into what he knew would be eight hundred
miles of stopping only to fill the tank, drink coffee, and pee.

6

Michael didn't remove the madstone until he arrived home. He hid it away on a closet shelf where it remained for some months until he came across it while packing for his lecture trip. The stone made several trips back and forth between closet and suitcase until it finally settled into a pocket of his utility bag.

Michael's first stop would be New York City. There was to be a reception in his honor at the Manhattan headquarters of the Pherendon Trust. His lectures in London are still a week away so Michael plans a side trip from New York to New Haven to visit his Yale mentor, Roger Clifford. Clifford had politely declined the invitation to the New York festivities "on the grounds of decrepitude," but had asked Michael up to New Haven for "lunch and a chat" the day following the reception.

Alfred Pherendon had called from New York to say that he would meet Michael's plane. "I'm quite sure that I shall recognize you from your photograph. I do own your books. Though I must be honest, I've not read them as yet. I'm looking forward to your lectures providing me a clue to what I am told is a rather complex vision."

Michael knew little more about Pherendon than that he had read comparative literature at Cambridge and had initially entertained some hope of becoming a poet whose early years of struggle would be underwritten by the Pherendon millions. But as is usually the case with an only child, he was destined not to be liberated but imprisoned by his inheritance.

"Let's play it safe, Mr. Pherendon. I'll be carrying a photograph of Tower Bridge."

"Really?"

"Yes, indeed."

"Right."

Michael had purchased *Bridges Over the Thames* only a few days before. He thought it might help pass the time on the rather tedious London flight. The front cover featured a photo of one of the visual clichés by which tourists learn to identify London: Tower Bridge. The bridge featured on the back cover interested him far more. Michael had lived at the foot of Albert

Bridge, on the south bank of the Thames, for some months during his first visit to London.

As he picked the book from its place on the shelf in preparation for his trip to the airport, he recalled his first passage over Old Albert. At first he had been unable to decide whether he liked the structure or hated it. It was garish by any standard and looked as if it had been iced rather than painted. Its colors—pastel blue and pink and yellow and white and green—illumined at night by strings of ordinary household lightbulbs, made the bridge appear to be some strange hybrid spawned by the mating of a birthday cake and a Christmas tree.

Very soon, however, crossing the bridge twice a day to and from the Sloane Square tube station, he yielded to its innocent charm. As much as he might condemn the Victorians in every other regard, he was prepared in this single instance to forgive them the baroque excesses of their architecture.

On his maiden voyage across the bridge, the taxi driver had responded to Michael's ambivalent remark, "That's quite a bridge!" with a phrase that had subsequently become a litany recited at his every transit, "Loveliest bridge on the Thames, I reckon."

7

The book wasn't necessary. No sooner had Michael emerged from the gate exit than he was approached by a very tall stoutly built fellow, discreetly preceded by his London accent. "Ah, Professor Evers. Good trip?"

Pherendon was likable from the very first. He was less nattily dressed than Michael had expected, more casual, in fact, than the stereotype permitted. He had obviously spent a great deal of time on this side of the Atlantic.

Pherendon's driver retrieved Michael's bags and they set off for the hotel. Michael was pleased when he discovered that he was to be staying at the Waldorf, a hotel he knew only by the art deco appointments of its lobby, and its elegant bars.

Michael had long made it a custom to visit the Waldorf's Bull and Bear Lounge whenever he was in New York. He liked to watch the display of stock exchange prices pass overhead and listen to the small talk of the brokers and businessmen. It was for him not unlike his visits to the Mexican *cantinas*, except that the ice (he trusted) was cleaner. The whores, however, were much the same. True, these Wall Street walkers stalked by day and received vastly greater fees for their services, but they seemed no less thin.

A few blocks from the hotel, Pherendon opened his valise and removed two books. Michael recognized one of the volumes right away as his own latest work. The other turned out to be a book by Pherendon himself.

"I'd like to give you this. A book of mine. As you see, I've inscribed it. The work is of no real consequence, of course. I only give it to you so that I might have an excuse to ask you to autograph my copy of your fine book."

Michael was embarrassed. Autographing books is normally reserved for writers with a commercial appeal much greater than he ever enjoyed. He took the work and examined the cover briefly. He was fond of this book, *The Meaning of Making*, a book on the relationships between culture and technology. At the same time he realized that his titles were infinitely more provocative than the contents they advertised. Nor was he very good, he now realized, at the art of spontaneous inscription. The best he could come up with was

> To Alfred, on the occasion of our meeting.
>   Michael

"Thank you very much, Professor Evers...Michael. Let me say again that I am receiving far more than I am able to offer in return. My poems are hardly more than pastimes, I'm afraid. But, perhaps you will find in this book a line or two that demonstrates my sincere interest in philosophic questions."

"You are kind to give me such a thoughtful gift. I know I will enjoy reading what you have written."

"At your leisure and convenience, of course."

"Of course." Nonetheless, Michael thought he had best have something to say about Pherendon's poetry when next they met.

They had reached the hotel. The driver removed Michael's bags from the car. Pherendon spoke briefly to the doorman, then turned to Michael and said, "Right. You'll be taken care of from here. I shall call for you this evening. I hope 7:30 will suit. The reception will be held at our Manhattan headquarters, only a few blocks from here."

"That will be fine. Thank you again."

Michael's room—a small suite, actually—was ideal. He immediately decided upon a long bath. The bathtub was one of the old-fashioned kind he remembered from his childhood home. Though its base was enclosed, he was certain the tub would be resting on round balls tightly gripped by the claws of eagles.

Michael stretched his body to the length of his soul. He thought that he might snooze. Later, he would read a poem or two.

8

AUNTIE/ŒDIPUS

Batten down the bedsheets.
Œddie has an itch only a mother can scratch.

What if mamas have always been momi.
(Dada-ist a momus, too.)

No matter were they all blowzy, steatopygous squabs.

Œddie is a myrmidon for mom.

Œedipal must must not breech family walls,
to rampage in unciphered wombs.
(Nothing in ex-cest.)
For of such stuff Deleuzians are made.

And Œddie would be civilized.

The horny band that raised its hand against the
Father infused his blood into the male-soaked times.

Givenness shaped by guilty wills,
Culture defeminate,

Homonotony.

Perhaps a callipygian aunt could have saved
Œdipus from becoming one.

What of auntie(,)Œdipus?

Michael was pleased in so many ways by this poem that
he hardly knew where to begin to think about it: In the first
place, though this was hardly a work of the caliber of a Yeats
or (to choose a character more closely analogous to Pherendon's
avocational status as a poet) Wallace Stevens, it was a well
constructed piece, and *he liked it.*

Pherendon had written his poems in what could only be
called the postmodernist mode, which in the case of poetry simply meant that, rather than depending upon imagery presumed
to be the common heritage of the sensitive, cultured reader, the
poem was an eclectic patchwork of obscure cultural references
and the arcane language that housed such references.

Even without access to reference works, Michael found he
could make sense of the poem. It took a while, but he finally
recalled the relevant slang meaning of *Auntie*—"aging homosexual." And though he had never seen the words *steatopygous*
and *callipygian,* his knowledge of Greek allowed him to figure
the meanings which, roughly, could be translated as "fat-assed"
and "owning a shapely derrière," respectively. *Momus,* he did
remember, was some sort of complaining individual. *Myrmidon*
puzzled him. He vaguely recalled its association with ants. But
that made no sense in its present context.

The likely source for Pherendon's allusion is the mythical
material which Homer used in creating *The Iliad*. There the
Myrmidons are characterized as a people who, with absolute
and unquestioning loyalty and obedience, fought beside
Achilles and Patroclus in the Trojan War. Though Michael has
read about the Myrmidons in *The Iliad*, the reference to them

freshest in his preconscious, the one he recalls indistinctly, is found in Ovid's *Metamorphoses*. There the Myrmidons are ants transformed into human warriors. The word *myrmidon* does, in fact, mean "ant".

The double *must* in the first line of the second stanza puzzled him for a time until he recalled that "must" can mean "animal lust" (specifically, "the rampaging behavior of a lusty elephant"). The references to Dada in the first stanza and Deleuzians in the second were historical and topical, of course. Giles Deleuze was the coauthor of a recent work entitled *Anti-Œdipus,* which apparently served as the occasion for writing the poem.

9

Pherendon's poem brought to mind a disturbing experience Michael underwent while staying at a newly opened Pacific island luxury resort. Here were, quite literally, miles of art-filled corridors, walkways which displayed objets d'art of the richest variety. But there was something very odd about these creations. Much of the art was immediately recognizable as done in the style of the great masters. However, something was amiss with respect to the use of subject matters. It took Michael some time to realize that a subject undertaken in the style of one master had been drawn from the repertory of another!

Thus, Michael noted that Van Gogh's *Sunflowers* had been executed in the style of his peerless countryman from a century before. A few steps down the gallery some Van Gogh manqué has returned the favor by transmogrifying *The Sortie of Captain Frans Banning Cocq's Company of the Civic Guard* into a (Starry) *Night Watch.*

This is clearly a greater assault upon the integrity of art than Duchamp's penciling of moustache and goatee on a copy of the *Mona Lisa.* Who could be comfortable with the skewed appreciation evoked by witnessing, as Michael had forced himself to witness, the vibrant broad-brushed planes of Cézanne's *Mont Sainte Victoire* dissolved into the miniscule points of Seurat or Monet's *Water Lillies* rendered into the vulvate swirls of Georgia O'Keefe?

This stroke of ironic genius must have cost hundreds of thousands of dollars. And to what end? Philistine tourists would miss the point of most of these artful pranks. Even the reasonably aware could not possibly catch them all. Is Bernini the inspiration for that copy of Rodin's *Kiss*? Has Turner's spirit been invoked to rework Gauguin's (now misty) *Brown Madonna*?

Though Michael thought he had successfully resisted, this grand prank worked its dark magic upon him. Only minutes after escaping the maddening corridors, he found himself engaged in enlivening the expressionless face of Rembrandt's *Old Self Portrait* (mercifully exempt from this roguish gallery), by overlaying the late self-portait of Van Gogh, crazy with anxiety and terror.

Michael's tour of this gallery of puns convinced him that the art of a Leonardo, Rembrandt, Turner, or Picasso could no longer stand alone. The great works must be seen as having dissolved into one another, each becoming a context or perspective permitting a new and intenser enjoyment of the others.

The protective fences built around works of art are now in serious disrepair, and there is little motivation to mend them. We have come to interpret *art pour l'art* as meaning all art is for the sake of all other art. Aesthetic creations dissolve kaleidoscopically into such an array of alternative contexts as legitimately to be all things to all persons for the sake of the gospel of postmodernity.

10

Minutes after arriving at the near-empty lounge on one of the upper floors of Pherendon Enterprises, Michael was encircled by guests appearing from every door. He thought that these celebrity well-wishers could easily have been delivered by the caterers along with the crisp cucumber sandwiches, assorted nuts and cheeses and the (surely robust) hazy punch that decorated the tables. The more prestigious looking of the acutely accented guests might have been uncrated with the strawberries which, Michael learned, had been sent on this afternoon's Concorde direct from Claridges.

Individually, the party extras seemed nice enough, but very soon Michael began to think how much, as a group, they resembled the swarm of grasshoppers he had once witnessed while passing through Yuma, Arizona. Having escaped his automobile, he was forced to stand for several hours inside a gas station as the host invaded the town. Michael had watched dispassionately as each insect satisfied its lilliputian appetite, as all ate their gargantuan fill. Finally, an even denser, lower flying cloud had made its way around the edge of a distant mountain.

11

During a brief respite from the staccatoed introductions, Michael started to go in search of a bathroom. (It's a "toilet," he thought. This is British territory.) But he was too late; Pherendon was approaching with the latest arrival.

"Jesus!" Michael said it aloud. Then he said to himself, smiling, "Well...I think he looks better without the beard."

"Hi, Mike."

"So, it's Mike now, is it?" Laughing, Michael reached out both hands in welcome, surprised that he was so intensely pleased.

Pherendon was laughing with them and paused only long enough to mumble an apology. "He *made* me promise, you see, that I *wouldn't* tell you."

"Ah, did he? And he told you how...where we met?"

Pherendon, apparently recalling that he was British, straightened himself a bit and said, "Yes, but you see, that is part of what I was not to tell. It was Peter..."

"Peter?" Michael grimaced. "Sorry...Pete—you'll always be A–K to me."

"I don't mind a bit. I grew genuinely attached to the name." Michael thought that he had been patient enough. "One of you must be ready to provide a full confession. Let's have the story."

Pherendon was the first to speak. "I must tell you that I am normally quite horrid at keeping secrets. It was Peter, you see, who...but, first, allow me: Pherendon took one step backward and from a rigidly erect stance proclaimed, "Professor Evers, this is Peter Haddox whom, though you know him better by an alias, you should in any case recognize by his real name as well. It is your real name, I assume, Peter."

"Ah, but reality is such a difficult concept, wouldn't you say, Michael?"

Michael looked into A–K's eyes and saw, beneath his smirk, that intense, hysterical fear. His beard, Michael now realized must have hidden the ever so slight twitch in his chin that now served to further ramify his anxious features.

Michael did recognize his name. Peter Haddox was an author of some notoriety. He was a journalist, though he had gained his recent celebrity by publishing a book on industrial espionage. Michael had thought of him as a much older man. He had just seen notices in *The New York Times Book Review* of an as yet unreleased work entitled *The Twilight of the Idols,* whose subject was the unforeseen emergence and equally abrupt decline of exotic spiritual cults over the last twenty-five years. Michael now knew the purpose of A–K's tour at Tilopa.

"But let me finish, gentlemen. Peter was largely responsible for your invitation, Michael. He brought your name to the attention of the Grants Committee, of which I should add he is a most distinguished and hard-working member. And you will be pleased to learn that Peter will be accompanying us to London."

Michael was beckoning toward an empty sofa, "Could we just sit down a minute and sort all this out before I become terminally confused?"

Pherendon nodded and said, "I am afraid you will have to do this without me. I've got to scintillate in another part of the room. I shall make every effort to protect you from the guests for a few minutes. But, Peter, you must talk fast. I can't fend the multitudes for long."

Michael and A–K each filled plates with pastries and cheeses, picked up glasses of champagne, and maneuvered themselves onto one of the black leather sofas that bordered the lounge, each spilling champagne in the effort. They laughed the casual laugh of old friends which, Michael noted with pleasure, they actually seemed to be. Michael reached for A–K's plate and placed it on the table next to the sofa. "Nothing to eat, A–K, until you confess. You might begin with the choice of your name."

"It was my way of nose-thumbing, I'm afraid. Juvenile, I know. A–K, of A–K and Associates? Aka? But I forgive you for not catching on; we were distracted by many other things—such as surviving."

"So you were set to write an exposé of Tilopa?"

"At first, yes. Though, I have to say, Mike, I was surprised to encounter some really worthwhile things at Tilopa. In fact, I didn't include Tilopa in my book, except in the most general and quite complimentary terms, as an exception to the rule."

"And Tilly?"

A–K squirmed in his chair, then sighed. "I know. I should have roasted that maggot, but that would have smeared Thögma indirectly, so I forswore. I guess I'm not as hard-hitting as my publisher advertises."

"Rinpoche knew about you, did he?"

"Oh yes. I had met him through a friend who had hosted him when he first came to this country. He had no qualms about my coming. He seemed altogether unconcerned about my opinions. But my, how Tilly must have suffered! I don't think he ever knew. But he surely must have suspected something."

"Have you kept up with Rinpoche since the retreat?"

"I saw him, in fact—briefly. He is back in Dharamsala now. I think he will stay there for good."

"His mission here is complete? Do you suppose he reckoned us unredeemable?"

"Well, if...Uh oh, Mike. You're in for it now. Here comes Alfie with two not-so-fun guys." A–K leaned close and muttered into Michael's ear, "Te-di-*ous*!"

12

Pherendon was smiling. "I trust you gentlemen have reached a breaking point in your conversation. Michael, I would like to present Professors John Springer and David Robinson. Professor Springer gave our lectures the year before last."

"Ah, yes, of course." Michael didn't wish to imply a greater familiarity with Springer's work than he possessed. He had picked up one of his books when he had learned of his participation in the lecture series. It was a work of literary criticism that Michael had thought rather superficial and tendentious and had only leafed through it.

"And Professor Robinson..."

Michael took Robinson's hand and said, "I have read some of your essays on the history of technology."

A–K shook his head. "You academics are an incestuous lot..."

Robinson interrupted. "But the family is not always a harmonious one. For example, I'm afraid Professor Evers and I would have a slight family quarrel over a number of issues. Wouldn't you say so, Michael? —If I may call you Michael."

"No doubt, but that would not diminish my respect for your work."

"No, indeed, nor do I mean to imply..."

"And, of course, you may call me Michael."

Pherendon raised his hand toward Robinson and said, "I by no means wish to be accused of incitement to riot, but I should like to suggest that we find a relatively private place for you gentlemen to chat. You may well enjoy a brief respite from discourse *en masse*. There is a small office just off the lounge foyer." Pherendon turned as he spoke, gesturing for the four of them to follow.

The office was not small. It was decorated with an odd collection of Victoriana and art deco appointments that spoke as surely as did Pherendon's poetry of the self-conscious eclecticism that had recently come to represent *haute* British culture.

Pherendon beckoned them into comfortable chairs. Bottles were removed from an antique oak cabinet. Pherendon and Michael had gin. The others asked for sherry. "This gin, you will notice Michael, is 'export strength'—much heftier than one gets in 'Jolly Old.' It's what we call 'Gin for the Colonies.'"

Michael smiled and raised his glass. "You Brits think to sog our brains—still hoping, I suppose, for a final advantage."

"Shame, sir! Surely you know the story of colony gin. In years past when ships took many weeks to reach the outlands, gin would lose proof en route. It had to be made stronger to survive the voyage. Apparently, no one has noticed that, what with tighter containers and overnight shipping, there is no longer that need. And I for one intend to remain silent."

Michael raised his glass. "To silence, then."

Everyone joined in the toast.

13

"To silence."

It might have been better had the sentiment of the toast been honored by the group, for immediately after sipping their drinks all hope of peace and harmony was compromised by the sort of petty dead-earnest cutthroat banter to which academics are given. Springer and Robinson set about to converse in the manner of two men who are mutually aghast that the other should have received renown in spite of the so obvious banality of his work. Pherendon meanwhile was bemoaning, in the contrived tone of cultured politeness, the "perhaps slightly unbalanced" series of articles on chemical waste A–K had recently written for a national magazine.

Michael, momentarily abandoned, was gazing out the open office door at the progress of the party. The scene appeared to him as a grotesquely slow-moving square dance, a series of allemandes and do-si-dos that sent the celebrants about the room, shifting and swirling from one fading conversation to another. He watched the guests, pairing off, leaning close, spilling drops of liquor on the roseate carpet as arcane insights were spread about the room in the manner of a viral contagion.

Michael's surveying eye paused, as anyone who knew him could have predicted that it would, when it encountered the glistening pale skin of a woman standing nearly in the middle of the room, perhaps some seventy-five feet from where he sat. She was standing beside a table filled with condiments and pastries and the obligatory tray of cucumber sandwiches. She had a drink in her hand, and Michael was curious to see what accompanying snack she might choose. As he watched, a man approached her. He must have addressed her because she turned slightly toward him in a somewhat detached, questioning manner. The man had an aggressive stance and carriage that Michael found immediately distasteful. There was no question, however, who would have the advantage in this encounter. Just before this mismatched pair drifted out of his vision, an involuntary wave of sympathy escaped from Michael and drifted in the direction of his soon-to-be-fallen comrade—a sympathy occasioned by Michael's detailed insight into what surely must come to pass...

Michael's confidence in the inevitability of what is about to take place may well be seriously overdrawn. Nevertheless, were he to compose a narrative of this incipient encounter, the pale-skinned specter would most certainly be its heroine and his account would probably read somewhat as follows...

14

...Distracted by her cleavage, he made what was for him a very serious mistake: he picked a almond from the dish (he hated almonds) rather than the cashew he had spotted a moment before. This was the way of the world, he thought: trade-offs, furtive pleasures purchased at the expense of unsurmisable pain. The moral order: There is a God, and he counts not only the fall of the sparrow but the casting down of one's gaze.

The faded echo of mushy ice cubes magnified his frustration. He recalled how, years ago, he had discovered his gin-doesn't-freeze-in-the-freezer argument for the existence of God. Mocked now by his wilting martini, he was moved to doubt not God but His steadfastness. Somewhere amid the fragments of what once had been the keenest of minds an answer to his dilemma could be found. Get it together. Focus. Near frozen gin...and cashews every time...these could be his. Not without sacrifice...but they could be. Purity of heart is to will one thing. But he was close enough to smell her skin. No perfume. Skin scrubbed clean and lightly oiled. Her breasts reached out to him with every breath. He synchronized his breathing with hers to increase the proximity. Did she notice?

She noticed.

It was time. "Which are your favorites?"

"Pardon?"

"I'm all too fond of cashews, I'm afraid."

"Ah, yes. Pistachios."

He hated her. A better life and pistachios could have been his choice. But they were such an awful pain to get at. He recalled his early experiences with pistachios. Delicious kernels, awaiting liberation. You have to use your thumbnail to retrieve the nut. But one is never enough. Another...and another. Always exquisite. Too exquisite. Promising more than they can deliver. Palate teasers. He wondered if she could accomplish what had been impossible for him: shell perhaps a hundred pistachios before eating a single one, then settle down for uninterrupted pleasure. He thought probably she could. And he hated her.

"Certainly a good choice—or so it might initially seem. But there is a problem with pistachios, you know."

"The shell."

"No, no, no. That's merely a question of delayed gratification. No problem, I should think, for the reasonably mature. The failing of pistachios is much more significant. It's nutritional, I'm afraid."

"Yes?"

"Yes. You see, pistachios are missing one of the essential amino acids. They are, I am sorry to inform you, unassimilable protein."

"A pity."

Was that pique in her voice? He was feeling better. "Tasty. Most desirable in the narrow sense of the word *desire*. But I should never commit to a food so totally without...integrity. 'T would seem immoral."

His eyes fixed hers. Soon she would be on the ropes.

Her breathing slowed. "But isn't it always a question of the lesser evil? Granting your judgment concerning pistachios, what about the sin attendant upon the consumption of cashews?"

He didn't like this turn. He particularly didn't like her use of the word *sin*. Why bring in theology for God's sake? His anxiety returned. Nothing to do but maintain at least the pretense of confidence. "Sin, you say?"

"Indeed."

He was hating her again. His breaths shortened. No

longer obeying the same rhythms, they were drawing apart.

"A man of your obvious wide learning..." She's mocking me. Mocking *me!* "could not possibly be ignorant of the manner by which we obtain cashews."

Vicious.

"What of it?" He hadn't the slightest idea where cashews came from. He knew she could smell his rising panic. Hold on. It's not over yet.

But, of course, it was over. He listened to the account of how cashews are farmed. He was appalled. Damn her. She was absolutely right. Sin was the only word for it. He was ashamed...

15

"But Michael would likely see it another way."

"I certainly don't see why he should."

The unwelcome voices insinuating themselves into his reverie made him shift his attention, but not without a final glance toward the woman who had inspired his fantasies.

Before Michael enters the argumentative ellipse at its more furious focus, we are determined to chronicle for him this creature's final victory...

It was like a halo, glowing red—the aura of humiliation she had so deftly occasioned. Calling up the final shard of dignity left him, he started to excuse himself. But he was not to be allowed even that. She beckoned toward the silver dish, her face displaying not the least trace of curiosity, turned her face from his and moved across the room.

"I agree with you both. David is quite right in believing that I would have a different view. And there is certainly no reason that you, John, should be able to see why I would." Michael was embarrassed by his own unaccountable petulance.

Encouraged by Michael's apparent support, Robinson sought to enlist him in the argument. "You had best come defend wisdom against the fury of the rhetorician."

Michael tried to soften his former expression of contempt by smiling as he said, "Modesty forbids."

Robinson and Springer paused long enough to honor the riposte, then continued their discussion without him.

16

"I'll certainly admit the philosopher to the higher echelons," Springer continued in the baiting manner he had been employing for the last several minutes, "but not the highest. A philosopher, after all, is on a par with the pedant. A pedant is one charged with the task of gathering information. He is an encyclopedia in the making. We are not concerned with the questions he asks, only with the data he provides—usually in his footnotes."

"But a philosopher is not a pedant, surely. Is he not, above all, concerned with questions and questioning."

Robinson had fallen into Springer's trap. Michael thought that he could construct the rest of the argument from here. But he wouldn't. These fellows needed no help in making fools of themselves.

Springer leaned toward Robinson with the slightest smirk and continued what Michael knew to be his well-rehearsed argument. "I said only that the philosopher and pedant are *on a par*. The pedant collects answers without concerning himself about the interest or importance of the questions to which they are relevant. Philosophers gather unanswered questions and proudly broadcast them to the unsophisticated—sowing barren seeds on rocky soil, acting all the while as if they are performing an invaluable service to culture at large."

Robinson was warming to the argument, and for the first time seemed to be taking the offensive. But it was, Michael knew, already too late. "Would you actually prefer the pedantic scholar who provides mere uninterpreted information? The philosopher's questions are certainly more interesting than any answer that might be given them. If we could say, for example, whether God exists or, if He does exist, exactly what His nature is; or if we could define true beauty once and for all, or say for certain what the good life is, then surely something would have been lost. We need these open questions to keep our thinking vital.

"Moreover, I'm not ashamed to say that the historian is philosophical to the extent that he remains sensitive to the dis-

tinctly different understandings of cause and law, of the nature
of institutions, of types of rule, of the meaning of happiness,
that have been presupposed in the different ages of the past.
As long as we do not attempt to say which of the many views is
true once and for all..."

"I don't doubt, David, that there are interesting questions
that ought to be protected from easy answers. But surely important questions ought to be made off-limits to all but a select few
who are prepared to think in a disciplined fashion. Were we
indiscriminately to hand questions over to philosophers, we
should never know whether they could be answered. The idea
that we should celebrate philosophers because they withhold
answers from the questions they consider is plainly silly."

"But you would not want to exclude all philosophers from
the community of the wise. That would surely seem a paradox.
Philosophy is the love of wisdom, after all."

"Ah, but, David, it is the philosophers who exclude themselves. It was Pythagoras who gave the name *philosophy* to the
discipline. 'We are lovers of wisdom,' he said. 'But we are not
wise. No one is wise save God Himself.' So it is with professional philosophers—they wish to exclude everyone from claims to
final wisdom so they are able to glory in 'thinking for its own
sake.' They needn't take the risk of claiming to possess the
truth. Their attitude is precisely that of the rejected suitor who
rushes to kill his beloved, shouting, 'If I can't have you, no one
shall!'"

"You seem to have a great deal more faith than I in the
answerability of our perennial questions."

"Yes, and there is a very good reason why I do. You see,
the answer to important questions is always, *ecce homo*. Jesus
said, 'I am the Way and the Truth.' The Buddha himself, not
his doctrines, was the true path. I grant you that the pedant
provides answers more interesting than any questions he himself might offer. I would even concede that the philosopher provides questions more interesting than the answers most of us
are prepared to give them. But the wise man is far more interesting than either his questions or his answers. Or better put:
he—or yes, as sometimes happens, *she*—is the union of question and answer."

17

"Then it is to the religious virtuosi that we should look for truth and certainty? How very odd!"

"No, no, no. Not at all. Definitely not. No, I was merely giving a few trite examples of those who claim to realize truth in their person and who have made that claim stick. It is the authoritative person who provides us with the signposts of truth. The philosopher as wisdom seeker glories in his inability to find truth. The wise man doesn't need to live by truths. He neither celebrates nor regrets the absence of immutable doctrines. He is sufficient in himself. And that sufficiency serves others as the source of their little truths."

"Who besides religious leaders could be said to have wisdom?"

"The wise emerge from among those who have suffered. That is why the young cannot be wise. Wisdom finds its nesting place in the cavities of regret. The young may be quick, even brilliant, but they may in no sense be wise. They are insufficiently decayed."

"Then the poets?"

"The poets, yes. Of course."

"But not the philosophers, and not the historians."

"Philosophers, no, for the reasons I have given. Historians, with all due respect, are also pedants. It is the artist whose greatness is born and nurtured from his creativity who is the source of wisdom. It is those who through fame achieve authority to whom we must look if we are to find wisdom."

Robinson smirked slightly as he spoke. "Ah, yes, I am beginning to see..."

Long overdue, Michael thought, but congratulations anyway.

"It is the authoritativeness born of fame that you hold to be the source of meaning and value. The historian would agree in part. Whoever, whatever is *important* determines truth. But how does your view differ from the might-makes-right doctrine?" Robinson must have anticipated Springer's answer, but as self-induced penance for his former dullness, he was allowing Springer to make his case.

"Politicians don't define values. Values are in the culture. They are the products of the poets, the makers. Rulers don't have authority; they possess only temporary, transitory power."

"Yes, but how do the poets and artists achieve authoritativeness? I have a suspicion that it is through the aegis of one of the classes of pedants that we ostensibly dismissed before. Is it by any chance the critic who determines the authoritativeness of the poet? Were I, for example, to ask for a list of the great poets, you would be glad, I'm sure, to provide one. If I challenged the list, you might tell me that, in all humility, you were better equipped than I to identify poetic genius. Your expertise authorizes you to make judgments that I couldn't rightfully make. So, it is the literary critic who decides which poets are the sources of truth, which poets are wise."

Springer seemed disappointed that Robinson had caught the train of his argument. "We must allow the experts, those who have read and studied the works, the right to make such decisions. Wouldn't you say?"

"I wouldn't say yes or no to that; I only wish to point out that you have admitted now what you seemed to deny before—namely, that it is pedants, in the guise of critics, who determine the nature and progress of culture. Critics serve as *éminences grises* for our poets and writers. They have approximately the same relationship to high culture as the rock star's manager has to popular culture. Both the critic and the manager know that their respective charges would not be successful on their own. How could the artist and critic avoid the temptation to feel contempt for each other?"

Springer was undisturbed by Robinson's claim. "Well, David, I must say that I am not responsible for the paradoxes that beset us. I neither revel in nor revile them. I merely consent to live by them. I should think that the relationship of the manager to the rock musician is one of mutual manipulation. But fame usually comes late for the poet, often after his death. So the critic and the poet are distanced in time. The mutual advantageousness is rendered impersonal.

"As for the pervasiveness of contempt as a cultural force, I confess sympathy with that view. Indeed, I am prepared to argue that something like contempt is the fundamental emotion underlying all human relationships."

"Surely, John, even your cynicism hasn't reached such profound depths."

"Cynicism? Hardly. Call it rather the benign acceptance of human limitations. Look at the evidence: Sexual relationships, friendships, even the presumed relation between God and man, all presuppose mutual insufficiency. Since contempt is merely the recognition of weakness and insufficiency in oneself, as well as in others, self-contempt and contempt for the other are the roots of every relationship. We can hide from contempt by pretending to sufficiency in ourselves. But that seldom works for long. It can only lead to *mauvais fois*."

"Purity of heart belongs to those who confess their contempt?" Robinson was shaking his head. Even Michael had not anticipated this turn.

"It follows. Of course, there are many quite subtle ways to manifest contempt. The finest flowers of civilization are expressions of the most subtle forms of contempt. Religious poetry is a perfect illustration. The Psalms are excellent examples of self-contempt and contempt for God. God needs to be worshipped. That is a need, however, we do not often acknowledge on His behalf, since to recognize this weakness in Him would be to challenge the basis of our dependency. The biblical poets recognized this need and advertised the honest contempt resulting from that recognition."

Robinson wasn't trying very hard to hide his own contempt for Springer's argument. "Yes, yes—we must be honest in our contempt."

Springer leaned back in his chair, blinked his eyes several times, as if to signal his waning interest in the conversation. His words were detached and pointedly condescending. "But we mustn't be altogether blatant. Pretense is often a valuable constraint on aberrant behavior. We shouldn't be too hard on hypocrites. Look at the sole nonhypocritical form of government—I refer of course to fascism. It is the most inhuman precisely because of the license candor permits."

18

Michael had marked every word of the discussion passively, inertly, without the slightest feeling of engagement. He could easily have played it back just as dispassionately. His self-serving pretentiousness aside, Springer made as much sense as anyone else. That ambition and contempt rule the world is no sillier a claim than that it is moved by sex and aggression.

But therein lies the problem. Once educated and cultured sensibilities are permitted to shape the course of a discussion, *any* argument seems as good as any other.

19

Michael had been looking out the office door, straining his neck and eyes without success. He thought to excuse himself, to go in search of her. Perhaps he would just walk to the door and see if she were still in the room. But he knew she was there. From the very beginning he had, or so he was persuaded, distinguished her fragrance from among all the other odors drifting into the office from outside. And yes, it was still as strong as ever, the musty piquancy broadcast from that pale, arrogant skin—dark promise promising nothing.

"Ah, Michael, you'll enjoy this." Pherendon was speaking. "You know Graham Andrews?"

"I know of him, of course, but we've never met."

"Good, then. You shall meet him first in London. He plans to attend your lectures."

"Really. I can't guarantee a sinologist will find much of interest in my remarks."

"Well, Graham is far more than an expert in Chinese grammar. He is, by his own description, a 'failed polymath,' though some of us wouldn't be able to say wherein the failure lies. In any case, he has told me that he has read your work and plans to 'hear you out.'"

"Hear me out? That has an ominous scent about it. But, It will be good to meet him, I'm sure."

Michael had long wanted to meet Andrews. He was by all accounts one of the last examples of the British scholar who had something intelligent to say on practically any matter.

"But you see, Michael, I was about to tell a story about Graham, and you will want to hear it. And you chaps," Pherendon had turned in the direction of Springer and Robinson, "can interrupt your refined banter for a moment to listen to some low-level gossip."

Robinson stopped talking in midsentence. It was a lame sentence whose completion would have added very little to its beginning. He turned his head toward Pherendon, raised his arm imperiously, and replied, "Of course. Let the gossip begin."

Left without a victim for the moment, Springer was forced

to attend as well, though by his expression and posture he was attempting to indicate that gossip was, of course, beneath him.

"I heard this on my last trip to London. It seems that when Graham retired from the University of London he simply walked away, leaving his office completely untouched. Apparently, he thought that if he didn't remove his things he would be permitted to hold on to his office. The trouble was that he left at the end of the term for a visiting position in Buenos Aires, with no plans to return for two years.

"Books, papers, and personal articles were left in the place that he had last used them. He is a bachelor, of course. There was no wife to clean up after him, and none of his friends was willing to accept the responsibility of disturbing his things. Further, no one even had the courage to contact Graham about the situation. After several weeks a visiting scholar of some distinction who had been promised the office finally had enough and demanded his due. The chairman then took it upon himself to resolve the situation. He asked a porter to pack up Graham's things, then persuaded three of his colleagues to shepherd the goods until Graham's return.

"One of the colleagues—it was she who told me this story—inherited a tea chest. For the longest time, so she vows, she resisted the temptation to look through the chest. Finally, she yielded. It seems that among several handwritten manuscripts in, she insisted, perfectly publishable form she found some notes on Chinese grammar, written on the backs of pages duplicated from a magazine of questionable stature. The pages were taken from an article on the female orgasm. The section on the 'G-Spot' had been underlined and annotated!"

The laughter that followed was the first sign of any real accord among the five since they had toasted silence. Springer started to speak. Michael wondered what he would have to add at this point. He would never know. Pherendon raised his hand as he continued to laugh, waving Springer's comment away. "Yes, but gentlemen, you see, there is more."

All faces turned again toward Pherendon, anticipating an even more salacious ending to the story.

"It seems that among the items left in his office on the occasion of his departure were Graham's slippers. No one is sure how, but the graduate students got hold of them. I can't but think that Graham would have been only too pleased with the manner of their disposition.

"There was an auction held at a local pub, you see. I am sure it was intended to be an innocent celebration of the man, but it got out of hand. Finally, to prevent what I am told could have easily turned into physical violence on the part of two of the bidders, the pair of slippers was split. One of them went to Graham's last graduate assistant—female, need I add. The other became the possession of a still nubile student of Chinese philosophy whose progress Graham had notoriously overseen for three years prior to his retirement.

"When the slippers were last seen they were marching deliberately in opposite directions, one held fast to the doubtless faithful bosom of the lovely graduate assistant, the other warmly nested in the purse of the degree candidate in Classical Chinese Philosophical Texts."

20

"I read your Œdipus poem, Alfred. It was wonderful. I suppose I shouldn't have been in the least surprised that your poetry was so solid since, as you know, one of the greatest of our American poets was an insurance company executive."

As if by way of justifying the comparison, Pherendon blushed with ruddy, twinkling delight, leading Michael to recall a line from his favorite Wallace Stevens poem:

> Let the lamp affix its beam.
> The only emperor is the emperor of ice-cream.

Michael's comment had caused Springer to pause in midsentence, long enough to clear his throat in a mildly exaggerated manner, roll his eyes over to Michael and back, indicating that he had recognized the allusion to Stevens. Only then did he complete his sentence.

"...facts are mobile, thought is hard; thought is bunched and chunky, events are fluid, dissolving. I've cleaned up the prose a bit, Dewey was a notoriously *bad* writer, but the point is well taken. The philosopher is here condemned out of his own mouth. The language of facts and of events, the language of the real world, is not the language of the thinker but of the poet."

"And the story teller," Robinson added, hoping in this instance to leave room among the elect for the historian.

"Of course," Springer replied dismissively, denying by his tone what his words seem to concede.

"Poetry, is it, Alfie? Why didn't you ever tell me?" A–K was annoyed that Michael knew something about Pherendon that he did not. "Tell me about this poem."

"The poet defers to his reader," Pherendon said, nodding toward Michael. He was obviously anxious to discover what Michael thought of his work. "Actually, A–K, I was planning to give you a copy of my poems, as well. It will be in your hands before you leave the city. But I must say I never knew of your interest in poetry."

"It's Mike. He brings out the finer part of my nature. Besides, Alfie, you know that I'm interested in anything you do. Now, *somebody* tell me about this poem."

Michael thought he was expected to say something now, so he began, "It's a parody but, I suspect, quite seriously intended." Pherendon leaned back in his chair, striking what seemed to be meant as a casual pose, but Michael noted how stiffly he was sitting. He has a great deal invested in his poetry, Michael thought. A curious fellow.

Michael continued, shifting his ground slightly, aware now that he had to be cautious. "One of the truisms of contemporary criticism..." Michael didn't pause or glance toward Springer, he didn't need to. He could hear the slight hitch in Springer's sentence and knew that it had been accompanied by a sidewise mini-stare occasioned by the word *criticism*. "is that it is quite difficult, if not impossible, to be creative in a period in which all of the recognizable styles of thought have been repeatedly rehearsed. All of the seeds have been sown, have sprouted and been harvested. The land lies fallow.

"And without seeds, we must be content with scraps. Cultural products are no longer sown, they are..." Michael made a stitching motion with his hand, "*sewn.*" Works of art are patch-works made of cultural refuse scrounged by the artist or arti-san. Creativity is found not in the character of the collected bits but in the idiosyncratic manner one goes about juxtaposing the various leavings gathered from the refuse bins of the past.

"What Alfred has done in his poetry, at least in his Œdi-pus poem...this is the way I read the poem...is to make a patchwork quilt that parodies itself and its subject at the same time. And because of the centrality of the myth in our cultural self-understanding, the poem manages to be a critique of our culture as well."

Michael continued in this manner for some time, occasion-ally glancing outside, seeing only party faces, becoming anx-ious that he might never see *her* face again. He once looked over at Springer, whom he knew had been monitoring his words, waiting for a chance to correct this or that point in Michael's presentation or to offer a withering aside which would suitably punish him for poaching upon the critic's land. On seeing Springer's discomfited posture and expression, how-ever, he realized that moment would never come.

21

A–K's arms had been draped over the sides of his chair, now they suddenly flapped up and down in apparent agitation. "Wait a minute. I haven't read this poem, but I'll wager that Alfie would be quite surprised to discover that he has done so much in so few lines. I have never known Michael to comment upon any sub-ject—from cabbages to...sealing wax—that didn't have general cultural import. What say, Alfie? Did you write a poem, or did you write an essay on the rise and fall of Western culture?"

Pherendon seemed amused by A–K's frustration. "A bit of both, I think. And though I confess I could not myself have characterized the poem so trenchantly, I am pleased to defer to my critic's interpretation."

Michael couldn't tell whether Pherendon's response to A–K was ironic. He begin to think that Pherendon might be sympathetic with A–K's belief that he had read too much into the poem. "I did wonder, Alfred, just how seriously you intended to forward the thesis of your poem. Do you actually believe that our culture is homosexual at its ground?"

"Oh, yes, indeed. In the broader and more fundamental sense of the word *homosexual*, yes. Certainly Plato is our teacher in this matter. He has Socrates coming home 'hot and horny' from the war, casting lustful glances at the thigh of young Charmides, then discoursing at some length upon the meaning of love in, shall we say, distinctly gay terms. Heterosexual love is sullied by the extraneous function of procreation. Only love between free and equal members of the same sex can be disinterested and therefore pure."

"That's the old 'women for procreation; boys for pleasure' line," A–K said, not hiding his disgust.

"And where do you suppose we got that line, Peter? It is our Platonic heritage."

"But Platonic love is nonsexual. Come on Michael. *Say* something." A–K was pleading for support.

"You gentlemen are doing just fine without me." Michael had been momentarily distracted by Robinson and Springer who were still acting under the illusion that they were adding to the store of human knowledge.

Springer was up: "Rousseau was not fooled. 'Where is the philosopher,' he said, 'who would not deceive mankind for his own glory?' But it is the Basque Miguel de Unamuno who must be awarded first honors for his, I believe insufficiently prized, bon mot—'Philosophy is wont not infrequently to convert itself into a kind of spiritual pimping.'" Springer's smile was more pronounced on the right side of his face—the side angled toward Michael.

"Well, Alfie, you wouldn't discount the value of romance. Love poetry was written to, for, and about women and men. Look at Dante and Beatrice, Petrarch and Laura...or at a more delectably mundane level, Boccacio and his 'Fiametta.'"

"I'm not surprised to discover, Peter, that you are a great deal more familiar with poetry than you are given to confess. But, see here. It's so very simple. The poetry of which you speak was all written with men in mind. It is, after all, men who set the standards both for passion and for the poetry that expresses it. Women are merely occasions for the writing of such poems.

"Thomas Hobbes was more acute in his understanding of the ways of things than was Freud (Michael recalled Rinpoche's having made the same point). It is not sexual desire per se, but the desire for fame that is fundamental. It is this that shapes culture and society. Freud's view was quite plebian, no more accurate than the ideas of Karl Marx, another thinker who pandered to the masses. Hobbes, a Tory elitist, understood the movement of the world much better.

"Cultural products, such as art objects, poetry, scientific theories, are not born of repression and sublimation. It is quite the reverse. Sexuality is a substitute gratification for those who are unable or unwilling to make the sacrifice that fame requires. Order, control, and stability are the primary needs of the crowd. Those responsible for realizing and maintaining stability will realize fame as well. They will set the standards for our politics and culture, for our passion, and for poetry."

"I don't hear you arguing for homosexuality, Alfie, but for asceticism, for nonsexuality. It is the renunciation of sex that you seem to prefer."

"Not so. Understand me, Peter. It is certainly not explicit sexuality that best characterizes things homosexual. Culture is what *men* decide it is. Love between men and women is shaped by a male consensus as to what it should be. The sexual competence of a man is measured by standards set by that consensus. So even the act of strictly heterosexual intercourse must be included in this homosexual interpretation. We are all concerned about 'what the fellows would say'. The so-called heterosexual act is performed—*by both parties, mind you*—as if the guys were watching. Technical competence in the bedroom arises out of the same competition among males that defines the rest of our cultural activity. In any case, it is success that we desire—and the fame that success promises."

"I won't say that I am persuaded by your argument, only that I am relieved that it takes the shape that it does. If by homosexuality you merely mean the sort of male bonding about which anthropologists have had so much to say, I can't say I am much disturbed by your views."

"Perhaps I am not being altogether clear, Peter. I am saying that sexuality itself is ancillary to the more fundamental desire for fame. Our aim is to look good in the eyes of our peers. Now, until things change, these peers are *male*. Those of us who engage in heterosexual activity are in effect using the female as a medium of expression of an act for which ultimately we are seeking male approval. What is really going on in perfumed boudoirs all across the planet is *between men*. And those goings on, vicarious and by proxy, are what eroticism is all about. That surely is *homosexuality*.

"We are left with the disconcerting implication that explicit homosexuality is but a more direct and honest expression of the priority of the masculine in the determination of cultural values."

22

Michael thought to add a final remark to the concluding debate but was momentarily stayed by the appearance just outside the office door of the deliciously upholstered flesh he coveted so. To his infinite relief she was alone. She had moved toward the wall nearest the entrance to the office and was staring at a painting Michael had noticed when he had first entered the lounge. It was Turner's *Snowstorm*. He had often stood before the original, housed now in the new wing of the Tate Gallery in London.

He might have guessed that she would be enthralled by Turner as well. And unquestionably, she would love John Ruskin, Turner's greatest champion and most sensitive critic. The thought of Ruskin gave Michael pause, for he suddenly realized that this creature, delicate and pale, her hair drawn back tightly against her head, resembled—no, more than that, was a replica of the unattainable Rose La Touche whom Ruskin had loved from their first encounter. His love, and the resonating love of Rose for him, continued to intensify, to diffuse throughout his spirit and hers, as Turner's light diffused throughout his canvasses, until dementia canceled her life and took Ruskin's sanity as well, bringing both of them nearer to their promised meeting (these are Rose's words) "face to face in that kingdom where love will be perfected."

Ruskin had believed Rose unattainable. And his genius, as is all genius, was nourished by this self-deception. True enough, Rose did seem to wear that veil of 'blissful autonomy' which, according to Proust, serves to mask every object capable of eliciting desire. But Rose La Touche was not unattainable; she was simply unattained. She might have been won had not Ruskin so badly needed an other to struggle for, to strive on behalf of, to serve as an occasion for his creative impulse. It was this that kept them apart. Their separation was neither by Rose's choice nor by the chance of her sad death.

23

Pherendon raised his hand and rose from his chair. "Gentlemen, this is unquestionably more amusing than what must be going on outside, but it is my duty to insure that Michael is available to all our guests, so I should like to suggest, if I may, that we remove ourselves to the lounge and perform our respective duties. Shall we?"

The conversations had begun to slacken, so there was little reticence to comply with Pherendon's suggestion. Springer and Robinson had moved from their discussion of the failings of philosophy and were in the midst of a consideration of unfinished masterpieces. These were not works left incomplete by their creators, but books which few (if any) readers had ever completely read. Professional scholars and editors aside, there were, the two agreed, many classic works which, for a variety of reasons, could not be read to the very end.

Robinson claimed "anything by George Eliot" to be uncompletable. Michael agreed. After some thirty pages or so of indifferent foreplay, *The Mill on the Floss* had sat virginal upon his shelves for years. The books of some other authors were simply too long to complete. Robinson mentioned *Clarissa*.

Just prior to Pherendon's invitation to vacate the office, Springer made what Michael thought to be his first intelligent remark—namely, that the greatest works of fiction belonged to a special subsection of the class of uncompleted books. These were books too intense to be encompassed in their entirety. He had instanced Canetti's *Die Blendung*. "A brilliant book.... Absolutely without peer.... But a work of total insanity.... Not a normal character or situation in its pages—or so one must surmise, judging of the whole from a part. One is so disoriented by the act of reading that it would be impossible for any sensitive reader to complete the work without losing his hold on the consensual world. Two-thirds, I should say, is the best any sane man could accomplish."

24

Immediately upon reentering the lounge Michael began to search for Rose. She was nowhere to be seen. He scanned the room several times in the course of the evening, but he never saw her again. He didn't really want to meet her, or to talk with her. All he wanted was some assurance of her continued presence, some stronger evidence that she was (that silly word again) "real."

25

Michael was tossed from one conversation to the next for the rest of the very long evening. Other parties may trade upon power and celebrity; here the currency was argumentative skill. And among academics, it is not sufficient to have a talent for witty repartee, sardonic asides, hyperbolic flattery, or withering insults—though these certainly have their place. The key to success at events such as this is dialectical prowess.

He was more at home than he wished to be. From the beginning he understood that in the kingdom of the witless, that is to say, among these smug-cum-silly party props recruited from the list of compulsive readers of the *New York Review of Books*, even a half-wit might reign.

For these were creatures who merely by virtue of living in Manhattan, or on Long G'Island, presumed themselves definers of the intellectual atmosphere of the nation. Almost all had, however, long ago traded any true sensitivities for the oily arts of cultural commentary.

"Ah, you live in Texas. It must be difficult to stay in touch."

"In touch with...?"

"I don't know what I would do without the...intensity of the city."

"You mean...?"

"The plays, the concerts...the theater."

Michael sighed inwardly...then aloud. "I see. Of course. Yes. Access to cultural digests is doubtless a real convenience for those who haven't the inclination to experience culture first hand."

Even more painful was the conversation with the author of a latest best-selling novel, a Gregory Selmon, whose work had been compared (in his publisher's copy) with Nabokov. Michael had read this "eerie, disturbing phantasmagoria" (his publisher's words again), skipping pages shamelessly after the first hundred. The work began with an awful pun (the title *Attic Intrigues* referred to the perverse activities of a minor faction of Greek gods manipulating the fictional fates of some of the classical heroes) and sunk rapidly from the attic to the subterranean basements of bad prose.

There were some good moments, as well. He knew that A–K and Pherendon would be his friends. He was especially pleased when A–K told him that he planned to attend his lectures ("At least one, Mike, I promise.... I wouldn't miss it.").

And there had been Rose...

26

Michael told Pherendon he preferred to walk the five or six blocks back to the hotel. Armed with Pherendon's caution about the hazards of late night Manhattan, he made his final exit.

The walk seemed interminable. The street stretched thin before him, causing the buildings to recede. Though he was walking quite rapidly, and soon began to increase his pace, he seemed not to be moving at all. The April air was pasty thick with chill and damp. The stars were his only comfort. Not that he could see them through the smog and city lights; he couldn't see a single one. But he knew they were there, his desert stars—warm, uncountable.

27

Less than twenty minutes after arriving at his hotel, Michael was asleep. But soon he was awakened by an awful throbbing in his jaw. It had taken several excruciating seconds lying in bed before he was able to recognize the pain as that of a toothache. He got up and fumbled his way across the unfamiliar room. Upon reaching the bathroom, he turned on the light and began to examine his open mouth in the mirror. He was shocked and offended by what he saw: a silvery crescent band stretching from one side of his mouth to the other. He moved his fingers over his teeth and gums on the right side of his mouth but was unable to decide which of two teeth was broadcasting the alarm.

Puzzled, he rested both hands on the tiled surface of the basin and began to give some thought as to how this could possibly have come about. His checkups of late had been...how long since his last visit to a dentist? He was remembering now. Almost all of the damage had taken place when he was an adolescent. He had neglected his teeth. In high school he had to have two back teeth pulled and since had, shamefully, worn a bridge. But he had thought the other teeth sound. Not so. There was hardly an unretouched tooth in his head.

Michael had almost forgotten the pain. He was absorbed by his reflections concerning how he might avoid a broader, deeper ache. He began to calculate his life expectancy. Since his father had died at eighty-nine and his mother was still living at eighty-one, he thought he would probably live at least into his early eighties. He performed the subtraction and realized that he had some thirty-five or forty years left with—or without—these teeth. He looked again at the silvered sepulcher opened before him. He shook his head.

The sudden dull-sick panic began at his feet and rushed up to his head gaining momentum along the way. He felt dizzy. Jesus! God! Even though he had not yet recognized the cause of this feeling, he knew that it was a *universal* sensation, one that announced a rite of passage as powerful as the one which relieved him from that aching pubescent itch that, no more certainly than this emotion, belonged both to him and to everyone.

This feeling lacked the mystery of the first. Michael had lived long enough to have heard it spoken of, read the various poetic commentaries which are meant to provide us opportunities to rehearse it in advance of its first and final assault. But how are we to be truly prepared by so indirect a revelation of such a forceful fact?

He had been depressed to think that he would lose his teeth. But his depression had been occasioned by the thought of outliving his teeth. Once he realized this, Michael was led to the only fact worth counting: I will probably outlast my teeth...but not by much. *I am going to die*! He was feeling sick. Meanwhile, his tooth, having served so well its function as Harbinger of Death, no longer seemed inclined to ache.

Michael reflected how ironic it was that he had spent so much of his energies developing complex strategies to defend himself against death's agonies—those dying in the hospital...Mr. Grodjah...the death...[the thought of Karla and Company almost made its way to consciousness, but was forcefully repressed] only to be caught unaware by a moribund tooth. For all the sadness of those deaths, however, they were different. Those deaths were not "My Death." The difference between "My Death" and the deaths of others is so great that there should be different words for these distinct phenomena.

Just before he fell into this new sleep, his first sleep infected by the sense of his own mortality, a sleep that he realized he was obliged to enter at least in part as a rehearsal for the longer, longest sleep, he let the tears seep from his eyes and blinked to scatter and to multiply them. Tomorrow would begin another life, one which he knew must yield itself to the color and the odor, the humming, buzzing sounds of death.

As do almost all reveries that immediately precede sleep, Michael's final thoughts had the character of clichéd bathos: Must mortality enervate the passions, mock desire, render all efforts frenetic and desperate? Where heretofore I have measured my life in seconds and minutes—the narrow dimensions of intensity—will I now be forced to accept the thinning calendar as the gauge, the measuring rod of all my endeavors? How many millions before and after had, would ask these questions? How many...

Apart from these unforgivable histrionics of the no longer

immortal Michael (the narration of which, for obvious reasons, will be abbreviated), there was justification for the thrill he felt. This would be a precious, wonderous sleep.

After, all would be changed.

28

Michael awakened early. Only while brushing his teeth did he recall his toothache of the night before. There was no pain now, at least none from his tooth. There was, however, a slight ache remaining from his initiation into the Realm of Mortals. But he was surprisingly sanguine about that pain, and its cause. He realized that it would be chronic and that he must learn to suffer it with dignity.

He finished dressing. There were more than two hours before his 9:10 train to New Haven. He decided to skip breakfast and take a walk.

Other travelers search out the scenic and sacred places of Europe, the Orient, and the Americas. Michael preferred pilgrimages to what he thought of as Irony Spots. These, though less acclaimed, and indeed often unnoticed by all but the most discerning, offer at least as much solace and inspiration. Though he had encountered irony spots all over the world, his favorite was discovered in his own city. In one of the seedier areas of his hometown, in the window of a used magazine shop, he had seen a sign drawn in dark pencil on an irregularly shaped piece of corrugated cardboard. To the truly discerning the message contained both an invitation and a warning:

TATTOOS UPSTAIRES

29

He was on his way to Bryant Park, the postage stamp sized park squeezed behind the New York Public Library. Since Bryant Park provides the locus of the first Irony Spot he had ever catalogued, this pilgrimage was a special one.

Michael discovered the essence of the poet's ruse when, on his first trip to New York City, he had come upon the statue of William Cullen Bryant in the park that bore his name. The statue was a meeting place for the druggies and gays. Behind W.C.'s back, in the space between the statue and the hedges that border the library, some of the raunchiest forms of transient sex were performed. But these were mere road-show renditions of the real productions that paraded themselves before Bryant's sculpted gaze: The poet's face was directed toward the sleaziest part of Forty-second Street with shops, arcades, and parlors smelling of spent semen, echoing the timid whimpers of franchised lust. On the base of the statue these words were inscribed, authorized no doubt by a savant with a dry wit and no great love for W.C.:

Yet let no empty gust of passion
find an utterance in thy lay

A blast that whirls the dust
along the howling street and dies away

But feelings of calm power and
mighty sweep

Like currents journey through
the windless deep

Myth, meter, and metaphor are the so-called poet's tools for attempting to fill their lays with substance and permanence, to avoid the empty gusts of passion of simply getting laid. The rhythms of poetry are artificial echoes of the sexual act. Doesn't this belie any intimate connection between poetry and love? Love knows nothing of rhythms and measures. Rhythms are purely sexual. Poetry, far from being the expression of our more refined sensibilities, is little else than metered lust.

Mythic themes are celebrated in the ritualistic repetitions preserved by meter. Metaphors relieve the tedium of repetition. But it is repetition above all that we seek. (Rocking chairs are for the very old and the very young—those nearest the termini of existence. Anyone else in a rocking chair looks out of place.) Meter is the substance of poetry so-called. Rhythm is everything. It is the promise of return, the security of sameness, the sham of permanence. It is the seductive stability of the façade we pray will hide us from the truth: There is no permanence, no true repetition—whatever truly is occurs but once.

Reality is unknowable not because our intellects are finite, or because we exercise our wills perversely and so judge falsely, or because the things-in-themselves are always masked by appearances. Reality cannot be known because it is not the sort of thing that knowing is meant to reach. We know things that persist. So much the worse for knowledge.

Aristotle (*solid* Aristotle) claimed that science considers "what occurs always or for the most part." When as a young man Michael had read this, he had asked himself, "Who or what considers that which occurs sometimes or perhaps but once? He had then immediately responded: the poets. But when he realized how meter dominates poetry, he knew that the poet is simply a slightly maudlin grammarian. Meter, the soul's peculiar syntax, is but the pale remembrance of the rhythms of the sexual encounter. Poetry is Epimethean, an afterthought.

And what does it all come to if the best a poet can do is to mock his own most intense sentiments? One might say that Bryant is receiving his just deserts. His punishment is to have some of the worser of his lines carved on the base of his effigy and to see them everlastingly mocked by his environs. So William Cullen Bryant is sitting surrogate for all poets, his fated vigilance making him an involuntary witness to the transience of passion, the very lesson his poetry was meant to discredit: Passion comes only in gusts and the gusts (like the *dharmas*) are always empty. Bryant does not deserve his fate because he was a bad poet, but simply because he, like almost all who call themselves poets, sought to participate in the desperate actions of the artificer.

Michael's first poetry teacher had been the statue of William Cullen Bryant. His second was one of the living immortals. Aldous Huxley, hardly a poet in the narrower sense but an effective teacher of poetics nonetheless, once came to Northwestern University to speak. Michael had attended. Huxley began his presentation with a brief, perfunctory apology. He had, he said, brought along the wrong talk and would be unable to give the requested address. He would instead read his alternative paper. Michael had felt insulted. A man of Huxley's intelligence and articulation could have spoken on the announced theme. But he was not a speaker, not a teacher— neither a philosopher nor a rhetorician. He was (why didn't he just confess it?) only a writer. Overwrought, polished, perfected, he sought the most precise term, the most appropriate metaphor, the finely turned, eminently quotable phrase. Michael had come to hear words precious not by virtue of their excruciatingly disciplined wroughtness but by their uniquely occasional character. He wanted words in passing. He wanted ephemera. Huxley owned only immortal words.

Writers suffer the *déformation professionnelle* of the poets; they simply do not have the means to touch the ephemeral; at their best they can only celebrate the irony of its claim upon the substantial. The ironists, those less polite and precious than Huxley, have very nearly escaped the poet's dilemma, but not quite. The greatest hope of the ironists is to catch their readers (their *readers*—they too are *writers*) in the tragicomic bind. If one takes the ironist seriously, he laughs. If one smiles knowingly at the ironic character of a statement, the ironist clucks his tongue and shakes his head in mock indication of the insensitivity of such a response. The mask of irony is the only true mask. It can be tragic to the comic and comedic on the face of the tragic sense.

30

Michael was sitting in the garden of his former Yale mentor, now retired, and his wife. They were having tea and home-made cakes, much as he remembered having many times over the years since taking his degree. As a student he was never entertained by Roger Clifford, except for one anxious luncheon taken at Timothy Dwight College, ten shortening days before his dissertation deadline. ("There is no reason why you can't make those few changes in time, Michael. It will likely come together. There is enough time to finish. Not enough time for panic, I'd say, but sufficient time for the work.") ("But I thought I was done...I...") ("You will be done. The changes are straightforward.") ("But, I had understood...") ("The apple com-pote is quite refreshing, Michael, even better than usual.")

He was the kindest of men, and the most exacting—a com-bination that makes genuine teachers. And he was exceptional in another significant way: Contrary to most of the philosophy faculty at Yale who sought to foster the student's ability to own and express his or her *v-yooze*, Clifford supported the develop-ment of clarity and cogency in thinking above all else.

Though Michael hadn't appreciated this as a student, Clif-ford possessed the rarest of professorial qualities: He spoke lit-tle. In the seminars Clifford conducted there would often be long, painful periods of silence which he and his fellow stu-dents would make every effort to fill with comments that at least approximated the level of articulation of which they knew Clifford was capable. They could expect neither praise nor con-demnation for their efforts. Clifford would never say, "very good" or "interesting point" or even "I think you have missed the mark here." No smile or frown or gesture of any kind would ever indicate what judgment, if any, he might be making.

Michael recalled the story of Clifford's attendance, as one of only twenty-five invited participants, at an International Seminar on Value Theory. Because of his reputation and the respect he had won at the sessions, he was, without his advance knowledge, offered the honor of bringing the proceed-ings to a close. At the end of the three-day meeting, the chairman had said, "Now I would like to provide Professor Roger Clifford the opportunity to make the concluding remarks of this symposium." Clifford, it is said, straightened the papers in front of him, rose from his seat and said, "Thank you, Professor Grieves. Colleagues, I really haven't anything to say." And took his seat.

Sitting opposite this professor who had withered before his periodic gaze, Michael felt more profoundly than usual the ritual shame that every student feels when in the presence of his teacher. Michael knew that he was neither as exacting nor as kind as his mentor. Though his sardonic use of the postures and gestures of irony fell far short of a killing cynicism, they precluded real gentleness with his students. Moreover, he had learned too well the need to have *v-yooze*. And he shared his *v-yooze* with his students in such an enthusiastic manner as to make it particularly difficult for them to have any *v-yooze* of their own.

"A credible approach to a very difficult problem, Michael. Your lectures will be worthwhile. I wish I could attend them."

Michael noted with some pain that the word had been *credible* and not *plausible*. He knew all too well how precisely Clifford used language. He wondered why after all these years he was still waiting for some unqualified praise from this man, and why he was so depressed to know that in a very little while he would be leaving without it.

31

Michael walked about the campus, making several turns for no other reason than to avoid passing in sight of the no longer mysterious structure whose wasted secret he now knew. He was remembering the overstuffed leather chairs in the college lounges and the comfortable, overstuffed minds, masters of their overstocked bookshelves. The scholars here had *arrived*. These annotated, nonrenewable minds seldom raided libraries for fresh knowledge. They consulted books now mainly to verify this or that incompletely remembered point. Nevertheless, fresh minds were consistently produced in this place.

Michael thought of a Ch'an Buddhist *kung-an*, or *koan*, he had encountered long after leaving this institution. The master asks his disciple, "What is the spirit of the Ch'ing Liang Monastery?" Unlike most *koans*, this puzzle has an answer: "When you go to other places, just say that you are on your way to Ch'ing Liang."

Looking now at the familiar buildings, hedged by the greenest of grasses in their first proud advertisements of spring, Michael understood that, by some unavoidable irony, the spirit of this place could not reside here, among those who *had arrived*. That spirit can exist only in those outside the gates of Ch'ing Liang, those *on their way*.

32

He had wandered away from the campus toward a residential area just on the boundaries of the Yale Divinity School. He had suddenly developed a desire to see the neighborhood movie house he had attended at least once a week while a graduate student, usually late on Friday evenings. The films alternated between low-budget horror films and even lower-budget semi-soft pornography. One week he might see Godzilla slogging about Tokyo harbor in a death struggle with the Smog Monster, the next week he would witness Bayou belles romping and frolicking with sex-starved escapees from the local chain gang.

These films would purge him and give him balance after a week of exercising the arts of abstract speculation. It was essential that the films be really bad. They had to have incredible (not just implausible) plots, incompetent actors, and production values approaching zero. After a week of thinking about the importance of thinking, Michael would feed his impoverished spirit with fantastic improbabilities and visions of the purest Bad Sex. Thus was he saved from the occupational hazard of the student of philosophy—Death by Abstraction.

33

As he approached the location of the theatre, he saw a vacant lot, with wild grass growing among the scattered brick and stucco ruins of what once had been the Lawrence Cinema. He paused at the edge of the lot, scanning the remains of the ruined monument. There was hardly enough material to work with, but supplemented by brick-and-plaster memories of this treasured edifice, Michael set about rebuilding the old movie house. Actually, he erected only a single wall, the back one, on which the screen had been mounted.

Michael checked his watch—there was still plenty of time before his train. Feeling only slightly silly, he positioned himself in such a manner as to focus upon the precise center of the imagined wall. He felt compelled to maintain his posture without knowing why.

Had he access to his deepest imaginings he would have realized that he had begun to send a chaos of images beaming forth toward the screening wall. These unrecollected memories formed a montage of real-life horrors and bad sex.

The ecstatic event of total recall occurs not only in the face of death but while confronting culmination of any kind. This is so since life has the syntax of a German sentence. The verb comes at the end. When one confronts death, or severe crisis, a search is initiated for the meaning of the convoluted life-sentence. One scans the jumble of nouns and adjectives and prepositions and adverbial phrases, subordinate clauses, dangling modifiers, and sadly split infinitives until the meaning-bestowing verb is found.

Michael had almost drowned once, off the coast of the Yucatan peninsula. At the instant of euphoria, the gateway to death, he had seen his life in its entirety, much as it was being projected now on this fast-fading screen for his blind eyes.

Life is tentative, or ought to be, until its very end. Few of us can directly experience endings, summings up, so we can never know the meaning of our lives. It is, of course, possible to take penultimate inventories (provided one has the unenviable talent for sending his experiences on a forced march past the inner eye).

On this occasion, however, Michael is unaware that he has become a blind witness to the *mélange* of his life, that he is taking inventory of the Vast Indifference of his inner world, the Blessed Multifariousness of his convoluted experiences. So he doesn't understand why he continues to stand fixed, staring at the image of a wall, feeling calmer than he should feel, happier, more contented. He doesn't in the least understand why he has no desire to move a single step in any direction.

VII

A Reluctant Avatar

1

Michael was walking into the main entrance of University College, London. He was somewhat skeptical. Having lived in London before, he knew that granting special favors to Americans was not a high priority among the British. Pherendon's call might well have been wasted. The porter, however, could not have been more congenial or more eager to undertake his special duties.

"Just this way, Dr. Evers. Professor Andrews called this morning."

He was surprised to hear Andrews's name. Pherendon must have contacted him. This was getting complicated. He was escorted down a hallway just off the main entrance and through a door opening to a set of narrow stairs. "The lift is under repair, I'm afraid. But there won't be many steps."

The porter was quite old. "You know" (he was breathing hard already), "the good gentleman...has...seen better days." It was "the good gentleman" Michael had come to see.

At the top of the stairs they turned left. The porter began to sift methodically through his keys, arriving at the correct key and the right door at the same time. "This is just temporary. We'll have him back in public soon enough. But, like I say, he needs a bit of work."

The porter opened the door with the subdued formality which serves the British as a substitute for reverence. The room was dark. Several seconds passed before Michael could see him. He was seated, dressed in formal attire, holding a walking stick, just as he remembered from several photographs he had seen over the years.

"How much time do you require, sir?"

"Oh, not long. Just a few minutes. I hope I am not being too much trouble."

"Not a bit of it. You stay as long as you wish. I have to go downstairs. I'll come up directly to see about you."

"Of course. I'll be ready when you return."

The porter took special pains to close the heavy door quietly. Michael was left standing alone in front of the glass case. "Hello, Jeremy." His words sounded louder than he had intended. "I've wanted to meet you for some time, you know."

Michael's eyes searched the shelf just above Jeremy Bentham's head. He was looking for a smallish black box which was supposed to contain the brain. He tried to anticipate the dimensions of the box, remembering that we almost always overestimate the size of internal organs—the heart, the kidneys, the bladder, the ovaries. Intestines are impressively *long*, of course. But only the liver and pancreas are larger than one might expect. Even the skull, stripped of its skin and muscle, seems quite small.

Michael couldn't find the box. He wondered what shape its contents were in. The brain of Albert Einstein, preserved at Princeton, was still in good condition. However, Bentham's equally prodigious graying matter was at least a hundred years older and could well be little more than gelatinous pulp or viscous ooze.

Bentham, a truly important nineteenth-century philosopher, was the first (and presumedly last) benefactor of certainly the oddest of his many proposals for social reform. Bentham had urged the preservation of the bodies of the "best" and "worst" examples of humanity to serve as positive and negative behavioral reinforcements. He had also suggested that individuals might wish to save the bodies of their deceased relatives, using them in place of trees or shrubs to line the driveway of the family estate.

Every attempt had been made to preserve the body of the University of London's most famous benefactor as per the explicit conditions of his will. Nevertheless, he *was* in rather bad shape. His head, which had lasted less than ten years, had been replaced by the discoloring wax substitute that now stared at Michael with the mocking indulgence he had come to expect from every Englishman.

Of course, the caretakers of these particular remains meant to preserve more than Bentham's mummy. They were acting in defense of the solemn right of every English gentleman to his peculiar idiosyncrasies.

2

No one questions that the British are the least spiritual people on the surface of the planet. Indeed, though Bentham was but one of a rather distinguished company of British citizens whose quest for immortality was decidedly this-worldly, the intransigent secularity of the nation was summed by the iconic presence of this mounted curiosity.

The skewed tradition Bentham represents was foreshadowed by Francis Bacon in the sixteenth century who experimented with the preservation of flesh by stuffing a chicken with snow. The experiment cost Bacon his life (he caught pneumonia and was dispatched posthaste), and as no one thought to stuff him with snow, he was lost to us.

A century later, Bishop George Berkeley, an Irishman, a gentleman of some philosophical and ecclesiastical importance, wrote a rather popular work entitled, *A Chain of Philosophical Reflexions and Inquiries concerning the Virtues of Tar-Water, and divers other Subjects connected together and arising from one another*. The Bishop's will confirmed his unqualified faith in the rejuvenating power of this gummy elixir, for in it he directed that upon his *apparent* demise no attempt at burial should be made until positive signs of putrefaction were evident. Berkeley fully expected that the doses of tar-water he had consumed over the years would afford him a prompter resurrection than otherwise might be expected.

By all accounts this was not so.

There are, of course, notable exceptions among the British to the secular quest for immortality. The corpulent Scotsman, David Hume, was cursed with ulcerative colitis which finally resulted in a gangrenous bowel. He actually began to rot before his death and suffered the vile fate of shitting himself away.

On the whole Bentham had managed the best of the lot.

3

Michael heard the porter approaching and stepped out into the hall to meet him.

"Yes, sir. Done, are you?"

"Yes, thank you. I hope I didn't interrupt your schedule."

"Not at all, sir. Not at all."

He was glad to get outside. The sun had removed its smudge-gray mask. It was a sunny April day. Michael's first breath of air tasted cold at the center, but seary hot on the surface, like a dish of Baked Alaska. He felt nervous, unsettled, vaguely apprehensive. He trusted the sun to make that feeling disappear. While visiting Bentham's corpse he had begun to feel giddy and mildly nauseous. His growing anxiety enveloped him like an ellipse with two distinct foci. Its other focus lay some several hundred yards away.

He moved through the revolving doors of the British Museum, automatically turned to his left and proceeded up the stairs. He was still feeling dizzy. Nothing seemed to have changed. But then why should it? The past, at least that portion of it displayed in a museum, certainly ought to be settled.

He closed his eyes for an instant, taking a snapshot of his memory. He was very near...*There*. As so often before, he avoided her face for a few moments. His eyes averted, he allowed the image to form. The image that drifted outward from the the time-layered darkness just behind his eyes was that he had last encountered at Tilopa, superimposed upon the painted face he now saw, and upon all of the remembered faces from years before.

48971-2   Mummy and coffin of an unnamed priestess
Thebes, XXIst Dynasty, about 1050 B.C.

He was saddened, as always. For he well knew that his priestess was not really without a name.

4

As he retraced his path up Malet Street past the British Museum, Michael began to look about for a taxi. He was rapidly surrendering to the sardonic, depressed humor against which he had been struggling since first catching Bentham's waxen eye. His mood was brought on by a growing sense of the omnipresence of decay—the ubiquity of rot.

He could certainly find no comfort in his present ambience. Everywhere about him he saw only decaying buildings and monuments decked with scaffolding. During his lengthy walks about the city he had often passed churches and cathedrals, monuments and mansions, office buildings, castles, bridges, and Underground stations—all enveloped by scaffolds. The entire city appeared to be wearing its gruesome skeleton on the outside, pinned to its corrupting flesh.

When he had lived in London before he had presumed the scaffolding temporary, erected for the purposes of cleaning and/or renovation. Now he knew the truth. Scaffolding goes up, but none ever comes down. These were not temporary structures to aid in the restoration of beloved castles and monuments; they were there to frame the historical relics, advertise their mortality, celebrate their decay.

This is not so shocking, perhaps, once one recalls that *scaffold* shares its Latin root with *catafalque*—a structure raised to hold the dead prior to burial.

There is something very *Eng*lish about the scaffolding, the catafalquery, that stands defiantly about London. The British are vengefully proud of their decay. The catafalque on which their past is laid is the scaffold from which it ignominiously hangs. This fact well illustrates the cranky ambiguity of the British sensibility. They love nothing that they do not also hate—Nannies, America, the Past.

Most assuredly, the past. And not just their past, but the past of others as well. The British hate the past of others as much as, more in fact, than they hate their own. This is why London is no proper place to store plunder from Egypt, Mesopotamia, Greece, and Rome. Cleopatra's needle stands rotting by the Thames. And the same industrial poisons that attack that royal obelisk assault the uncrypted bones of a no-longer immortal priestess, whose name has been lost to time.

Michael half-wished he'd never met the Mummies of Malet Street—the anonymous priestess moldering behind her wooden mask and the waxen philosopher, stubborn icon of sec-ularity, rotting in an upstairs closet. In their corruption he was forced to confront the gloriously incessant decay of monu-ments; he was made to smell the meaning of history itself.

5

Michael's decline into morbidity might have become serious were it not that he suddenly recalled his visit some years before to the exhibit of medical oddities at the Montpellier School of Medicine.

When Michael had lived in London before...

A caution is in order here: One shouldn't make too much of Michael's interest in visiting body parts (that is to be the subject of the following vignette). He has, admittedly, gone some distance out of his way in his travels to visit famous bones and brains. And once he had thought how convenient it would be if all the various body parts of the famous dead were collected in a single place. But in defense of Michael's slightly aberrant mode of tourism, it should be said that plan-ning one's travels around the sites of famous body parts can be culturally rewarding. Erasmus's skull is in Geneva. Dante's bones...still in Florence? (Michael thought he remembered them having been stuffed inside two large envelopes and stored in a filing cabinet in some library clerk's office.) Until recently, one could have found the bowels of Henry V in a pot in France (They had been dug up in 1978, and in 1984 were reunited with the majority of His Highness already at rest in Westminster Abbey.)

The Roman Church of the Capuchins (yes, the same one

celebrated in Hawthorne's *The Marble Faun*) is certainly worth a visit. Standing on the Via Veneto, not far from the Piazza Barberini, its crypt has rooms piled high with skeletal monk parts. There are vaults and niches where huge mounds of skulls glow with the light of candles mounted upon yet other bones—femurs, tibias, and perhaps, here and there, a cardinal's coccyx.

A most rewarding tour of Europe could be arranged by visiting nothing other than prepuses—Holy Foreskins. These tiny divine mementos, each confidently warranted to be the most sacred of shreds, the holiest of scraps—each, that is to say, asserted to be authentic splinters of the One True Penis—are scattered throughout the cities and villages of France, Italy, Germany, and Spain. (It is probably safe to ignore the rather questionable one in Prague.) Doubtless such a tour would edify the spirit. And there is nothing, after all, preventing one from taking in a few of the more tradition-al sights along the way.

6

...he had received an invitation from a friend teaching at Paul Valéry University. He had taken a ferry across the channel and a train from Boulogne to Montpellier, pausing in Paris only long enough for a Yawning Tour of the essential sites. Parisian monuments were not yet consigned to the scaffold. But this was, of course, misleading. Had he examined them closely at the time, Michael now knew, he would have seen the cracks and felt the crumble—wrinkles, furrows, in Lutetia's lovely face. Soon. Decay would visit Paris soon.

Michael's colleague had met him at the Montpellier sta-tion. They immediately drove to his apartment near the center of the city. Minutes later they were off on a walking tour. At the edge of the city square they came upon one of the oldest medical schools in Europe. Wandering about the buildings and courtyards, they happened upon a large room that served as a museum of medical rarities. There, on display in thick glass jars of eighteenth-century vintage were grotesques of every variety.

Fetuses.

Abortions, spontaneous and otherwise. Most seemed fully developed but without a hint as to the goal from which they had fallen so far short.

Human scraps.

They stared at one of the oversized fetal freaks, its sepulchered flesh so tightly confined that it appeared to be wrapped around, almost turned inside itself. No one had cared to tend its obscene eyes. One was open, staring. This single eye pressed hard against the glass...what did it see?

The creature looked like a scaleless fish, a baby shark, but with arms (or what in a better world might have been arms) that stretched outward from the torso like bony strands of flesh, bending at the limit of the glass. The arms reminded Michael of the stringy growths of ginseng roots he had seen in the windows of herbal shops in China and Korea.

Michael squinted at its...his...*her* almost face. There was no nose. Not really. The emotion growing inside of him was, he supposed, no less or more monstrous than the misshapen flesh that occasioned it. He wanted to press his face against the glass...for a closer look...to comfort and to be comforted. He wasn't able to identify his feeling, would not have been able to express it, and so was grateful when his friend (it was his first visit here as well) spoke for both of them.

"Horrible, eh? And so human. It is humanity, is it not? The part we never see. The rest of it."

The rest of it.... Yes. Beneath their ghoulish fascination and the cruel ecstasy of relief at being on the outside of that jar, it was love that Michael and his colleague felt. Love, for sure. Not (of course, not) in its normal form. It was a monstrous, leftover love—some scraps of love which he, they, had not needed until that moment since neither of them had ever encountered beings alien enough to call them forth. Michael thought just how indiscriminate, finally, is the love of our fellows, the love of mankind. It is the love of whatever, at whatever conceivable extreme, is human.

Returning to Paris by train, Michael snuggled into his seat and into the strange, soft silence of the streamlined rails. On the very edge of sleep, as his mind's eye opened wide to feast upon his monster one last time, he yielded to the desire he had so shamefully repressed. He leaned toward the jar...nearer. Its surface was warm against his lips.

Yes, the quasi-human seed that blossomed into refuse presents humanity, too.

The rest of it.

7

Raising his arm brought an immediate response from a passing taxi, lowering it signaled his memory's fade to black...

He watched as the Mummies of Malet Street staggered, zombielike, into his reverie and stood beside the monster in the jar. He smiled, at first without knowing why, but soon he understood the reason for his somber ecstasy: unlike these two crumbling monuments to the past, the aberrant creature born from some skewed dimension half-in half-out our world, the gruesome, strangely coveted flesh resting in its glass amnion, blanketed by everlasting namelessness...would never decay.

8

He gave the driver directions as succinctly as he could and entered the back seat of the cab. If he could control his breathing, he would be all right. Still, his nausea was becoming more severe, and he was shivering in spite of the warm sunshine seeping into the cab windows. He hoped the driver hadn't noticed his condition. He smiled abstractly, wondering just what his condition might be.

Across Albert Bridge and to the corner of Parkgate Road: He paid the driver and climbed the single flight to his rooms several steps at a time, challenging his cramping stomach to do its worst. Once inside he went directly to the bathroom and started to fill the bathtub.

His nausea was passing. He felt calmer. Still, there was something wrong. He left his clothes on the floor and climbed into the cast-iron tub. The water was very hot. It should have been too hot, but it wasn't. Michael immersed himself to his neck. His shivering got worse. Then he realized he wasn't shivering; he was vibrating, resonating to some frequency source that had captured his body and was in the process, for all he knew, of shattering it into its molecules.

Michael had at least a vague knowledge of what was happening. He had had it for some time now, long before he had climbed out of the taxi and leapt up the stairs—before, in fact, he had left the museum. And in the vaguest sense, he had known from his first sight of Bentham's mummy. There had been no choice but to fool himself, persuade himself that he hadn't any idea what was going on. But now he was safe in the bathroom. Now he could acknowledge what he had known from the very beginning—and by that acknowledgment bring it to pass.

9

"Hi, Michael."

It wasn't at all as if there had been the breaking of a cord, or the collapsing of a bridge that connected him with his familiar, substantial world. Nor was he visited as before—silently invaded by a friendly force outside his imaginings. He was in a boat. It was a small, perhaps fragile, rowboat. It was leaking slightly, but only slightly. He had pushed the boat from shore and was drifting, without oar or motor, toward the middle of a lake. It was not a huge mountain lake, a mile deep and a mile to shore. No. The shore was near enough and he thought he could swim if need be. Perhaps the lake was not so deep either. He might find that he could stand upon its bottom at no more than shoulder's depth.

The boat neither rocked nor glided, was still. Michael felt a little sad. There should be pain. He knew that was so. Pain that accompanies dissolution merely certifies loss (a word perhaps more innocent and pale than the grander term "damnation," but even awfuller for that), but to experience pain in the act of creation is redemptive. There should be pain. Unless...unless he was mistaken in believing himself to be creator rather than created, artisan instead of artifact. There would be pain then, but not in him.

Floating free on the surface of this safe lake, regretting the absence of effort or its pain, Michael was one moment's reflection away from a truth that he would realize in practice before it would ever burden his understanding: There is always pain. The mother takes pain upon herself in order that her child can enter the world in innocence. In every other instance of creativity, there is a distribution of pain. The pain of artistic creation is neither in the clay nor in the fingers of the artist but in the spirit that animates both.

"Hi, Genie."

She was sitting on the toilet seat, barefoot, her dress pulled well up above her knees. It was that same dress, muslin with laced hem, green and purplish-blue flowers embroidered on the bodice. When he had last seen the dress it had been ripped and wrinkled with red (orange in the moonlight) clay stains. Now it was crispy fresh and clean. He waited for the odor of hickory and pine to touch his nostrils.

Do spirits, poor rural ghosts as Genie is, wash and iron their clothes? Do they boil their laundry in blackened cast iron pots, shake and wring the water out, hang it to dry on sagging strands of wire strung between two small fruit trees, wire that must be wiped clean of soot and rust before each use, fix each item to the strands with wooden clothespins cracked and splintery from rain and sun?

Genie's legs were spread slightly and Michael's eyes drifted to that vagrant thigh, returning almost immediately to her face. She was wearing her hair pulled back, but on both sides wisps of brown were hovering around her cheeks. Michael started to speak and realized that he had nothing to say. It was enough that she was here, that she was smiling, seated near him, looking at him with neither anxiety nor expectation, just looking at him...and wearing that dress that sent forth—yes, he could smell them now—the distinct odors of hickory and pine.

Michael wanted to be closer to her. He thought to get out of the tub but settled for leaning over the side, resting his arms and chin on the rounded porcelain surface. He thought that Rinpoche should be present. He should be seated in the corner on his smelly cushion. He wanted him to see what he had accomplished. There she was...his *yi-dam*, his *dakini*.

Michael rehearsed Rinpoche's words, seeking reassurance he did not really require: "Your White Tara will not appear as our White Tara." Indeed. Michael much preferred his freckled faced, brown-haired Tara. He would like to be able to say to Rinpoche at this moment that the truth has lost nothing in translation.

You don't have to be a Buddhist to be a buddhist.

10

Genie leaned forward, wrapping her arms around her bare knees, raising her feet several inches above the floor. She began to rock slowly back and forth. "Well, here we are in London, England, huh?"

"Yes. Here we are." Michael looked into her eyes, still sparkling from the smile that faded only slightly when she spoke. He wanted to say to her, "Genie, why don't you tell me why you have come." He realized that he was still expecting some sort of message—a sibylline oracle, a siren's song, a rousing speech from Diotima come again to teach a philosopher of love and wisdom.

Genie stopped her rocking. She wrinkled her forehead in concentration, looked at Michael with a fresh new smile that answered his question before he was able to ask it aloud. Smiles are never enigmatic. They always say exactly what they mean to say. Genie's smile said, "Nope."

The water was getting cold. Michael laid back, put both feet on the front of the tub, placing his arms under the water. He was floating free. If he had wanted he was certain he could have seen the shore off in the distance.

But he didn't bother to look.

11

Michael had been scheduled to stay at The Russell, a hotel only three blocks from the site of the lectures. But his love for Albert Bridge and Battersea Park compelled him to request lodging in Battersea. He could not have been more pleased when he learned that his rooms were within half a block of the place he had lived before.

He thought he might have strained the boundaries of propriety by urging that they dine in his old neighborhood. For he knew well that there were some Londoners who were loath to venture south of the Thames.

"There is an interesting place at Albert Wharf, near my rooms. We could meet there."

"I must say, Michael, that you are doing very little to impact the trust's rather large treasury. I do hope that you will give some thought to exhorbitantly overpriced dinners after the series."

"Alfred, I know I'm being a bit of trouble. It's just..."

"Say no more, say no more. No trouble at all. It will be an adventure. Though I should confess that it will not be altogether novel. You see, I have eaten at Ransome's—that is the restaurant, isn't it? A charming place. I wonder if seven o'clock would be too early?"

"That is very considerate of you. I was hoping to get a good night's sleep."

"Yes, well, of course. But, you see, it was more out of consideration for another of our guests that I chose the hour."

"Oh?"

"There will be just the four of us. Peter, of course...and our surprise guest, Graham Andrews."

"Really? That will be wonderful."

"Yes, quite. Especially so since we shall be dining at an early hour."

Michael was puzzled. He waited for Pherendon to clear up the mystery, which he did in a rather involved fashion, the gist of which was that the earlier they ate the more sober Andrews would be. And though he was altogether too much when completely sober, he was equally overwhelming if drunk. He was at his absolute best when only half-polluted.

12

"In the realm of practical affairs, true genius lies in the ability to anticipate all of the important contingencies and to respond imaginatively to them." Michael remembers having read that, or something like that, in high school study hall while suffering detention for some long-since forgotten offense.

Graham Andrews was generally conceded, even by those normally unimpressed by intellectual achievement, to be a genius. That he would have contrived to meet the challenge of an early dinner hour in an imaginative manner did not surprise Michael.

"Hallooo." His voice was muffled and scratchy coming through the lobby phone. "Graham Andrews. Thought you might like to have a chat and a drink before dinner. I've taken the liberty of bringing the bar."

Michael looked at his small travel clock on his working table. It was 4:30. Quite an early start, he thought. "Well, of course. I'll ring you in. I'm just at the head of the stairs."

Andrews stood for a moment at the door before entering. He was neater than Michael had expected, though he subsequently realized that Andrews's legendary sloppiness must be more a function of the *choice* of his attire rather than of its cut or condition. Andrews's brown top coat was open, revealing his suitcoat and vest. The vest was a tartan, woven of a red, blue, green, and yellow pattern which clashed dramatically with the lapels of his dark blue pin-stripe suit. Michael thought that such an obvious offense against the standards of reasonably good taste had to be by choice. Andrews was purposefully opting in favor of the pleasures of style over the safe comforts of class.

There was no opportunity for shaking hands since Andrews was fumbling in both of his coat pockets, simultaneously drawing packages from them, holding them out toward Michael, one just after the other in a vaguely familiar gesture. Almost instantly Michael recognized the moves. They had the same sequence and tempo as those of Marshall Matt Dillon when he drew his six-gun at the beginning of each episode of "Gunsmoke." No one draws his firearm like Matt Dillon—a graceful, deliberate, sweeping movement up and out of his holster that always looked slower than it should, but accomplished with such authority that everyone knew what the consequence had to be.

"Didn't know what you would drink, so I brought a selection. There is Jack Daniel's for you—and for the American in me. And if there is any British—any Scot—in you, we shall nurture that as well. It's Glenlivet."

Michael had given up the idea of a handshake or any other sort of introduction and proceeded to the kitchen with the bottles. Andrews had already removed his overcoat, leaving his scarf hanging about his neck. "Sit down, Professor Andrews. What will it be? The Scotch for you?"

"Do you have ice?"

"Ice?"

"Ice, yes."

"Yes, I do. You would like ice in...?" The one certainty Michael had grown to depend upon with respect to the English had just been challenged.

"Well, you see, I've always wanted to have an opportunity to say this (Andrews was still standing, now he spread his legs slightly and struck a formal posture): 'I'll have a boourr-bon on the rrrocks.'"

Michael laughed. "You do that quite well." He reached inside the small freezing compartment for the single ice tray. He thought it might be profligate of him to open the Scotch for himself and so decided to share the bourbon. He poured himself a small amount, without ice.

Andrews was pacing about, examining all of the objects and furnishings in turn. Michael, still standing at the kitchen portal, was examining Graham Andrews.

Andrews's face was trapezoidal. Michael thought that, were he to wear a dunce cap his head would form a perfect cone. His straight brown hair (very little hint of graying) was extremely thin. Pasted tightly to his scalp it offered the appearance of a comb with several teeth missing.

He had to be approaching seventy. But his carriage made his age difficult to assess: most people bend slightly forward as they grow old. Andrews, on the contrary, had so obviously stood and sat rigidly erect for the greater part of his life that as he had begun to grow old he was increasingly bent backward. When he stood directly in front of anyone, he would be unable to present his face full-view. The first thing one would see would be the bottom of his chin, over the horizon of which one would have to look to see the end of his nose and, finally, a glint of the eyes beyond. Talking to Andrews would be an unusual experience, since instead of "looking him in the eye" Michael knew that he would be forced to speak into his nostrils.

This would likely be less disconcerting than attempting to look at his face directly, for it was becoming clear to Michael that Andrews did not have a face in the truest sense of the word. When he spoke (especially when he uttered what Michael soon learned was an habitual response, "Hmmm... yessss..."), his mouth could not but stretch thin over his teeth. This would have the effect of greatly distancing his nose from his mouth, which in turn would cause his face to dissolve into a set of comically dissociated features.

Only when he had his drink in his hand did he sit. Michael took a chair opposite Andrews at the small dining table. He had set both bottles between them. There would be no further call for Michael's services as bartender. Nor was there any further need for ice. Without asking, Andrews lit a cigarette. He decided to use the small glass coaster Michael had supplied with the drink for his ashes.

Andrews smoked fitfully and with a strange, initially unidentifiable rhythm that Michael finally decided was the consequence of unfocused motivations. He seemed to have two equally powerful reasons for smoking. His first hard drag on his cigarette was for pleasure, the second was caused by anxiety over the potentially deadly consequence of his first. And so he would rapidly consume his cigarettes until, reaching the end, he would pause in anticipation of the final drag which would occasion a defiant ecstasy that canceled for a short time the knowledge that his habit was a killing one.

And Andrews drank with the same sadomasochism with which he smoked. Before long, Michael will come to think of Andrews as the fullest manifestation he had ever encountered of the struggle between Eros and the Death Instinct.

13

"Ah, yes, well, you see, I've read some things of yours. *The Rhyme of Reason* was quite fascinating..." Michael was impressed. Here was a Englishman who required neither formal introductions nor small talk. This might be fun, after all. "Though I must say both your recommendations concerning the putative limits of language and your own peculiar use of language in that work struck me as innocent of the constraints of grammar and syntax."

Michael sipped his bourbon, stretched his legs out a bit and prepared to settle into the conversation. "I hadn't thought to abandon grammar; I only wished to expand the language a bit. Surely that is necessary at times."

"You are being too modest, Professor Evers. I distinctly recall reading this sentence in your work: 'Communication is best when it is most allusive?' That's stretching it more than a bit, I'd say. Must we give the world over to the metaphoricians? Why, bless my soul, that would put me and my kind out of a job."

"There will always be a need for the grammatically sensitive author and translator. But we must worry about the need to protect language from being reduced to its presumedly literal significance."

"I could have some sympathy for that worry of yours were I to believe that there is an alternative to accepting the literal meanings of words as the norms for deciding significance."

"Sometimes, often, we are at a loss as to how to use the literal language. What are we to do then?"

"I have no objection to abandoning language in certain situations. If we cannot find words, then we shouldn't speak. I only oppose the half-hearted abandonment that you seem to suggest. There is no excuse, as I see it, for mucking about with the language, stretching it beyond its legitimate bounds, celebrating its paradoxes and ambiguities as a means of undermining the authority of literal discourse, then making a desperate appeal to metaphor to save the day. It is hardly wisdom, only an abuse of language, when one claims for poetic discourse some authority above that of the literal."

While speaking, Andrews's forehead had wrinkled to the severest. His lips had almost disappeared beneath the tight grimace, leaving his two irregularly shaped nostrils dangling in space. Having used his face to its expressive maximum, he now seemed to be searching about for some supplemental gesture that would intensify his expression of distaste for what he took to be Michael's views. Not finding one, he was silent.

Michael replied in a conciliatory tone. "It would be good were we to have greater resort to silence in the face of the limitations of language. Unfortunately, few of us know how to be silent. Silence is as much abused as speech. When it is the consequence of simply refusing to speak or of lacking the imagination to formulate an articulate reply or is a calculated avoidance of language, then silence is a tool of the irresponsible, the uncaring, and the unaware. As the Ch'an Buddhist has it, 'A donkey does not achieve silence merely by refusing to bray.'

"But there is a second point at which we shall perhaps find common ground. Language, or so it has always seemed to me, functions as both signpost and barrier. It both indicates that something lies beyond and prevents further penetration in the direction of that something. I believe the difference between us is largely due to your far greater faith in the character of words as signs, while I emphasize the allusive function of words because I feel that first, and most fundamentally, words serve as barriers."

"Hmmmm...yesss..." Andrews finished his second (or was it his third?) drink and reached for the bottle as he spoke in a slightly deprecating manner, "Then I suppose you would grant that grammar is a comfort to us by virtue of its serving as the main foundation of the wall that prevents access to a territory which in any case shall always remain beyond our reach."

"To tell the truth, Graham..." This was the first time Michael had used Andrews's first name. It sounded good. He felt close to this man. "I can't see what comfort linguistic rules of any sort are going to give anyone who pauses to wonder about the meaning of words. Words are altogether too ambiguous to provide us any assurance that communication, when it happens, is a result of the words themselves."

"Doubtless there are problems. And that is why some of us strive to provide reasonable assurance that literal meaning is carried by the words we employ."

"Look at the words you just used however. Take that innocent sounding word *strive*. Isn't it ultimately a single-term oxymoron?"

Michael's statement brought Andrews up short. He seemed to feel seriously challenged for the first time. He sat even straighter, raised his upper lip high upon his face, which brought his nose down, almost hiding the tip of it, then sent his lip back into tight formation against his teeth, the thin line of it stretching across his face once more like the rapid closing of a surgical wound. "That would be interesting if it were so. Tell me where the contradiction lies."

"Well, it seems that any cogent meaning of 'to strive' must include the senses of 'desire' and 'effort.'"

"I should think that would be so, yes."

"But it appears that what is striven for must be lost. It's the old Platonic argument. One cannot strive to attain what one already has. Striving would cease at the very instant one attains what is desired. One would no longer desire what has been attained simply because one no longer lacks it. Surely, if one knew that his effort would be in vain because the desire would be canceled at the moment of attainment, he would hardly put forth any effort at all. It is only because we remain ignorant of the meaning of the word *strive* that we permit ourselves the activity of striving."

"Hmmm...yesss...I suppose one might say that there is a meaning of striving that does not include desire. We could say that effort does not, as previously conceded, include the notion of desire at all. The act of disciplined effort is consistent with the meaning of duty...and dutiful actions may not be accompanied by...Ah, but I suppose you would say there must be a desire to perform one's duty...and that would put us in the same fix again. Hmmm...yesss.... Are there any more of these single-term oxymorons that plague you?"

"I'm afraid I am at a loss to discover any words that do not function in this manner."

"Examples? Of course, you would say 'to love' since it is shaped by desire as well. Likewise, the verb, 'to know.' One must desire knowledge and that would be so only if one possessed not it but its opposite, 'ignorance.' But, then, what of the copula? 'To be' seems safe enough. Ahhhhh...But no...You would obviously say..."

Michael was amused at Andrews's having suddenly taken over both sides of the argument and equally impressed by his ability to stay clear-headed while consuming such quantities of alcohol. Michael had been sipping slowly and had accepted a refill from Andrews only once (or was it twice?) yet already he was beginning to feel fuzzy headed. He was dreading the evening to come.

"...that being is a temporal activity, that by the time one says 'I am,' it could only mean 'I was.' Yesss...Then what about...No, No. Ah, let's say articles and conjuncts—'an,' 'but,' 'this.'"

The wrinkles in Andrews's forehead seemed permanently in place now, and when he wasn't speaking his lips would disappear altogether by virtue of the incredible stretching out of his grimace. "But that won't do—that would lead us to the initial arguments of Hegel's *Phenomenology*. 'This' refers to anything. But what is it meant to refer to? To some particular. But it refers to any, every, particular. Hmmm..."

Andrews leaned backed, his nostrils opened and closed two or three times. "Then, according to your position, language is, alas, without exception, pointedly foolish."

Michael tried to interrupt in order to qualify Andrews's inference, but there was no time, the argument would be concluded without his intervention.

"The meaningfulness you deny to language does not exist in some mystical or even metaphorical beyond. It exists, you would have to say, between the communicants in a dialogue."

Michael had no time to reflect as to whether or not he agreed. Andrew was on the track of the argument and was racing now to its conclusion.

"And if meaning must be found between the members of a relationship, then neither member has any real value apart from the relationship. Ah, yesss.... I believe that one of the existentialists, bless their souls, said that very thing, 'To be is to *be with*.' (It was Gabriel Marcel, Michael thought).

"Sooo, all events are collaborative and have meaning only by virtue of this collaboration. Let me see if that makes sense. Hmmm.... The author must have a reader, I suppose.... But that is trivial.... Ah! You *do* have a point.... Yes, you do."

Michael tried to think what his point might be—the one that Andrews had discovered in the argument which, without once indicating any agreement, he had carried to such lengths. Though Michael would certainly accede to the correctness of everything Andrews had said so far, he would somewhat grudgingly have to admit that he had never considered his own views in quite this light.

Andrews waved his hand to prevent Michael from speaking. "I want to be fair to your position...and I don't think I have quite reached your true conclusions. I am thinking now of Plato's *Seventh Letter*. There, it is said—I can only paraphrase:

In benevolent disputation without jealousy, through question and answer, suddenly a flame arises—it is the flame of philosophic wisdom.

Plato believed that whatever meaning there was to be found was located not in the grammar of the claims and counterclaims, nor even in the specific content of the doctrines espoused by either party, but between the communicants in a dialogue.

"The conclusion—your conclusion, with Plato's help—is clear enough now. Meaning is achieved through collaboration, often quite involuntary collaboration I might add. Where would Jesus be without Judas, or Faust without Mephistopheles? How impoverished our sense of Hamlet's wimpish character if—it was Turgenev who called this particular collaboration to mind—we lacked the single-minded Man of La Mancha with whom to engage him. Either Socrates or Plato without the other...or..." Andrews smiled his uniquely grotesque smile—but, mercifully, it lasted only an instant, "Tweedledum without Tweedledee."

"But, Graham, there is this point…"

"Sorry…" Both of Andrews's hands were raised this time. "We're almost done. The trick of using language correctly is to recognize that words are suggestive gestalts—no more. And metaphor is purposefully ambiguous in order to avoid the degrading contradictions into which grammarians must fall by ignorantly affirming the literal significance of words. Whatever meaning there is comes into being between the collaborative elements of an event. The meaning lasts as long as does the event.

"God save us, you will finally say, from the meaning squeezers who would attempt to maintain faith in the literal significances of words. For they believe that we can get along without others, that we can create meaning independent of relationships."

Michael, exhausted by Andrews's tour de force, managed only a weak smile as he said, taking far more credit than he deserved, "You rest my case."

In the few moments of silence that now supervened, Michael found himself uncomfortably indifferent to the *v-yooze*, his own *v-yooze*, so cogently presented by Andrews. He was beginning to think his position somewhat tendentious and absurd. He wondered if Andrews had any interest in trading opinions. It might be better could he be like this frenetic scholar who had long ago given up on other human beings and had found the meaning of his life in the comforting spaces guaranteed by grammatical injunctions.

14

"Bless my soul, Michael, I confess I am beginning to feel sober.
A dreadful experience!" Andrews reached for the Jack Daniels
and gave it a shake. It was nearly empty. He passed the bottle
to Michael.

"Oh, no. You'll have to finish it off. I've got to get dressed."

Andrews's hand paused in the air and he held the bottle
for several seconds, then he lifted it to his mouth, holding his
lips firmly around the neck of the bottle as the contents
drained. Michael reflected how ceremoniously slow his movements were, solemn and trancelike, performed in the manner
of one who knows what it is to mourn the passing of pleasure,
who has mourned before, who understands the meaning of
finality, who knows that this will be his final act, who turns
the weapon toward his face, places the barrel in his mouth, fas-
tens his drying lips to the tight cylinder, tastes the acrid blue-
steel surface, squeezes, waits, hears, but never feels the pain.

15

Comforted (ever so slightly) by the fact that the scotch had survived unopened and further reassured by the almost certain memory of Andrews having demanded several more refills than he, Michael told himself as they walked the two blocks to the restaurant that the chilly air would quickly clear his fuzzy head and that this would in turn allow him to straighten his gait and unslur his speech.

"Here we are." They walked inside the courtyard at the back of which stood Ransome's Restaurant. Inside they were immediately met by a hostess far more casually dressed, and a great deal more chatty, than one might expect in a London establishment. A–K and Pherendon had not yet arrived, so there was no choice but to sit in the lounge.

Andrews ordered drinks, and tapped impatiently on the table until they arrived. Then, hearing Pherendon's voice at the entrance of the lounge, he immediately downed his bourbon and exploited the arrival of A–K and Alfred in order to have yet another round. By the time they left the bar, Michael was feeling as he had feared he might at the *end* of the evening. Even Andrews was showing the effects of the alcohol.

Nothing good can come of this, Michael thought, as the four followed the hostess to their table.

16

But the evening was rather pleasant. Or so Michael would think when, now and again during the course of the meal, he would struggle to focus his mind and to make an assessment.

Dinner conversation focused upon the inevitable topic in mixed British and American gatherings: Fast food, parking lots, and all-night supermarkets—that's America to the British, Andrews had said. Michael had replied that his primary impression of Britain, having lived for the most of his tenure in London, was scaffolding.

"Look here," Michael said at the beginning of one of his several forays into cultural criticism, "London is a wonderful place. But it is a *museum*, not a city. It is the birthplace and nursery of the Industrial Revolution—and there is greatness in that. But all of the niceties of classical architecture and the Victorian age are insulting to anyone with a sense of context. One doesn't place classical structures in sooty cities. They simply do not wear well there. Nothing ages better than Gothic buildings and so your university towns—Cambridge is the best example—are pleasant places overall.

"Britain has become the wrong sort of paradox. While holding onto its past for the wrong reasons, it actively denies the excesses of industry, again for the wrong reasons. Meanwhile, the rest of the world enjoys the fruits of industrialization while the country that holds the patent drowns in its own ambivalence.

"You've an island mentality that continues to separate you from the other Europeans. You have just enough socialist sentiment to heighten the dissatisfaction of your workers but not enough to change anything. You are suffering for your colonial sins: so many different sorts have invaded your complacent shores that you can't presume the comforts of traditional continuities to save you. There is no consensus, nothing that from some standpoint, cannot be considered cricket. The sweet reasonableness you have always thought would see you through is dissolving into bigotry and rancor."

The evening did eventually wind its way toward lighter

conversation. A–K got into the act with his sexual classifica-
tion of European culture. "The French consume only French
culture. They are an incestuous lot. But all things considered, I
must say I prefer the French perversion to British pederasty
and American auto-eroticism..."

Michael, under the numbing inspiration of alcohol, skirted
on the edge of bathos with this final assessment of his host
country: "Perhaps I'm romanticizing," he said, "but the character of the British seems to be summed up in John Ruskin's
autobiographical confession: 'I was whipped whenever I cried.'

"Tears come for two reasons: either as the result of pain
and loss or because of the experience of inexpressible tenderness and beauty. For most children, it is the former stimulus
that makes one cry. But the child-Ruskin was different. He was
too sensitive. He saw too well. His were ecstatic tears for
which, as he said, he was always punished. What must become
of a child who cries first from ecstasy and then is made to cry
from pain? Ruskin's sensitivity was a curse.

"Many of the British, I admit, are not so plagued by sensitivity. They are starchy stiff and, in most instances, emotionally
flat. Perhaps it is because they were whipped whenever they
cried and, unlike Ruskin who had no choice but to continue
shedding tears, they have given up sentiment as unproductive."

Michael was looking at Andrews as he said this and wondered what the owner of the stiffest lip on record must be thinking. There he sat—stoic, dutiful, his expression indicating that
the last thing he had any right to expect from Michael's words,
or the words of anyone else for that matter, was comfort.

17

Apparently, A–K had not intended to leave with Pherendon, for
when it was time for farewells he moved toward Michael.
Michael had refused Pherendon's offer of a driver to take him to
his lectures day after tomorrow. ("Humor me," Michael said.

Pherendon acceded. "Very well, then, I shall. But, please do not—not even for nostalgia's sake—attempt to take a bus at that hour!")

Andrews was extremely drunk, as his posture showed. He stood so stiffly by way of compensation for his loss of equilibrium that his back was bent into a severe arch and, from where Michael stood, only his chin and the tip of his nose were plainly visible. Promising that he would be present at Michael's lectures ("Each and every one"), Andrews held out his hand to Michael with the same slow sweeping movement he had made before.

After Pherendon and Andrews had driven away, it became even more apparent to Michael that A–K had something to say to him. "You want some coffee? My flat is just down the street."

"No, thanks, Mike. I can get a cab on the corner. I just wanted to say a few words in private." A–K seemed nervous, and Michael was becoming a bit uneasy himself.

"This is my place here." Michael gestured toward his building. "Come on up."

"No, No...you've got to get to bed. It's a nice night. Let's just enjoy the air for a minute."

They had reached the corner directly adjacent to Michael's building. Michael stopped and leaned against the low iron fence that bordered his building. The entrance to the Battersea Park was just a few yards away. The silhouettes of trees were visible against the sky.

A–K was leaning against a lamppost directly opposite Michael. The light from the lamp illumined only half his face so his psyche, normally hidden so well (except for his terrified eyes) was now brazenly revealed. A cheerful side—the left side of his face—and a somber darkening side—the right one. His features advertised an individual at once sad and bright, fearful and ebullient.

"It's been great seeing you again, Mike," —this from the left. And from the shadow: *This is really very difficult for me.*

Michael returned the compliment, and nodded to the shade.

"I hope you'll come to New York soon. I'll show you how a hard-hitting journalist unmasks corruption and all that..." *I want to ask you...I want you to tell me something.*

Michael said that he certainly would, and, etc., but that there was plenty of corruption in Texas and why didn't A–K come down there. Then he leaned forward, offering his silence as food for A–K's hungry phantom.

A–K laughed and said that there certainly was and, etc....

The phantom was unyielding.

Finally, Michael addressed the shade. "What's up, A–K. *Tell* me."

A–K slumped against the lamppost. His face no longer captured the light. He took a deep breath and held it for several seconds before releasing it along with the words. "It's silly, Mike. It's just that you are...different. Something happened... at Tilopa...or after. Ah, Mike, I'm sorry.... I don't know what I'm talking about..."

"*No.* I think you're right." Michael was puzzled, but he tried to encourage A–K to talk.

"I guess it isn't you so much.... It's Rinpoche..."

"Yes." Michael thought that he understood.

The words that streamed from A–K now were familiar to Michael. He realized as he listened that he could be saying much the same thing. "All my life, even before I became a journalist, I've had a special gift for seeing the sleazy side of things. Now I make my living writing about power addicts and their greedy pimps.

"It doesn't take much insight to know why people like me exist. We are all looking for honesty and innocence, more than half-afraid that we will find them and have to own up to our own shortcomings. Still we look.... All we finally want to find is someone who isn't..." A–K smiled and shook his head, bemused by his own next words, "a bad person."

Michael couldn't help himself—he laughed. At first, it was in the manner of one indulging the comic disappointments of a child, but he soon found himself laughing as one shocked by an obvious truth recognized for the first time as his own.

A–K continued to shake his head. He was laughing now, as well. It wasn't clear whether the tears in his eyes were born from sadness or hilarity. The two men giggled and guffawed, each rocking back and forth on the low iron fence. Michael thought that they were like drunks coming home after the bars closed. Then he realized, and this added to the intensity of his laughter, that they *were* drunks coming home after...

Look at him, Michael thought. That frightened, sad, precious man, searching for a *good* person and all he has to do is to turn the lantern upon himself. A–K shifted his posture, his head turned to the side and the remainder of his laughter drifted into the park. Meanwhile, the spirit that promotes the harmony of metaphor and circumstance had guided him out of the shadows and into the light.

"Jesus, A–K. You *are* a wonder." Then, imitating the pouty manner of A–K's last words, Michael added, "Poor guy...all those 'bad' people."

18

The two men had finally recovered and were standing comfortably in silence. A–K spoke first.

"We're much the same. I think we *are*. That's why it's so hard for me. I wasted my time at Tilopa. You didn't. What happened to you? Something happened, something for the good. Something I missed. It's not that I have a taste for the spiritual stew they served up there, but Rinpoche was something else. I was there to find out what was rotten, and for once.... I have to say that, for once, I came across someone who wasn't hiding. But by the time I realized that, it was too late. I can't be sure that I'll have another opportunity. That may have been it for me, you know. Then Rinpoche sent you that.... Remember?"

"The stone figure (Michael had almost said madstone). Yes. It was an image of the *dakini* belonging to Padmasambhava. But you knew what it was."

"Sort of. I had seen things like it before. I couldn't be sure. But I knew what it meant. It meant that Rinpoche thought you were special. I was...jealous. Then, when I saw you in New York, I realized he had made the right choice. You were different.

"That's true, A–K. It seems we both came to scoff but stayed to pray."

"No. I'm afraid I scoffed past the point of no return."

"Remember the words of the dying Buddhist, A–K." Michael was trying to be light.

A–K smiled sardonically as he muttered, "Maybe next time.... Yes I remember.... Well, Mike.... The point is.... I have a message for you..."

"Oh?" Here it comes, Michael thought, without the slightest notion what "it" could be.

"I told you that I had seen Rinpoche some weeks ago."

"Yes."

"I wrote to him soon after I had finished the book. I wanted him to know that I hadn't dumped on him or Tilopa—not that he cared one way or the other. He replied. I was surprised. He said that he was going to be in New York to lead a meditation just prior to leaving for India. I went to the meeting and, after, he invited me for tea and for 'the conversation we never had.'

"We talked about...this and that..." A–K waved his hand vaguely. "Anyway, I told him of the trust's invitation to you. He just nodded and smiled. Well—not then but later—he said that I should give you a message.... There was really no opportunity at that choreographed cliché we endured in New York.

"It's not much of a message, I'm afraid, though it will likely mean more to you than to me. He said to tell you.... 'Tell Michael this,' he said—'Not every gift must be treasured.'"

Michael immediately thought of the madstone, as he was sure A–K had. But he hoped he would get away with changing the subject.

"Hmm...I.... You...don't think Rinpoche will return?"

"Not in *this* life. I think he went to India to die."

The conversation had ended. Both men turned to face the street. Several minutes passed in silence before an available cab approached. A–K leaned inside the cab to tell the driver his destination, then turned back to Michael. "I'll be there, Mike."

"Thanks, A–K." A–K climbed into the cab. Michael said a second thank you to the back of the taxi as it drove away.

19

Michael supposed it was named Battersea Park because of the type of wall that bordered it along the Thames. The wall was "battered"—inclined from the perpendicular in order to withstand the force of the ocean's high tide which would send the river well up the side of the embankment. The park touched the foot of Albert Bridge at one end and Chelsea Bridge at the other—a distance of about three-quarters of a mile—and extended approximately the same distance away from the Thames. The grounds offered a boating lake and tennis courts, a running track and miles of walking paths winding through a rich and robust variety of trees and shrubs.

London parks don't open until seven-thirty, but when Michael had lived here before, he often climbed the low wooden fence that bordered the park on three sides. The earliest birds would begin to sing by at least four in the morning, to be joined at discreet intervals by their tardier comrades, cheerfully unaware that their late entry into the songfest would seriously compromise their chances for worms.

He didn't have to climb the fence this morning. Even though it was only six o'clock the gate nearest the bridge was open wide. As he approached the entrance he saw Albert Bridge stretching itself in the morning sunlight. The small, intricately molded turrets that decorated the tops of the bridge supports looked like miniatures of the gazebo he and Genie had shared at the Court of the Dove. Then his eyes scanned downward to the base of the bridge entrance. Yes, the sign was still there. It had been fixed to the bridge entrance under the authority of the (now defunct) Greater London Council. Its message was printed in the stark commanding print familiar from propaganda posters of the two great wars:

ALBERT BRIDGE
NOTICE
ALL TROOPS
MUST BREAK STEP
WHEN MARCHING
OVER THIS BRIDGE

Albert Bridge, like its namesake, was rather delicate. It had been saved from destruction several times by those who realized that London was a museum and its artifacts must be preserved, whatever the inconvenience.

Michael walked inside the park along the embankment in the direction of the Peace Pagoda, a gift of the Japanese Buddhists to London. A Buddhist monk, downy robe and shiny shaven head, was crouched beside the structure. He looked to Michael like a bald-headed duck as he moved around the circular pagoda on his haunches picking up leaves and bits of paper and placing them, one item at a time, in a small cloth refuse sack.

Michael nodded to the monk, hardly expecting any response, thrilled when he received one. It was a smile, mostly toothless, and benign at first. But something in the smile seemed ominous. Smiling and grimacing at the same time, the monk made his message quite clear:

I am human like you.... And harmless. But, please, under pain of...(whatever) do not seek any further contact with me.

Michael complied.

Just past the pagoda, Michael turned away from the river and moved in the direction of the lake at the far end of the park.

"I feel the grass greenly." He said this aloud, just as his feet touched the edge of the large open space separating the embankment from a dense wooded area two hundred yards or so distant. The words were from a work by a modern philosopher. "In Spring," he had written, "one feels the grass greenly." Michael had never had that promised green feeling until this moment. Now, try as he might, he was unable simply to *see* the grass; he felt it pouring into him, coloring him green.

20

The lake was empty. The ducks and geese and swans had not yet made their morning entrance onto the water. They were mingling on the grassy *plaisance* that bounded the lake's shore. Sounds of pleasure (now of warning) accompanied the dancing (now scurrying) of the birds this way and that. Michael sat on the bank at the very edge of the lake. The ground was damp. He sat next to a large tree, using the knotted roots exposed by the wash of the lake as a stool.

The roots were hard and uneven. The pressure, almost pain, felt good to him, reminding him of other roots he had sat upon or scrambled over as a child in the Louisiana bayous. Sometimes they had been large enough to form crevices and hiding places, secret caches for treasures—true or pretended. The pressure, almost-pain, he was feeling now was so much like the sensation he was remembering that perhaps it *was* that original feeling. His body was recalling in sympathy with his mind and the growing ache in his buttocks had a cause now years and miles distant from its effect. The poignant pain layered over the one whose cause was here and now was the one he felt most, best.

How many levels, layers, must there be?

The shadow of the tree under which he sat extended into the water, but did not remain a shadow on the surface of the lake. It was a reflection now. Where had the shadow gone? Had it vanished? *Could* it vanish? And if the shadow remained, layered somewhere beneath the reflection, then why couldn't the soil along the water's edge that carried the shadow of the tree hide its reflection as well? Only the absolutest darkness, the very substance of shadow itself, would be unable to send forth reflections. And where could such darkness be found? Only the smoothest, sharpest, brightest mirror could fail to hold a shadow. But no such mirror could, or ought, exist.

Michael was sitting quite still. A swan on its way to the water was passing close to him. He had never paid attention to swans out of water before. They had such big feet! Should he feel sorry for them?

"I got big feet, too." She was still not wearing any shoes. Leaning against Michael's tree, she held her feet out for inspection.

"Genie, aren't your feet cold?"

"No sir. It's only tiny feet that get cold. I never had no trouble with my feet. My feet feel real good and warm. Touch 'em."

Michael shifted his position on the bank and was now resting his knees on the moist earth. He took both of Genie's feet in his hands, his fingers traced their arches, felt the warmth through the mud and crumbled leaves that caked their surfaces. He rubbed each foot in turn, removing mud and clay and leaf residue, transferring the bulk of it from her feet to his hands, along with that precious warmth.

What did he feel? Her feet or his hands? The warm feeling was in his hands as surely as the mud and the rotten leaves and sandy clay. I feel my hands, he thought. The feeling is there. The thought exhilarated him...and made him sad.

It is love's unpublishable secret, realized but never told by conspiring lovers. Romeo's hand seeks that of Juliet; Antony's lips would touch those of Egypt's queen. They share the same lament: Hand touching hand, it is *my* fingers that I feel; mouth on mouth, I feel *not her* lips but my own.

Love remains always outside, else there could be no love at all. There is no difference between Dante's unattainable Beatrice or Boccaccio's oh-so-attainable "Fiametta." To be an object of love, whether physical or ideal, is to be outside. In fact, *to be is to be outside.*

There is freedom to be found in this truth. It renders all beings on a par with one another. Each is singular and solitary. Whether that solitude occasions painful loneliness or liberation depends upon whether one attempts to hide from the truth.

Loneliness is born with the realization that one's desire to be mingled and joined is futile. But the sense of solitariness that, by grace, sometimes supervenes comes from the further recognition that to be so joined, so mingled, is the supreme delusion of vanity.

It is religion falsely so-called that most often permits us to hide from the truth of solitariness, the truth of the emptiness of things. 'God' is a device to make us feel that we are not alone. But who keeps Fat Dharma company? He who has all things can share nothing. We who have nothing but our emptiness need not be lonely. We are solitary centers always existing outside. We are nothing but our outsidedness. But since there is no *inside*, we cannot be cut off from others or from ourselves. That Bloated Overseer has no such good fortune. He is Fullness Itself, the only Insider. Fat Dharma suffers a terminal disease with no comforting terminus.

True religion, when it exists, as rarely it must, does not hide us from solitariness but teaches us to celebrate it. All comforts but the harsh comfort of solitude are born of panic and unrecognized despair. The artist and the poet, the scientist and the historian, are all condemned to tell an untrue story, provide a flawed image, a blurred accounting of the reality of solitariness and so insure the sad victory of loneliness over solitude.

Michael had little hope when he made the request, but he made it anyway. "Tell me something about yourself, Genie. Please?"

"Well, I got feet like a swan."

21

They were walking in the direction of an old stone bridge erected at the opening of the park in the late nineteenth century. The bridge crossed one of the many narrows in the lake and from that point the view was of the trees and water and hillocks that formed the ambience of this quaintest of London parks.

They walked more slowly than Michael was accustomed to walk. He noticed many things he had not seen before. These paths had served him as an exercise route during the months he had lived here. He had run through the park, and though his pace was slow by any decent runner's standards, it still had been too fast to permit him to see what he was now seeing, to enjoy what he was enjoying now for the first time.

They were silent. This was not the silence born of an absent partner, that fruitless dead calm that nibbles at any pleasure one might feel, but the real silence that exists between two people who know that they can bring sound to it whenever they wish but who choose for this moment not to speak—the silence that encircles every sound, giving words both limit and meaning.

Two ducks were standing beside the path. They remained

motionless as he and Genie passed, trapped between the edge
of the path and the picket fence that bordered the lake shore to
their right. The fence was made of narrow, unpainted hand-
hewn slats of varying sizes. Near the foot of the bridge the
fence had fallen, its wire frame and weathered gray wood had
been twisted into a long graceful spiral that formed a pleasing
complement to the single arch of the stone bridge which had
just come into view.

One always tends to be cautious in crossing a bridge. But
this particular bridge was made of large, irregular stones in a
rustic pattern that boasted of strength and promised endurance,
inviting one to stomp carelessly across it. Even if there be Trolls,
Michael thought, we shall have nothing to fear.

"Look, Michael." He assumed Genie was looking at the red
cedar tree just to their left. It's delicate bark was peeled away
just above head height. The tree was purest white underneath.
Michael stopped and walked toward the tree for a closer look.

"No, Michael. There!"

It was a tree several feet from the first that had excited
Genie, and now Michael. The tree was jet black, one side of its
trunk almost completely covered in yellowish green lichen. The
trunk was still damp from the morning mist drifting from the
lake. The sun, boring through the thick woods, had caught the
tree in the exact center of a hazy tunnel of light.

What had Genie seen? Was it the glistening black skin of
the tree that, contrary to the nature of dark surfaces, reflected
the sun's light sharply into his eyes? Or was it the furry, yellow-
green scarf that wrapped the trunk, protecting it from the early
morning chill, its separated hues—the yellow and the green—
rich in compatibly intense ways? It could be that she saw, as
Michael now saw on the upper portions of the trunk where the
lichen was translucently thin, both visions in a single unassess-
able portrait, the light both reflected and absorbed—the black,
the yellow, and the green interfusing and playing to and fro on
the tree's moist skin.

Michael looked at Genie standing transfixed by her vision.
He approached her, his eyes cast down. She looked at him and
smiled.

"Feet like a swan, huh?"

Michael looked up into her face. "Yes, like a swan's."

22

"The water's so pretty and smooth, huh?"

Genie was staring at the water as hundreds of insects glided, skimmed, and skated along its smooth surface, still undisturbed by geese and swans. She was watching the mist rising toward the sun, no longer able to hide in the spring-thickened brush along the banks, no longer able to pretend (by stretching itself to a molecule's thickness and distending over the surface of the water, by becoming the very thinnest of thin transparent masks) that it was actually the surface of the lake and ought by rights be permitted to remain awhile.

The mist was rising. On the bank to his left, almost hidden beneath the thick foliage, Michael recognized a group of sun dew plants. They were too far away, but he knew that were he closer he would see the drops formed on them by the touch of the sun. Soon these drops would rise as well and would begin their futile trek, dissipating millions of miles short of their destination. Should he be sad?

Mist doesn't only rise, he thought. It sinks as well. This return journey, not nearly so distant and never so futile, would take it into the tops and roots of trees and plants, through earth and sand and rock, until sinking at last to the core, it would be transformed into an even finer mist as it touched that second sun in that other center.

It is a mistake to believe that in the beginning there were creating, conquering star-suns. Rather, all things come from the misty firmaments always yielding, having yielded and returning to yield again. Michael looked straight into the face of the boasting, pathetic sun and laughed.

Genie was staring at the water's surface. Not at the surface itself—she was, rather, looking into it at the reflections of the trees which, before they reached the water, were not reflections but shadows. Why shouldn't she be fascinated? She was herself the reflection of a shadow. Michael looked with Genie's eyes and saw what she was seeing: not trees reflected in the water, not the reflections of trees in the water, but the reflections of tree shadows. They saw the opposite of what the sun was seeing. The reflections of the shadows displayed the other side, the underside. It was the bottoms of the leaves they saw reflected in the water, the branches and bark that faced away from, not toward, the sun.

There was no doubt as to which of them saw correctly. It is never the object but its image that we see. Or its shadow.

Or both.

23

Michael and Genie were watching the shadows of trees reflected in the water, witnessing the water yield itself up to mist, feeding the voracious rays of the sun. Each saw what the other saw, what neither could have seen before. Michael could share Genie's vision, he could watch with her eyes because there was a meeting place, a point of intersection. It was the surface of the water.

One doesn't think much of surfaces. They are places to stand and from which to leap. They are serviceable storehouses of images that signal not their own value but that of the objects they serve to ground or to reflect. They deflect the sun and give us sight. They are the bases from which mists rise, upon which shadows fall and images rest. But we don't think much of surfaces. Michael had long shared the general bias, reinforced in his case by training in the abstract arts.

Thales of Miletus, the first to be called by the name *philosopher,* had been mocked by a Thracian servant girl because, intent upon examining the stars, he had fallen into a well. And so all the practical people laugh at philosophers for being so anxious to learn about the heavens that they fail to notice what lies at their feet.

Socrates had praised Thales saying that philosophers must realize that only their bodies are earthbound. Their thought must take wings and fly, as Pindar said, "beyond the sky, beneath the earth." But what if the truth lies not beyond or beneath but simply *on* the surface? What if the surface is the truth of things? What, after all, does a thinker do? He reflects. And what is it that reflects if it isn't surface? Ideas are born from and borne by surfaces.

Michael looked at the surface of the water. His image and its shadow stared back at him. He couldn't make out Genie's reflection any more than he could see the shadow of the trees on the lake. But she was there. This time he would not, as always before, fall into the error of Narcissus. It was neither his reflection nor even its shadow that he loved.

He loved the surface that joined them.

24

For the greater part of the day Michael stayed at the flat, reading the text of his lectures, marking possible inelegances, straining after inordinate lapses in clarity, noting phrases or clauses that needed special stress, occasionally taking time to wonder what effect this or that turn of the argument might have upon his audience, sympathizing with them in advance when he read over a particularly demanding passage. He didn't like having to read his lectures. He much preferred a casual style of delivery. But the tradition here demanded formal presentation. So the words he used had to be selected in advance; they had to be his final choices. He could not pretend to be a poet; he had become, he was forced to admit, a *writer*.

As he read he kept hoping that his interest might increase, but by the time he approached the end of his lectures he was feeling almost despondent. Ten hours had passed. It was nearly sunset. He needed a break. When it was dark he would take a long walk. Earlier the BBC news reader had said "Lights on at 9:13." What was the time now?

Michael reached over and turned the clock toward him. It was the small buff black travel alarm that often accompanied him when he traveled. The clock said 8:53. But the *way* it made its announcement troubled Michael. The clock seemed...apprehensive.

Though he knew better than to share this information with anyone, Michael had a special relationship with this clock. It had kept him company over several years. Clocks are worthy companions. The clock has a face and hands, all that is really necessary for conversation. Apart from another human being, what could be more expressive than a clock? In fact, clocks are sometimes more revealing since their hands can never be used to hide their faces.

It was a German-made battery-operated clock with a luminescent dial and a sweep second hand. It's most distinctive feature was its voice-controlled alarm. Michael only used the alarm when he had traveled distances great enough to disturb his otherwise well balanced biological rhythms.

Whenever he was awakened by the electronically generat-
ed beep that grew louder and more insistent when ignored,
Michael would raise up in bed and look politely in the direction
of the clock's face with the expression of one who is forced by
his innate decency to prolong the tedium of a monotonous conversation and say, "Sag mir noch mehr, bitte." (Out of deference, he would only speak German to his clock.) Hearing no
reply, he would continue, "Ich bin wirklich fasziniert. Sag mir
noch mehr." Then, finally, "Ist das alles, was du zu sagen hast?
Bist du fertig?"

As reticent as his clock was to speak when spoken to,
Michael nonetheless learned a great deal from it, particularly
about the topic of its expertise. The clock would not lecture him
on grand chronological or historical themes; rather, it whispered the secrets of passing moments measured in hours and
minutes and seconds.

The most important lesson his clock taught him concerned
the intersection of clock-time and personal time. Once, when
his gaze had thoughtlessly drifted toward the clock and its face
had come accidentally into view, he thought the clock had
stopped. The second hand seemed motionless. Then it finally
made a click and moved forward one space, thereafter proceeding apace. Subjective time flows faster or slower depending
upon the complexity of one's experience. It is continuous. Clock
time is discrete. In this instance Michael's personal time had
been racing faster than his clock and had to make a dimension-
al adjustment when intersected by the steadier rhythms of the
machine.

Michael was never offended by his clock, as well he might
be, for interrupting the smooth continuity of temporal passage,
calling him from personal time to the time shared by the consensual world. He rather liked the idea that the clock made
demands upon him, told him when he was behind schedule or,
on rarer occasions, ahead, or on the rarest of occasions, that he
had altogether too much time and had to find a way to fill it.
And since he had occasion to be so often in alien time zones, he
increasingly relied upon the comforting discipline of his most
constant companion.

That he should find himself talking to the clock at odd
moments during the day—not simply to quell its alarm, but to

confide a doubt, a frustration, to announce the birth of an interesting idea, to beg its hands to slow their pace—never troubled Michael. He firmly believed that anyone who lived alone must surely develop some exotic habits.

Alone now with time's referee, Michael paused in his emendations long enough to pick up his clock, hold it in his left hand, raise it close to his mouth and to reveal, in the slowest of whispers, his first serious doubts, doubts that he knew would soon magnify into such proportions as to require actions of an appropriate magnitude.

He had been reading a paragraph from his final lecture:

> Some few still struggle to believe that the sciences enlarge and enrich our lives; that ethical and political institutions secure and protect individual rights and freedoms; that art sensitizes and enobles the human being while underwriting quality leisure pursuits. But the voice of modernity narrates the soul at war. It is a story of self- and world-alienation, an account of the contradictions of art, morality, and science which yields finally the gifts of a denatured science bound by the rigors of purposively rational technology and an uncultured art whose insipid creations neither result from nor encourage any constraints to the moral sensibility.

He slumped back in his chair, resting his chin between the palms of his hands. "Oh me," he groaned, adding aloud, "he groaned" by way of descriptive commentary. "Worte sind mein Geschäft," he announced to his clock.

The clock ticked and sighed.

"Dann bin ich offenbar arbeitlos."

No answer from the clock.

With awful resignation Michael then said, "Das ist unmöglich."

The clock understood.

25

After he finished shredding both copies of his lectures (he had gathered three or four pages at a time, ripped them down the middle, continuing to tear the sheets until they were no larger than about two square inches), Michael gathered the pieces into three piles and carried the piles one by one to the bathroom.

In the beginning he had felt some guilt, as if he were getting rid of a dismembered spouse. But it didn't take long for him to get into the rhythm of the enterprise. In less than twenty minutes he had flushed all of the paper down the toilet. He felt relief. When he returned to his work table he glanced at the clock. He thought he saw approval on its face.

Whimsically, he had decided to save one copy of the title page. It lay face down almost exactly in the middle of the table, an embarrassing, oddly symmetrical stain.

26

The lectures weren't *bad*, it's just that Michael had written what he thought he should rather than what he really believed. And he knew why he hadn't written his own thoughts. In simplest terms it was because he had written the lectures by the calendar and not by the clock. That is, he had written with the thought that it was the season for him to make a mature statement of his *v-yooze*. That's an old man's way for sure. How could he have fallen so far without recognizing it?

Old men struggle with calendars, fearful of the decreasing number of pages they will turn. Young people are at odds with clocks, counting seconds, hours—always with energy and passion remaining at the end of the day. The young struggle with the minutes that race past them while in the presence of the objects of their passions. One may bend time and distend it if the units be hours, minutes, seconds. A month, a year, is too distant, too abstract, ever to be disciplined.

The young are teased and goaded by clocks; old men look askance at calendars and have their glances vengefully returned. Michael realized that he had lately begun to pay more attention to calendars than to clocks. He seldom yearned for seconds to accelerate so that he might the sooner be united with a face, a hand, a voice—or that moments be prolonged that he could remain in the presence of that voice, that face, that hand. Instead, he had begun to look wonderingly at calendars, mourning the demise of years he had hardly known, nor could have known, since they had passed in impatient celebration of the minutes and seconds which in the thousands and the millions are seen by old minds' eyes as the invisible, inaccessible atoms comprising those dead years.

Desire feeds upon seconds and minutes one by one. Minutes and seconds become countless, uncountable; they may only be *recounted*. Time then no longer serves to invigorate but to enervate one's spirit. And memory is forced to gnaw upon bony-cold leftover years.

Life's most frenetic battles are shaped by singular drops of time—near-mortal wounds inflicted at an instant. As long as a wound is open, skin still torn, blood oozing bright from the body which in its vigor renews both itself and its healing source, there is the hope that life guarantees. Scars are dead, desireless wounds. Death is the scar tissue that finally closes the living wound of desire.

The false virtue accorded maturity (the first step toward old age) is the virtue of patience. Patience is the forced flowering of inertia. The passions no longer seeth; the furnace is dampened. And because the reward is past enjoyment, the stakes are no longer deemed worth the risk. Seconds, minutes, hours pass unheralded while years race and mock and dwindle.

Only some clocks have alarms. But for the old, every calendar sings its song of warning.

It takes the sort of fool each of us must prove himself to be to waste the gift of memory in the dissection of year's-long cadavers from the past, morbid now and impervious to alteration. And only the sort of fool no one of us has the courage to play could know that memory is meant to shepherd the still warm, just passed moments while they may yet serve the builder, conscious of his craft and aim.

Michael wasn't really obssessed with the battles waged with time and by time against us. But he cared. And since he did, he decided to make a vow. Holding his little clock in his hands, moving its face directly in front of his, he pledged that nowhere, neither at his office nor in his home, would he ever again display a calendar.

After he had spoken (he made his pledge out loud), the clock merely said, "9:31." He winked at his companion. "Neun Ur, ein und dreizig. Gut. Es ist höchste Zeit, zu gehen."

He reached for his shoes.

27

Michael turned right a block past Ransome's and crossed over Battersea Bridge. He looked in the direction of Old Albert. Its suspension chains were lighted now. Most of the bulbs near the railings of the bridge, those within safe reach, had been removed, probably by budget-minded flat-dwellers from the neighborhood. Others, higher up, had burned out. The total effect, Michael thought, was to give this so-quaint structure the look of a rickety Ferris wheel at a cheap three-day carnival. Having already fallen permanently under the spell of this bridge, however, this judgment merely served to enhance his appreciation of shabby carnivals.

He proceeded down the Embankment, across to Cheyne Walk at the head of which sits the statue of Thomas Carlyle, less than a hundred yards from the house in which he died. Not that he paid much attention to these familiar landmarks, he was simply enjoying the rhythm of his steps. He retraced old wanderings on King's Road and through the dimmer streets of the pretentiously named "The Royal Burrough of Kensington and Chelsea." It took several thousand steps to clear, and finally to empty, his mind.

The bridge was visible at the end of Oakley Street. After he had recrossed the Embankment, he stood at the foot of Albert Bridge. The Ferris wheel paused to let him board. He thought he could hear the struts and bands and chains that held the structure aloft creaking and groaning as he was swept forward, stopping at the highest point. Neither the crisp, singing breeze nor the absence of traffic sounds would tempt him to yield himself to the night.

He stood looking neither at the water nor at the outlines of the bridges silhouetted on either side. He was nesting his hands at the intersecting point of the suspension chains, precisely at the center of the bridge. His hands felt the cold steel. The incipiently rusting frame scratched him through the several thick layers of paint.

He thought that, if he wished, he could shake this structure at its center, could bring it down, giving it its overdue rest on the river's bed. Or, if necessary, he could clasp his hands tight and hold the edifice in place, saving it from an ignoble collapse into the water that had so ignored it as it passed beneath. It would have been his choice.

Then he remembered an occasion on which there had been no choice....

28

Bayous...moss...ghosts...hidden, haunted terrain. At night.
But during the day, nothing was more inviting than this place.
In spring and summer, on this one special pond in the wooded
area just before the edge of the swampland, there would be
lilly pads spread all the way across the water, a distance at the
narrowest point of about forty to fifty yards.

Beginning in his seventh year, Michael and two of his
friends would enact their springtime rite in this place, a rite he
learned how much he loved only when that love was rendered
futile. Twenty- to thirty-yard running start, leaping from one
lilly pad to the next, never letting go of your momentum. If you
were running fast enough at the beginning, and if you tripped
lightly enough, you could cross the pond without getting wet.
Three years in a row, only three, he and his friends took to the
pads—scattering frogs and beetles and dragon-flies in their
paths as they skipped and skittered across the pond.

Michael was heavier than his friends, so the inevitable
visited him first. Just at the middle of the pond, on his fourth
spring outing, a pad gave way under him and he sank straight
into the grassy mud at the bottom of the pond. Of course, he
tried again but he knew even before sinking a second and, yes,
a third time that the game was over for him.

He had grown up.

There are two sorts of growing pains: the pains of growing
up and those of growing old. Each involves the sense of irrevocable loss. Not long before Michael sank beneath the weight of
his few but still too heavy years, a philosopher of some note
would become even more noteworthy by conceiving the
apothegm, "Youth is life as yet untouched by tragedy." Michael,
standing on the bridge, sitting in the Ferris wheel, sinking on
the lillypad, could have reflected that the truth might be better
expressed as "Life is youth as yet untouched by tragedy."

Though the tragedy of growing up may seem identical
with that of growing old, there is a difference. The difference is
that the main crises of growing up are experienced as chasten-
ing, sad surprises while the pains of growing old (since each of

us is trained in advance to fear them) have all been anxiously rehearsed. The tragedies of growing up are only experienced well after the fact by one who is already bending and sinking under the weight of old age.

To be young, to be the innocent carrier of innocence, is to be prehistoric. A life story begins with perplexity over the loss of one's youth. Its denouement arrives with the struggle to retrieve one's prehistoric past. Michael's first baptism had demanded of him that he grow up. His second would allow him to grow old.

And so Michael was standing at the center of the bridge, hands on the still-point that balanced the weight of the structure, holding the bridge aloft, the lilly pad groaning and bending, yielding beneath him, groaning and bending, sinking.

This is life, he thought. This is real.

29

Same dress. No shoes. Once again Michael had been halved and doubled, made whole. He gazed upward at the suspension chains and thought how a puppet might feel if, freed by its master, it could look upon the impelling strings so recently detached from it. Would he, would she be afraid that release had been bartered for death? Michael knew that if there were fear it had to be in the air, in the sky, in the no longer indifferent currents escaping to the sea—anywhere but in himself.

Michael looked directly into the face of his freckled ghost. This was no *yi-dam*, no *dakini*. This hybrid spirit had been born from impure doctrine. Still, how could he complain? Genie, he knew, was serving him well by serving him right.

He was remembering the words of...Where had he heard this?... "Names are the lies we most like to tell." There is no face behind the mask since without a name there would be no single set of features which needed to be hidden. Behind the faces shaped by masks there is pure surface. This is the naked, maskless, faceless face of the nameless and unnameable.

But if from lust and ignorance one imposes a name, cancels chaos, steals the robust emptiness of the surface, the result is a rancid, stale, unfecund *something*...

Michael said the name he wished had never been said and which he so wanted to unsay..."Adrienne." The nameless in him mourned her as he spoke.

A phantom name, a name no longer, the word rebounded like an echo from his lips. He thought the sound might never fade, yet the silence, when it came, was lovingly complete.

"Hoo-ray, Michael."

He looked one last time into the freckled face of his redeemer—impassive it was, but not without love.

"Hoo-ray," she had said.

Michael reached his hands around Genie's neck and untied the madstone. Her hand held his as together they reached out over the edge of the railing. The figure slipped from their fingers and fell silently toward the river, vanishing in the darkness of the night before disappearing once again into the water.

Not every gift must be treasured.

Hurray, Michael. No more hauntings. Genie has joined Adrienne. An eye for an eye...

30

He leaned against the railing, thinking of nothing in particular. It was not until he felt the bridge lights go out that he made his way across the other half of the river.

31

Michael has no intention of returning to his flat right away. He will probably walk for a long while. He will surely begin to wonder what he should do now that he has shredded his last best wisdom and flushed it into the sewers of London, now that his fragmented *v-yooze* are oozing toward the river to be received, ultimately, by the immense indifference of the ocean.

He might even laugh at his dilemma. Perhaps he will find the courage to stand before his audience and echo the words of Roger Clifford, "Colleagues...I really haven't anything to say."

It could be that he will sit at his table and begin again. Will the clock's expression be stern or apprehensive when it is forced to say something like "7:22"—which will mean, "Zero minus twelve hours more or less and counting"?

There will not be time to formally prepare for this evening's event. If, however, Michael decides to wing it, as well he could, he might say what he really wants to say. He would, of course, have to speak of Fat Dharma, and of the Vast Indifference of Chaos. And he would tell of history as the detritus of passing time. He could hardly omit a presentation of his proof, though in a slightly more ironic and whimsical fashion than once might have been the case, that all apparently living human beings may be classified without remainder into the categories of vampires, zombies, and ghouls. It would be essential that he vigorously assault Plato's Hoax and Goethe's doctrine of the Eternal Feminine, speculate on the value of voluntary ignorance and defend the use of physical constants as reminders that nothing important ever comes out even. And though by now Michael certainly recognizes the serious limitations of the device, he would probably detail his technique for controlling future events through the meticulous rehearsal of all undesirable possibilities. Finally, depending upon his mood, he might even be willing to reward his audience, and himself, with a celebration of the hope that in the end the Blessed Multifariousness shall receive us all.

At the moment, however, he is not thinking about any of this. He is feeling easy, free. Sunrise is approaching. He turns toward Old Albert, grins and says to himself, then once more speaks the words out loud, "Loveliest bridge on the Thames, I reckon."